Monitoring the EU Accession Process:

Judicial Capacity

COUNTRY REPORTS

BULGARIA
CZECH REPUBLIC
ESTONIA
HUNGARY
LATVIA
LITHUANIA
POLAND
ROMANIA
SLOVAKIA
SLOVENIA

2002

Published by

OPEN SOCIETY INSTITUTE

Október 6. u. 12.
H-1051 Budapest
Hungary

400 West 59th Street
New York, NY 10019
USA

EU ACCESSION MONITORING PROGRAM

Október 6. u. 12.
H-1051 Budapest
Hungary

Website
<www.eumap.org>

ISBN: 1-891385-27-5

Library of Congress Cataloging-in-Publication Data.
A CIP catalog record for this book is available upon request.

Copies of the book can be ordered from the EU Accession Monitoring Program
<euaccession@osi.hu>

Printed in Budapest, Hungary, September 2002
Design & Layout by Q.E.D. Publishing

Table of Contents

Acknowledgements

The EU Accession Monitoring Program of the Open Society Institute would like to acknowledge the primary role of the following individuals in researching and drafting these monitoring reports. Final responsibility for the content of the reports rests with the Program.

Bulgaria	Yonko Grozev,	*Helsinki Foundation*
Czech Republic	Miroslav Krutina,	*Helsinki Foundation*
Estonia	Jaan Ginter,	*Tartu University Law School*
Hungary	Ágnes Kövér,	*ELTE Law School*
	András Medgyesi,	*Medgyesi & Nagy*
Latvia	Kristīne Krūma,	*Riga Graduate School of Law*
Lithuania	Linas Sesickas,	*Bernotas & Dominas GLIMSTEDT*
Poland	Łukasz Bojarski,	*Helsinki Foundation for Human Rights*
Romania	Monica Macovei,	*Helsinki Committee for Human Rights*
	Ioana Cornescu,	*Independent Consultant*
Slovakia	Jozef Malý,	*Detvai Ludik Malý Udvaros*
Slovenia	Boštjan Zalar,	*University of Ljubljana, Institute of Social Sciences*

ADVISORY BOARD MEMBERS

Károly Bárd	*Central European University, Hungary*
Giuseppe di Federico	*Superior Council of the Magistracy, Italy*
Rosa H.M. Jansen	*Utrecht district court, the Netherlands*
Ernst Markel	*Supreme Court of Austria; European Association of Judges*
Peep Pruks	*Tartu University; Open Estonia Foundation*
András Sajó	*Central European University, Hungary*
Renate Weber	*Foundation for an Open Society-Romania*

We would also like to thank the following individuals for their invaluable contribution to the reports in the form of research or review and critique of draft reports: Lucie Atkins, James A. Goldston, Stephen Humphreys, Valts Kalniņš, Ignat Kolchev, Katri Paas, Birgit Punison, Janja Roblek, Petr Smolik, Daniel Šmihula, Marek Tulipan.

THE EU ACCESSION MONITORING PROGRAM

Rachel Guglielmo	*Program Director*
Henrikas Mickevičius	*Legal Advisor*
Timothy Waters	*Legal Consultant*
Andrea Gurubi Watterson	*Program Assistant*
Andrea Kiss	*Program Assistant*

Foreword

The publication of this volume on judicial capacity complements that of the volume on judicial independence issued in 2001; there is an obvious and close link between the two notions. Justice is a public institution, designed to serve valuable social functions. The way the members of the judiciary and the staff under their authority are selected, promoted, trained, evaluated and disciplined; the way they perform their duties, both individually and collectively; and the way courts are managed are the constituent elements of judicial capacity.

At the same time, each of these areas carries with it an element of *power*, and hence is linked with independence: which persons, which institutions shall control the judiciary? The number of political and social actors is limited: the executive – that is, the Ministry of Justice – Parliament, National Judicial Councils, and the judiciary itself, including its Supreme and Constitutional Courts (as shown by the recent decisions of the Czech and Hungarian Constitutional Courts on judicial reforms) and court presidents. Who decides, and according to which procedures?

In any country judicial reform is bound to be fraught with obstacles, difficulties and delays – and the more so in Central and Eastern European countries, after half a century of Communist rule during which the judiciary, the courts and law itself were debased and used as mere instruments of power. Their rehabilitation in public opinion, and their attainment of real autonomy, require both time and tangible achievements – proofs of their effectiveness and accountability – beyond the black letter of the law. Hence a somewhat disturbing query: who, today, is asking for judicial reform?

The valuable studies contained in this volume are a vivid illustration of a number of paradoxes: profound structural reforms are needed in all these countries in order to provide the judicial system with the capacity to fulfil its constitutional mission according to the requirements of a democratic society. Such reforms require a strong and lasting political will from Governments and Parliaments – but one may ask if such a will really exists, or even how consistent the European Union itself has been in calling for such commitment.

Political actors are naturally reluctant to abandon the many means, legal and *de facto*, by which a judicial system can be influenced or made sensitive to external pressure. The pages that follow contain many concrete and compelling examples of undue discretion, lack of transparency and opaque procedures; equally importantly, they document the need for clearer standards so that States – both as candidates and later as members – can know what they must do in a democratic society. Governments and Parliaments need to be praised when they try to overcome these obstacles – and encouraged to be bolder and better when they do not.

Last, but not least, attempts at comprehensive reform may meet with another kind of resistance, that of corporatism: the temptation of the judiciary to become an insular and conservative guild opposed to change and accountability – and under the banner of independence.

Advocates of judicial reform face a difficult but necessary task. The useful studies in this volume tend to show that the start has been somewhat late in some countries. 2002 has seen a spate of reforms, perhaps in view of the forthcoming European Council in Copenhagen, when the admission of these countries will probably be decided. One thing, however, is clear enough: much will remain to be done once these States are admitted, especially in selection, training and evaluation; the obligations these States undertake are not obligations of accession, but of membership.

The pages that follow will be a valuable guide for all those involved in this essential field; the Open Society Institute's European Union Accession Monitoring Program and the authors deserve to be praised for making available such a wealth of useful information and assessment. But more importantly, their findings deserve to be read, and acted upon by anyone who is interested in what the Union will become.

Roger ERRERA
Professor, Central European University,
Conseiller d'Etat (hon.), Paris.

Preface

The Open Society Institute's **EU Accession Monitoring Program (EUMAP)** was initiated in 2000 to support independent monitoring of the EU accession process.

In keeping with the broader aims of the Open Society Institute, EUMAP has focused on monitoring governmental compliance with the political criteria for EU membership, as defined by the 1993 Copenhagen European Council:

> Membership requires that the candidate country has achieved stability of institutions guaranteeing democracy, human rights, the rule of law and respect for and protection of minorities.

EUMAP reports are elaborated by independent experts from the States being monitored. They are intended to promote responsible and sustainable enlargement by highlighting the significance of the political criteria and the key role of civil society in promoting governmental compliance with those criteria – up to and beyond accession.

In 2001 EUMAP published its first two volumes of monitoring reports, on minority protection and judicial independence in the ten candidate countries of Central and Eastern Europe. In 2002 new and more detailed minority reports (including reports on the five largest EU member States) have been produced, as well as reports on judicial capacity, corruption and – in cooperation with OSI's Network Women's Program/Open Society Foundation Romania – on equal opportunities for women and men in the CEE candidate States.

EUMAP 2002 reports on judicial capacity assess both the ability of individual judges to perform competently and efficiently, and the organisational efficiency of judicial branches and courts.

The EUMAP methodology for monitoring judicial capacity (available at www.eumap.org) was developed by EUMAP with input from an international advisory board. The methodology provides for the compilation of an original report drawing on existing research, case studies, legislative analysis, and interviews conducted by country reporters. Country reports do not purport to constitute an exhaustive or scientific examination of the specific areas covered; their principle advantage lies in the consistent application of the same methodology to all monitored countries. EUMAP assumes full responsibility for their final content.

Monitoring The EU Accession Process: Judicial Capacity

Table of Contents

OPEN SOCIETY INSTITUTE 2002

I. INTRODUCTION

This Overview and the accompanying country reports assess the state of judicial capacity in ten Central and Eastern European countries seeking full membership in the European Union.[1]

In 2001, the EU Accession Monitoring Program published reports on candidate States' efforts to comply with certain aspects of the political criteria for membership.[2] Those reports focused on issues relevant to judicial independence in particular as a fundamental aspect of the requirement that members States of the Union ensure stability of institutions guaranteeing the rule of law and human rights.

The current reports examine judicial capacity as a complement to the 2001 reports.[3] They are intended to bring to the attention of candidate State Governments and judiciaries, civil society and the European Union issues that still need to be addressed if candidate State judiciaries are to achieve the capacity essential to fulfil the obligations of membership.

The expansion of EUMAP's monitoring efforts from judicial independence and impartiality to other elements that distinguish an autonomous and capable judiciary is a result of the evolution of judicial reform in the region. Although in principle judicial reform should address all relevant components comprehensively, the legacy of the communist period made the emancipation of judiciaries in the current EU candidate States a particularly urgent task.[4] Independence is inherent in the concept of adjudication – there is no adjudication, properly speaking, without an independent and impartial adjudicator; since the previous regimes by their very construction rejected the judge's fundamental independence and impartiality, a special emphasis on this particular element

---

[1] In these reports, the term "candidate States" refers to the ten States in which EUMAP has conducted monitoring – Bulgaria, the Czech Republic, Estonia, Hungary, Latvia, Lithuania, Poland, Romania, Slovakia, and Slovenia – and do not include consideration of Malta or Cyprus; nor does it include consideration of Turkey. References to the situation in specific candidate States in this Overview are generally made without citation; full citations are included in the accompanying country reports.

[2] *See* EU Accession Monitoring Program, *Monitoring the EU Accession Process: Judicial Independence* (Open Society Institute, Budapest, 2001), available at <www.eumap.org> (hereafter, *EUMAP Reports 2001*).

[3] The present reports are designed so that they may be read independently, or in conjunction with the 2001 reports; many of the theoretical and practical arguments about reform – and especially judicial independence – that are mentioned in the present reports are discussed at greater length in the 2001 reports. *See* EUMAP Reports 2001.

[4] *See, e.g.,* Lucie Atkins, *The Shifting Focus of Judicial Reform: from Independence to Capacity,* available at <www.eumap.org>.

in Central and Eastern Europe has been justified. Today, although a number of problems related to judicial independence remain – and are discussed in this year's reports – the impressive progress achieved in the majority of the States over the past twelve years in this area[5] makes it possible to consider other elements of judicial reform that complement and counterbalance judicial independence.

This expansion of focus is not only possible but also necessary because of the ever-increasing relevance of the European judiciaries in political, economic and social life and the resulting public demands for professionalism, efficiency and accountability. This is especially relevant with regard to the candidate States; the dramatic political change from totalitarianism to a European Union based on democracy, a free market, human rights, and the rule of law and the concomitant growth of legal instruments as a means of social regulation, have led to a considerable increase in the quantity and complexity of cases brought before courts. This new challenge requires judges and judicial administrators to acquire and maintain new competencies and to develop efficient and transparent work methods. If judicial reform is socially unresponsive, public trust in the legitimacy of the judiciary will be put at risk.

Following on the work initiated with last year's reports, the present reports discuss major changes in each State's constitutional and regulatory framework or practices affecting the judiciary that occurred between August 2001 and July 2002, including changes that affect judicial independence. The central objective, however, is to ascertain the effectiveness of existing mechanisms and standards in ensuring that the quality of judges and supporting institutional infrastructure guarantees the *capacity* for an independent, competent, accountable, and efficient judicial process.

A. THE CONCEPTUAL FRAMEWORK: HOW IS JUDICIAL CAPACITY ENHANCED?

The concept of judicial capacity may be understood as incorporating four mutually reinforcing notions: independence and impartiality; professional competence; accountability; and efficiency.

Independence and impartiality. This report focuses principally on judges' capacity to adjudicate, but it is clearly an essential condition for adjudication that individual judges be guaranteed real independence in exercising their core decision-making

---

[5] *See, e.g., EUMAP Reports 2001*, p. 21.

functions.[6] More broadly, however, judges or the judiciary as a whole often require a level of peripheral independence ensuring that they may administer their own affairs.

This is not because there is any inherent right to independent administration as such, but simply because experience has shown that direct and formal guarantees of independence are often insufficient if there are indirect or informal ways in which outside actors may influence judges. Outside control over the judiciary's budget, administration, or disciplinary apparatus, or over judges' career paths may jeopardise judges' adjudicative independence even in the face of formal guarantees. When circumstances require or allow it, the judiciary should form a separate and autonomous (that is, self-governing and self-administering) branch, or at the minimum, should have a meaningful level of participation in administering its own affairs.

In the candidate States in particular, the legacy of the judiciary's subordination and dependence and, more broadly, the lasting cultural effects of political dictatorship, may require institutional separation and institutional guarantees of judicial independence that are more far-reaching then in countries with an entrenched culture of judges' independence or a tradition of decision-making based on consensus and negotiation. But any present or future member State which does not provide its judiciary with a reasonable level of autonomy in administering its own affairs ought to bear the burden of explaining why such a deviation from the norms of Union membership should be accepted.

As argued in EUMAP's 2001 reports, judicial independence is not an absolute right vested in judges, but a structured strategic decision by society to accord judges a measure of freedom for the purpose of ensuring access to meaningful justice for all. In that sense, it is part of a broader range of strategic choices society makes to ensure such access; that broader range of choices encompasses what these reports call judicial capacity. Independent governance and administration may be equally well understood as an aspect of judicial independence or of judicial capacity – indeed, formalistic, definitional distinctions are less helpful in formulating policy than a pragmatic appreciation for the real effects different approaches to structuring the judiciary's activities may have.

Professional competence. Adjudicative and even administrative independence may be essential, but they are insufficient; it makes little sense to make judges independent if they are nonetheless incompetent. Unless judges are individually and collectively capable of rendering timely, effective determinations that broadly comport with,

---

[6] *See, e.g.,* Art. 1 of the Universal Charter of the Judge, adopted in 1999 by the International Association of judges: *"The independence of the judge is indispensable to impartial justice under the law."*

reinforce, and advance society's sense of justice, there is little gained by society affording judges a broad measure of independence.

The professional aptitude of individual judges is therefore a crucial element of judicial capacity. Judges must have sound judgement, professional erudition, and skill to render judgements effectively in accordance with the law and their own conscience. To ensure this, judges should be selected in accordance with clear procedures that verify their personal and professional suitability for the strenuous demands of the profession. Judges' advancement in the profession, likewise, should bear a reasonable, measured relationship to their demonstrated abilities, and they should have the opportunity and, perhaps, the obligation to continuously refresh and improve their professional knowledge and skills.

There are various models for ensuring that individuals with a high level of professionalism enter into and advance in the judiciary; these include both the civil-service model that draws young professionals into judging and the common-law tradition of appointing judges somewhat later in life. All the candidate States – like the majority of member States – have adopted some form of the civil-service model, but both these major models have advantages and drawbacks, and reform in this area should be undertaken with a comprehensive view. For example, the emphasis that many States place on probationary periods for new judges – an evaluative method that necessarily places their adjudicative independence at risk – is often a direct consequence of the recognition that new judges have little experience; this in turn is a direct consequence of a system that hires recent university graduates as full judges.

Accountability. Guarantees of judicial independence and measures to promote the personal and institutional aptitude of individual judges must be set within the context of mechanisms to ensure judges' collective and individual accountability before society as a whole and to other branches of the State, as well as within the judicial branch itself. Indeed, as EUMAP's 2001 reports argued, accountability and independence are actually complementary expressions of society's decision to grant a limited measure of autonomy for particular common purposes, and an independent judiciary must therefore be ultimately accountable for its decisions and operations.

As a practical matter, without clear mechanisms for establishing accountability, the judiciary will ultimately fail to secure public confidence in its ability to deliver effective justice and safeguard social, economic, and democratic values. Throughout Central and Eastern Europe, increased independence has often been perceived as having unduly diminished reasonable controls needed to detect and correct abuses of power within the judiciary. Although it is always necessary to insulate judges from the political process in order to ensure their adjudicative independence, mechanisms of accountability should nonetheless ensure that judges are professionally and publicly accountable for their performance.

Some of the mechanisms for locating judicial independence within a framework of accountability include ensuring transparency and creating channels of non-controlling communication between judges, the other branches, media, and the public;[7] these mechanisms will obviously enhance the judiciary's professional capacity as well by providing feedback concerning judges' performance. In particular, judicial accountability requires that reasonably transparent mechanisms for selection of judges and for assessment of their performance be introduced, and that the judiciary's internal operations be conducted in accordance with pre-established rules subject to some measure of non-controlling external scrutiny. In the first instance, therefore, judicial accountability requires transparency and answerability, rather than formal legal liability and sanctions which always carry with them risks to judges' adjudicative independence.[8]

Organisational efficiency. Society grants judges independence not as an abstract right, but as a pragmatic privilege to ensure the public welfare; to continue to merit this status, judges and the judiciary as a whole must prove capable of resolving disputes and delivering justice in accordance with the law and in a timely, efficient manner. Indeed, enhanced administrative capacity and a new operational culture within the judiciary are important – although often overlooked – elements of meaningful judicial reform.

Although skilful judges are essential, they are not sufficient; an inadequate organisational structure will thwart the best efforts of even the most capable judges. To achieve an adequate level of systemic competence over time, the judiciary as a whole must be organised in such a way that competent and accountable judges can thrive within a supportive operational framework. Such a framework requires a strong and transparent organisational structure, qualified and highly skilled management, and adequate human, financial, and technical resources on both the national and court level.

Administrative operations of the judicial organisation should be arranged in a manner respectful of court clients' time and expense. Courts should have access to adequate levels of information processing technology and research materials, and judicial administrators should held accountable for their performance, just as judges should be. Above all, an ethos of responsibility and competence needs to be fostered – an

---

[7] *See EUMAP Reports 2001,* pp. 19–20.

[8] Consequently, issues of criminal and civil liability and professional discipline of judges, as well as corruption, judicial ethics, and conflicts of interest, although of considerable importance, are not the core focus of the 2002 reports, and will be considered only in connection with other issues. Corruption in the ten candidate States, including its serious effects on their judiciaries, is considered at length in a parallel series of reports: EU Accession Monitoring Program, *Monitoring the EU Accession Process: Corruption and Anti-Corruption Policy* (Open Society Institute, Budapest, October 2002), available at <www.eumap.org>.

especially important element given the traditionally low status of the judge in the system that formerly dominated in the candidate States.

Interrelatedness of reform efforts: These four principal elements of any meaningful judicial reform are closely interrelated, and indeed even overlapping. For example, the methods and standards for judicial selection and promotion are crucial both to protecting judges' independence and to ensuring the quality of the corps of judges.[9] Training increases judges' range of knowledge and skills – essential to their professional competence – and in the process gives them the means to be more independent, both through their increased knowledge and through autonomous management. Judges' performance evaluation in turn is a form of professional accountability, but also a means to encourage enhancement of professional skills and knowledge, and thus independence. More broadly, institutional arrangements may either support or hinder judges' independence, professional competence, accountability, and efficiency.

Ideally, any change relevant to the judiciary should be mindful of all elements of judicial capacity and should approach reform in a complex and comprehensive manner. An unduly narrow focus on one single aspect of reform, however important in itself, at the expense of the others might not lead to improved judicial performance. Indeed, it might be harmful to the judiciary's overall capacity to deliver timely, quality adjudication.

For example, exclusive attention to efficiency in terms of the speed with which cases are processed might be harmful because an effective but subservient judge compromises the very concept of neutral adjudication. Alternatively, an imbalanced emphasis on judicial independence, without regard to the broader range of factors affecting the judiciary's work, may lead to the abandonment of efforts to monitor judges' activity, and in turn to a decline in professionalism and performance.[10]

---

[9] *See, e.g.,* UN Basic Principles on the Independence of the Judiciary, Art. 10 available at <http://www.unhchr.ch/html/menu3/b/h_comp50.htm>, (accessed 8 October 2002), which directly links judicial independence to professional and personal qualities of judges: "Persons selected for judicial office shall be individuals of integrity and ability with appropriate training or qualifications in law."

[10] For example, reform efforts in Italy have shown that when judicial independence is pursued at the expense of other important values, such as judicial accountability and guarantees of professional competency, reform may prove self-defeating and ultimately even detrimental to judicial independence. *See* Giuseppe Di Federico, "Judicial Independence in Italy: A Critical Overview in a (Non-systematic) Comparative Perspective", in *Guidance for Promoting Judicial Independence and Impartiality* (United States Agency for International Development, Office of Democracy and Governance, Technical Publication series, January 2002), available at <http://www.usaid.gov/democracy/pdfs/pnacm007.pdf>, (accessed 8 October 2002).

Even more importantly, these reports do not mean to suggest that there are purely technical solutions, however comprehensive, that can ensure the effective, accountable, competent, and independent adjudication of legal disputes. The act of creating a truly independent and capable judiciary – or reforming an existing judiciary in accordance with the principles of judicial independence and capacity – is a complex social phenomenon not readily reducible to static formulae, nor is success or failure in such reform ever merely a matter of numerical evaluation or ranking. Even more than financial or technical resources, successful reform requires social and political commitment; it requires, more than anything else, an atmospheric change. Society – the populace and its governing officials – need to view the creation and maintenance of a truly independent and capable judiciary as an important shared good in the common interest, and one worthy of high priority. This is a shared goal that the Union and all its members can jointly foster.

B. The Role of the Union: Clarifying Standards for Continuing Membership

The accession process has generated an unprecedented momentum for judicial reform in the candidate States, and has demonstrated the importance of the continuing role played by the European Commission. The Commission has placed great emphasis on the ability of judiciaries to safeguard citizens' rights, contribute to a favourable business environment, and implement EU legislation,[11] as well as, more recently, on the judiciary's adjudicative and administrative independence.[12] In 2002, for example, the Commission launched an Action Plan for each candidate State's judiciary, accompanied by special financial assistance, to reinforce its administrative and judicial capacity.

Encouragement and incentives from the Commission have proved quite effective in promoting reform of the judiciary; during the last two years constitutional amendments affecting the judiciary have been adopted in Slovakia, while new comprehensive laws or significant amendments to existing ones came into force in Poland (in 2001), in Bulgaria, the Czech Republic, Estonia, Lithuania, Slovakia, and

---

[11] European Commission Strategy Paper 2001, available at <www.eumap.org> (noting that "[a] predictable and efficient judicial system is… essential for the citizen and business;" [and candidate states] "need an adequate level of… judicial capacity to implement and enforce the acquis [ ]").

[12] For the first time, in 2001, the Commission's Regular Reports all noted the importance of safeguarding judicial independence. *See* European Commission, *Regular Reports on Progress towards Accession 2001*, available at <www.eumap.org>.

Slovenia (all in 2002). Numerous specific changes have been made in all States and some Constitutional Courts have proclaimed important decisions affecting the judiciary.

In most of these States, however, the newly adopted legal acts have yet to be effectively implemented, and in many cases a number of serious flaws in existing reforms need to be rectified. The recent public and political priority given judicial reform needs, therefore, to be sustained beyond the initial legislative phase, and indeed, will only prove effective if it continues beyond the date of accession into the period of full, continuing membership.

The importance of clear standards extends beyond the current candidates for membership, however: current member States are also engaged in ongoing reform efforts aimed at enhancing judicial capacity, as the recent creation of judicial councils throughout Western Europe – in Ireland (1998), Denmark (1999), Belgium (1999), and the Netherlands (2002) demonstrates. Western European judiciaries face problems similar to those experienced by the candidate States in the East. The well-documented Italian case shows that lopsided reforms, in which only one element of judicial capacity is addressed, may lead to a situation in which the judiciary becomes a closed, unaccountable, inefficient and self-perpetuating professional guild.

In this context, the European Union, including its current members and applicants for membership, needs to ensure that the standards candidate States are called upon to meet are themselves clearly defined, rationally related to the requirements of the Copenhagen criteria, and, of course, consistently applied across the Union, to both members and candidates alike. To date, however, the accession process has shown that the Union itself needs a more comprehensive approach to the reform question. There are few standards on how the judiciary should be organised and how it should function, and the existing expert support system is often uncoordinated and ineffective.

There have also been instances when the European Commission has sent mixed signals to candidate States.[13] On occasion, the direction of judicial reforms in different countries has been dependent on expert advice from EU member States; in the absence of EU-wide standards, pre-accession advisors and representatives of twinning institutions have often simply encouraged the adoption of specific solutions imported from their own States. In some instances, their advice has arguably not been in accord

---

[13] For example, the Commission repeatedly recommended that Slovakia abolish probationary periods for judges, but has not made similar recommendations in other cases, even though several other candidate and member States use such systems, and one candidate – Slovenia – is presently considering introducing a five-year probationary period.

with clearly preferable practice or international standards.[14] Different approaches by different twinning institutions and EU-employed experts are also partly responsible for uneven reforms throughout the region. Candidate States cannot reasonably be expected to bring their judiciaries into line with standards that are themselves not defined.[15]

Judicial reform – like legal reform more broadly – will perhaps inevitably always have a highly particular, national character, given the strongly domestic focus and divergent traditions of different States' legal systems. Indeed, considering that the Union embraces members with both common-law and various civil-law systems, there will always be broad scope for choice in how States wish to organise their judiciaries – even to the point that what may be seen as essential to a just system in one may be thought antithetical to justice in another. Yet although the scope for choice may be very broad, it is not infinite; there are, and properly ought to be, areas of agreement. To the degree that the Union and its members do wish to create a community of shared values, some measure of common standards should be identified that constitutes the minimum membership requires.

One of the most valuable services the Union and the Commission could provide is to identify those common minimums, and to assist States in realising their common interest in seeing those standards met throughout the Union. Such standards, while minimal and largely reflective of existing practice in member and candidate States, should nonetheless have a prescriptive quality; they should be properly understood as expressions of the political commitments made in the Copenhagen criteria and consequently continuing obligations on all members.

The process of clarifying and defining such standards will likely require that the EU itself engage in further monitoring, much as it has done during the candidacy phase through the Commission's Regular Reports, which have proven useful tools in promoting reform. The act of monitoring – as EUMAP's own reports have sought to demonstrate – is itself a spur to the clarification of unvoiced yet commonly accepted standards. Such monitoring – whether done by the Union itself or by outside groups that have the Union's cooperation – should itself be truly independent, well-staffed and stably funded, and its findings should have political support.

---

[14] In Latvia, for example, the EU's pre-accession advisor proposed employing judges in the Ministry of Justice as a means to increase the efficiency of the Ministry, although this practice raises serious risks to judicial independence.

[15] In Slovenia, for example, the Government has claimed that certain controversial measures that tend to limit judges' independence – such as a five-year probationary period and mandatory dismissal for certain misbehaviour – are *necessary* for accession to the Union – a claim that suggests the need for the Union to clarify what it believes the content of the process and the political criteria to be.

Most importantly, standard-setting and monitoring should have consequences supported by all members. The Copenhagen criteria should be understood as vital, continuing obligations. Any deviation from the minimum common standards the Union defines for itself, whether by a candidate or a member, should be justified, not by mere assertion of privilege, tradition, or unique history, but through reasoned, convincing, and – where necessary – continuing evidence that the deviation neither violates the Criteria and the values underlying them nor the legitimate needs of an independent and capable judiciary in particular.[16] Ongoing adherence to commonly defined minimum political and democratic standards should be a *sine qua non* of membership; the power to derive those minimum standards, and to continuously monitor member States' compliance with them, is a logical and necessary function of a vital Union.

II. Overview of Country Findings

The remainder of this introductory Overview largely parallels the structure of the accompanying individual country reports and surveys their findings, providing theoretical and practical justifications for the issues they examine in detail, drawing generally applicable observations from them and highlighting particular problems of note. The country reports should be read in conjunction with this Overview, which places each report's findings in both a theoretical and regional comparative context.

---

[16] *See* Council of Europe Recommendation No. (94) 12 on the Independence, Efficiency and Role of Judges, Principle I, Art. 2c., available at
<http://cm.coe.int/ta/rec/1994/94r12.htm>, (accessed 8 October 2002),
Universal Charter of the Judge, Art. 9, available at
<http://www.iaj-uim.org/ENG/frameset_ENG.html>, (accessed 8 October 2002), ("Where this is not ensured in other ways, that are rooted in established *and proven* tradition, selection should be carried out by an independent body, that include substantial judicial representation.")(emphasis added).

A. Recent Developments Affecting Judicial Independence and Capacity – Summary of Country Findings

1. General Observations

Although generalisations about ten countries with significantly different legal systems, levels of economic development, histories, and social organisation is inevitably problematic, it is nonetheless useful to identify some trends in which all or some of the States partake. Most States have afforded some greater measure of autonomy to their judiciaries in recent years, although the degree varies greatly and some have yet to make any meaningful changes.

One interesting trend is that in those States that have afforded their judiciaries extensive autonomy, such as Hungary and Lithuania, the principal concern now is not threats to judicial independence as such, but rather the risk of an insufficiently accountable, insular and corporatist judiciary. Mechanisms for ensuring that society has non-controlling access to information about the judiciary's decision-making and administrative processes can help limit this novel risk and also help ensure that the judiciary develops its professionalism.

In other States, the risk to judicial independence remains real, as the executive continues to exercise undue influence over the administration of the judiciary and judges' career paths. This is especially true in Bulgaria, Latvia, and Romania; in the Czech Republic, this system has recently been discredited by the Constitutional Court, but no replacement has been developed. These executive-centred systems – as well as the nearly universal tendency to afford the judiciary only the most minimal involvement in budget planning – also limit the judiciary's ability to develop its professionalism by fostering continued dependence on outside expertise.

Beyond these structural concerns, there is broad scope for improvement in administrative procedures. All the States, whether or not they have devolved autonomy onto their judiciaries, continue to employ selection, evaluation and promotion procedures that are insufficiently transparent and objective. Few have adequate training systems, and none provides the kind of training in technical or managerial skills that an autonomous judiciary will need to ensure its professionalism.

2. Country Summaries

Brief summaries of each candidate State's progress and deficiencies in ensuring judicial independence and capacity follow:

It is now widely acknowledged that the many serious problems confronting **Bulgaria**'s judiciary – such as lack of clear operational standards, opaque selection and promotion, and ineffective performance evaluation – require a comprehensive, committed solution. In 2001, reform of the judiciary emerged for the first time as a central political concern. Recent legislative amendments could provide a good basis for an overall reform effort; it is now essential that they be implemented in full and in a manner fully consistent with the principles of judicial independence and judicial capacity.

Certain amendments, moreover, would actually further jeopardise the position and professionalism of the judiciary, and should be reconsidered. Beyond that, the amendments fail to address a key issue: the need to reform the Supreme Judicial Council, whose current composition unnecessarily limits judges' independence and their ability to improve the judiciary's professional capacity.

Judicial reform in the **Czech Republic** remains in a state of flux, following the Constitutional Court's recent invalidation of important parts of the new Act on Courts and Judges. In abolishing the new Act, the Court made it clear that an executive-centred model for governance and administration of the judiciary must be revised.

The Court's decision is itself a welcome corrective to a flawed piece of legislation, but courts are still in an uncertain position. The willingness to engage in serious debate about judicial reform that the political branches demonstrated in passing the Act is itself an important and welcome change; the Government and Parliament should return to the still-outstanding question of how to shape an independent, accountable and efficient judiciary.

Estonia has made significant progress in establishing and supporting an independent, capable judiciary. Courts are increasingly staffed with capable, trained professionals; reform of judicial and administrative structures is given priority on the political agenda.

The new Courts Act potentially represents a major step forward in strengthening the judicial system if its provisions are effectively implemented, especially those on the new Council for Court Administration. In particular, further progress is needed to integrate the judiciary into the budget process, to clarify judges' selection process, and to develop a comprehensive system for performance evaluation based on clear standards.

In **Hungary**, the independence of the judiciary as a separate branch is well established. Generally, the structures of judicial self-government and self-administration function efficiently. A recent ruling by the Constitutional Court has helped ensure that basic questions about the organisation of the judiciary are protected from politics.

At the same time, the continued involvement of the executive in the budgeting process for the judiciary has resulted in consistent under-funding that weakens its independence and capacity. More broadly, the very success the judiciary has had in asserting extensive autonomy makes it imperative that it continue to increase judges' professionalism and to avoid creating an insular and unaccountable institution that lacks public trust and support.

Latvia lacks a comprehensive approach to modernising and strengthening its judicial branch. Judicial reform has proceeded, when it has, in an *ad hoc* manner in response to specific problems, and has failed to establish effective systems for selecting, training, evaluating, and administering judges. The problems that plague the judiciary's operations are largely a result of consistent under-funding.

Recently proposed amendments to the laws governing the judiciary promise some improvement, but there does not yet seem to be sufficient political will to ensure that the amendments can be effectively implemented; at present the amendments even include elements that will likely do nothing to improve the judiciary's position.

Lithuania has taken a decisive step towards ensuring judicial independence; new institutions of judicial self-governance enjoy broad powers that can ensure adequate representation of the judiciary's interests and needs. Certain areas still require attention: the system for selection and promotion of judges needs to be made more merit-based and transparent; consideration should be given to developing a system of periodic assessment of performance; and training still needs to be placed on a stable and sustainable footing.

More importantly, expanded institutional autonomy makes it imperative that the judiciary also ensure its accountability, in part by acquiring specialised expertise in public administration, and enhancing the transparency of its operations; early signs suggest the system may be tending towards insularity and resistance to professionalisation.

Poland has made important progress in judicial reform in the past year. Two new Acts have introduced procedures and professional staff posts that – if properly implemented – could enhance courts' ability to manage themselves professionally and autonomously.

However, reform efforts need to be pursued more vigorously. Although courts have gained considerable autonomy, reform has proceeded piecemeal, and there have been reversals. Last year, the Ministry of Justice imposed austerity measures that demonstrated the risks to the judiciary's autonomy that exist when the executive retains fiscal or administrative supervision over courts. Whatever body retains the authority to administer the courts needs to be more transparent and to develop regularised, inclusive procedures.

Romania has made little progress in realising greater independence or professionalisation of the judiciary. Several major structural problems – such as the Ministry of Justice's continued administrative authority, and the Superior Council of Magistracy's mixed composition and joint jurisdiction over judges and prosecutors –

have not been addressed, preventing the effective and independent functioning of the judicial system and contributing to the high level of public mistrust in the courts.

Government, Parliament, and society as a whole need to commit to comprehensive and sustained reform of the judiciary's internal structure and its relationship to the rest of the State, if judges' independence and their professional capabilities are to be fully realised.

In the past two years **Slovakia** has made significant progress in clarifying the equality of the judicial branch and in strengthening the independence, competence, and efficiency of courts. Comprehensive implementation of the new Act on the Judicial Council would do much to further enhance the autonomy and efficiency of the judiciary.

Still, further improvements are clearly needed in several areas, including overly discretionary selection procedures and serious delays in case resolutions. Although recent constitutional and legislative changes have transferred certain powers to the new Judicial Council, the Ministry of Justice retains extensive responsibilities for the operation of the judicial sector. Whatever body ultimately exercises administrative control over the courts needs to develop more professional administrative capacity and expertise.

Slovenia has made considerable progress in establishing an independent and capable judiciary. Professional and political commitment has kept improvement of the judiciary at the top of the reform agenda. Legislative efforts to address discrete areas of concern – budgeting, selection procedures, evaluation, and case flow – are currently underway.

However, recently adopted legislation and proposed constitutional amendments would actually reduce the scope of judicial independence. In particular, the proposed five-year probationary period, mandatory dismissal of judges in cases of constitutional violations, and the system for setting judges' salaries should be reconsidered.

B. PROFESSIONAL COMPETENCE OF JUDGES

One of the foundations for a capable and legitimate judiciary is the professional competence of individual judges; indeed, access to professionally competent adjudication is considered a human right of court service users.[17] The most relevant tools to ensure that competent judges serve in the judiciary are those addressing judges' career path and acquisition of skills – that is, the systems for selection and promotion, performance evaluation and training. If poorly designed, these systems may allow unskilled, incompetent and unmotivated individuals to populate the bench and may discourage the development of professional standards. By contrast, rationally designed methods and procedures promote merit and stimulate the continual renewal and development of a professional and motivated cadre of judges, which in turn will ensure that society has access to more efficient and timely adjudication of its disputes.

1. Selection and Promotion

The quality of individuals selected and appointed to perform judicial functions is crucial for the capacity of the judiciary to deliver high quality services. International standards recognise the significance of objective criteria for selection and promotion,[18]

---

[17] International Covenant on Civil and Political Rights, Art. 14 (declaring the right to a competent, independent and impartial tribunal), available at <http://www.unhchr.ch/html/menu3/b/a_ccpr.htm>, (accessed 8 October 2002).

[18] Council of Europe Recommendation No. (94) 12 on the Independence, Efficiency and Role of Judges, adopted on 13 October 1994, Art. 2c, available at <http://cm.coe.int/ta/rec/1994/94r12.htm>, (accessed 8 October 2002), (declaring that selection and career of judges should be based on merit, having regard to qualifications, integrity, ability and efficiency); Universal Charter of the Judge, Art. 9, available at <http://www.iaj-uim.org/ENG/frameset_ENG.html>, (accessed 8 October 2002), (declaring that selection and each appointment of a judge must be carried out according to objective and transparent criteria based on proper professional qualification); Judges' Charter in Europe, Art. 4. (declaring that selection must be based exclusively on objective criteria designed to ensure professional competence, and judicial promotion must equally depend upon the same principles of objectivity, professional ability and independence).

and pay significant attention to the procedures employed, including what body controls the process and how is it composed.[19]

It seems incontrovertible that, as a minimum, the quality of justice directly depends on the quality of the individuals chosen to be judges; organisational systems can only do so much to improve the skill and capacity of the individuals initially chosen and promoted. The importance of the quality of judges for the overall strength of the judiciary requires that applicable criteria and procedural rules be crafted and applied in a manner that ensures clear, rational and objective selection and promotion so as to prevent cronyism or other unmerited preferences in admission to the profession or in subsequent promotion.

While in the first instance the most important considerations are that selection and promotion criteria be fair and transparent, it is of equal importance in practice that the judiciary exercise some measure of autonomous control over the process. The degree of autonomy which judiciaries exercise in selection and promotion ranges from almost absolute in Hungary and Lithuania, to minimal in Romania.

Several States still afford the executive considerable latitude in determining judges' career path, which inevitably affords opportunities to interfere with judges' adjudicative independence and tends to discourage the development of autonomous capacity within a still dependent judiciary. Where the executive still controls selection and promotion, judges' independence is stifled, and, moreover, opportunities for professional development of the judiciary as a whole tend to be more limited, because

---

[19] Council of Europe, Recommendation No. (94) 12 on the Independence, Efficiency and Role of Judges, Principle I, Art. 2c., is perhaps the most specific:
The authority taking decision on the selection and career of judges should be independent of the government and the administration. In order to safeguard its independence, rules should ensure that, for instance, its members are selected by the judiciary and that the authority decides itself on its procedural rules. However, where the constitutional or legal provisions and traditions allow judges to be appointed by the government, there should be guarantees to ensure that the procedures to appoint judges are transparent and independent in practice and that the decisions will not be influenced by any reasons other than those related to the objective criteria… These guarantees could be, for example one or more of the following:
i. A special independent and competent body to give the government advice which it follows in practice; or
ii. The right for an individual to appeal against a decision to an independent authority; or
iii. The authority which makes the decision safeguards against undue or improper influence. *See also* the Universal Charter of the Judge, Art. 9 ("Where this is not ensured in other ways, that are rooted in established and proven tradition, selection should be carried out by an independent body, that include substantial judicial representation.").

the entity with decision-making authority over judges' careers inevitably has institutional interests that diverge from those of the judiciary itself.

All candidate States have introduced novel procedures for judges' selection and promotion in an attempt to realign them with international standards. Admission to the profession and subsequent promotion are based on legally defined minimum requirements and procedural rules of various degrees of specificity. Despite unquestionable improvements, there are several aspects that are in need of reassessment from the point of view of rationality and efficiency of selection and promotion criteria and procedures. If not addressed, they will continue to undermine the credibility of the systems. There are three aspects in particular in which improvements are still needed: rules that unnecessarily limit the scope and quality of the pool of candidates; a lack of objective criteria; and an unduly closed and opaque process.

a. Unnecessarily narrow pool of qualified candidates. There is a clear tendency to narrow the pool of lawyers who are able to join the bench. Following the typical continental tradition, all the candidate States have introduced a civil-service or career model that gives preference to new law graduates or young professionals,[20] who are then gradually promoted throughout their careers. This system effectively bars – or at least strongly discourages – experienced legal professionals from entering the profession;[21] in turn, this limits the pool of qualified candidates. Although previous legal practice *per se* is no guarantee that a candidate will be a good judge, there seems to be no reason to discriminate against those who would like to bring to the bench their professional knowledge and life experiences. Indeed, diversity would not only strengthen the judiciary professionally, but would also increase its democratic legitimacy.

Moreover, when judges control the selection process without effective input from outside the judiciary, the career model may even contribute to the development of a closed and hierarchical institutional culture that is unfavourable to valuable innovation

---

[20] For example, Poland and Slovakia give clear preference to judicial apprentices – in Slovakia, a public tender for a vacant entry level position is announced only if no apprentice can fill it – and thus even judicial aspirants with extensive legal experience may be excluded in favour of less experienced apprentices.

[21] It should be noted, however, that there is a tendency to make exceptions for holders of academic degrees. In Lithuania, for example, holders of Ph.D.s with a certain number of years of pedagogical experience are eligible to join the bench. The rationale behind this exception is unclear; it is certainly questionable whether pedagogical experience is more relevant or useful than, for example, a practicing lawyer's courtroom experience.

and social responsiveness.[22] This risk is especially acute in the Czech Republic, Hungary, Lithuania, Poland, and Slovakia, and to some degree in Bulgaria.

The practice of some other States has shown that certain quotas reserved for experienced legal professionals can mitigate this drawback of the judicial career system; simply opening up the examination process to applicants of all ages and of greater experience without prejudice can likewise improve the overall quality of candidates.

b. Overly general and discretionary criteria: In a majority of the candidate States the criteria for judicial selection and promotion are overly general. The criteria typically include requirements of citizenship, legal education, civil capacity, minimum age, and either a clean criminal record or moral integrity. These requirements are frequently too minimal to guide officials and bodies responsible for making decisions about who is an adequate candidate; instead, such open and general guidelines simply allow for overly broad discretion unrelated to candidates' merit.

In Bulgaria, for example, the process of identifying, selecting and nominating candidates for judgeships is largely left to the discretion of court presidents, who submit proposals for appointment to the Supreme Judicial Council together with a statement describing the professional experience of that person. There are very few formal requirements: Bulgarian citizenship, a law degree, a clean criminal record, and a certain number of years of professional experience; candidates must also have certain undefined "required moral and professional qualities."

In Romania, judges are appointed by the State President upon the proposal of the Superior Council of Magistracy, but only following the recommendation of the Minister of Justice; the Council may not consider a candidate not recommended by the Minister, who thus has an effective and uncontrolled discretionary veto power over any candidate.

In Hungary, the powers of court presidents to determine promotion of serving judges to higher instance courts are almost entirely discretionary; in such cases, court presidents are simply entitled to select judges to fill vacant positions.

Selection and promotion criteria need to be further elaborated beyond mere formal eligibility requirements. Slovenia has taken steps in that direction, by developing more specific criteria to assess ability to perform judicial functions, such as conscientiousness,

---

[22] This issue is also an excellent example of the need for comprehensive reform: while the judiciary ought properly to have autonomous control over, or at least significant input into, the selection and promotion of judges, unrestrained or non-transparent control may, as noted here, discourage accountability and actual lessen incentives for increasing professional competence.

diligence, oral and written expressive ability, and ability to communicate and work with parties.[23]

Judicial examinations, which are a condition for admission in all candidate States except Slovenia, are generally narrow in scope and only test applicants' technical legal knowledge. While such knowledge is of course important, it should be equally important to examine an individual's personal or psychological suitability for the profession;[24] if personal abilities are not subject to verification, this may lead to the selection of 'good lawyers' who nonetheless do not have the personal maturity and sobriety needed for impartial, socially responsive adjudication. Tests should therefore aim to assess more than merely technical legal knowledge; psychological tests, such as are used in Hungary, are a step in the right direction.

The standards for oral examinations in particular need further clarification with an eye to verifying the personal qualities of candidates. Oral examinations are particularly valuable in determining the personal qualities of applicants, but they are also, by their nature, more discretionary and more open to abuse than anonymous written examinations. This trade-off is perhaps unavoidable, but States could do considerably more to ensure that oral examinations are as impartial as possible.

For example, oral examination boards should always consist of multiple members, preferably drawn from and selected by more than one organisation.[25] Interviewers should be trained, and should have clearly elaborated, written guidelines for conducting the interview. They should have to file a written assessment of each candidate; whenever possible, candidates should have the right to review and possibly appeal those assessments, which should also be available to internal assessors.

---

[23] It is not always clear, however, how these characteristics are verified.

[24] The value of the judicial examinations is also attenuated by exemption clauses existing in all countries. The rationale for such exemptions is not always clear, and they often give an unjustifiably broad discretion for the Minister of Justice. In Romania, for example, the Minister of Justice is entitled to grant an exemption to former Members of Parliament and political appointees of the Ministry.

[25] In particular, the practice of allowing the president of an individual court which has a vacancy to constitute the examination committee should be discouraged; new judges should be competent to adjudicate anywhere in the country or jurisdiction, and should consequently be selected according to standards that are, to the extent possible, reproducible anywhere. Court presidents' right to select judges for their court should, in most instances, be restricted to selecting from among candidates already approved to serve as judges anywhere in the country or jurisdiction by some other body.

Standardisation of procedures is especially needed in Latvia, where oral exams constitute the entire assessment process.[26]

c. *Unduly closed and opaque process*: The process of selection and promotion is insufficiently transparent and lacking in opportunities for outside input. In all candidate States judicial selection and promotion procedures are opaque and are confined to a small number of officials, mostly untrained judges or officials of the Ministry of Justice who are granted considerable discretion. Many details about screening procedures and determinations about individual candidates are not made public.

To minimise undue discretion and alleviate the risk of abuse, conditions for promotion and vacancies should be widely advertised, candidates should be publicly introduced, and the broader legal community – judges, lawyers' associations and legal academics – should be given an opportunity to express their views on candidates' suitability.

Procedural transparency and outside input are especially advisable for judicial systems that have achieved a high degree of administrative autonomy, such as Hungary and Lithuania. If these systems are to secure public support for their newly acquired and far-reaching independence, they must constitute their membership in a manner that is transparent and reasonably open to outside input and scrutiny. Opaque selection and promotion procedures will only contribute to suspicion of abuse and consequent public mistrust, which remains high in most candidate States.

In sum, it is inevitable and acceptable that a certain measure of discretion and confidentiality is left to members of selection committees. However, when a lack of clarity in how untrained selection committees reach decisions is combined with a lack of input from legal professionals or representatives of civil society, the value of oral interviews as a legitimate means of verifying professional aptitude is diminished, and opportunities for arbitrary or even biased selections are increased. Inclusion of representatives of legal professions and academicians in the process, better preparation for members of selection committees, and more transparent proceedings are all advisable.

---

[26] In Latvia, candidates must complete an examination before the Judicial Qualifications Board. The examination, prepared by the Courts' Department of the Ministry of Justice, consists solely of an oral interview testing the candidate's legal knowledge. There is no written component, assessment of legal reasoning or writing skills, or psychological assessment to determine the candidate's suitability for a judicial post, nor do there appear to be any grading criteria or procedures. In addition, the Board consists exclusively of judges who have received no additional training to prepare them for evaluating the suitability of judicial applicants.

2. Evaluating and Regulating Performance

Monitoring and evaluation of individual judges' performance is a relatively recent phenomenon. Increased reliance on the courts and the greater complexity of cases have resulted in higher workloads and longer proceedings, which in turn have increased public demand for competent and efficient courts. This in turn has led to the recognition in many candidate States that a system of evaluation based solely on the appeals system and the traditional administrative supervision of judges' performance is insufficient to ensure the continuous improvement of judicial performance. Lack of feedback may lead to professional stagnation and a decline in standards. In career systems periodic evaluations are especially important to ensure performance-based promotion.

Systematic assessment of individual judges' performance in accordance with pre-established standards is a form of individual accountability. Because assessment also provides a form of periodic feedback about the quality and efficiency of their work, it assists in further professional development and can also be a valuable tool in improving judges' overall capacity, especially when integrated with training programmes.

There are two principal issue areas in which candidate States' practice requires improvement: in a smaller number of States, judicial independence concerns are raised by the continuing influence of the executive over evaluation, in some cases in a manner linked to disciplinary sanctions or promotion prospects; and more generally, in all States that have evaluation systems, there is a need for greater clarification and sophistication in the standards employed.

a. Accountability and independence in the evaluation process: A primary consideration in designing any evaluation system is that it must not intrude on judges' independence or exercise of their core adjudicative function, especially where evaluation is linked to promotion or otherwise to regulation of judges' status or behaviour. This does not mean, however, that no evaluation may be conducted, or that evaluation may not have any consequences; society's legitimate interest in an accountable, efficient judiciary does provide scope for inquiring about judges' performance.

Where sanctions or significant professional consequences do attach to the outcome of evaluation, then allowing the executive to retain the power routinely to sanction judges through evaluative or disciplinary processes unnecessarily introduces serious risks to independence; the requirements of judicial independence strongly suggest that in such cases discretionary or determinative authority should reside with the judiciary or with a truly independent body within which the judiciary has meaningful participation.

Generally, as a result of the drive for greater institutional independence, the trend in the region has been to assign responsibility for evaluating judges' performance to the judiciary itself. Thus, responsibility for evaluations has been variously assigned to court presidents (Hungary, Romania, and Slovakia), special commissions composed of or controlled by judges (Latvia and Estonia respectively), court personnel councils (Slovenia), or to judges of higher courts (Poland, Romania[27]). Commonly, other individual judges – usually at the appellate level – and bodies within the judiciaries such as court councils participate in the process.

In general, the ability of judges to evaluate the professional side of their colleagues' work is certainly greater than that of outsiders, and this trend is in general a welcome development. However, if given an entirely free hand, judicial institutions may prove less attentive to legitimate concerns with judicial efficiency and accountability for misconduct than would external bodies. The case of Italy has already been cited as an example of the harm to both judicial accountability and judicial independence caused by a bias towards an overly independent and insufficiently accountable judiciary.[28]

Where judicial bodies have an exclusive or nearly exclusive authority to evaluate judges' performance, they must endeavour to demonstrate to the broader society that they can undertake this task with professionalism; non-controlling mechanisms for making evaluation procedures transparent can help ensure that the judiciary does not lapse into insular or self-serving institutional behaviour.

In certain States, however, the opposite concern still predominates: in Latvia and Romania, the Ministry of Justice has retained – and in Bulgaria, recently acquired – inspection powers that bear, directly or indirectly, on performance evaluations. In Romania, for example, there have been reports of general inspectors from the Ministry extending their evaluation to the substantive reasoning of judgements under the rubric of verifying how the law is applied in particular cases; many judges have expressed concern that the Ministry is using inspections to control the judiciary.

In Bulgaria, the Ministry of Justice's powers are even more considerable. In 1998, the Ministry acquired the power to submit a motion for disciplinary proceedings, in an attempt to overcome the reluctance of court presidents to discipline judges from their courts. Clearly, it is not desirable that the Ministry, as a branch of the executive, has

---

[27] Romania has established a system of monitoring and evaluation in which the Ministry of Justice, appellate courts and court presidents all have extensive inspection and evaluation powers.

[28] *See, e.g.*, Giuseppe Di Federico, "Judicial Independence in Italy: A Critical Overview in a (Non-systematic) Comparative Perspective", in *Guidance for Promoting Judicial Independence and Impartiality* (United States Agency for International Development, Office of Democracy and Governance, Technical Publication series, January 2002), p. 88. ("In Italy... evaluations, although still required by the law, have been de facto eliminated by the CSM [Superior Council of Magistracy], whose composition and electoral system is such as to favour the corporate career expectations of the magistrates[ ]").

such considerable powers both to propose disciplinary proceedings and to conduct what inevitably is the principal investigation.

In principle, there is nothing wrong with another branch being involved in evaluating judges, bearing in mind society's legitimate interest in judicial accountability. However, having in mind the region's legacy of executive domination of the judiciary, and the fact that the powers of Ministries are often not precisely circumscribed, this practice seems to contradict the principle of judicial independence and should be abandoned altogether.

Where organs of the executive nonetheless retain inspection powers or are otherwise involved in evaluation, there should be a clearly discernible firewall between those evaluative powers and any exercise of disciplinary power or of discretionary authority over judges' career paths – powers that, in any event, should be limited or removed as likely to be antithetical to judicial independence.

Nonetheless, a democratic system of governance does imply a principle of judicial accountability: a middle path, therefore, is to entrust evaluation to independent bodies, composed of judges and representatives of other public and private institutions, bar associations, and law schools, and which might include Ministries of Justice. Judges may have majority representation on such bodies, but other groups are also represented, and proper procedures would ensure that no one individual or one group's representatives can totally dominate the process.[29] This would inject some measure of public participation into the process, and lessen legitimate concern about corporatist bias.

An additional way in which society's legitimate interest in ensuring judges' accountability can be assured is to provide the general public with opportunities – even if only indirectly – to express its opinions about judges' performance and to have legitimate remedies for judicial misconduct. Mechanisms to encourage public input are especially important in candidate State societies that do not have a tradition of public scrutiny of the judiciary through civil society organisations.

In part, these social demands can be met by establishing effective complaint mechanisms that allow petition for action against judges for misbehaviour. Besides serving as a mechanism to initiate disciplinary procedures, public complaints can be a valuable source of information that can spur improvements in judicial performance, provided the procedure incorporates remedial as well as punitive sanctions. At present, however, no candidate State has developed a comprehensive complaint mechanism; either they are entirely absent, as in Lithuania, or lack clear guidelines and procedures

---

[29] For example, the power to initiate an evaluation for disciplinary purposes may be separated from the power to actually conduct such an evaluation; or again, evaluation and imposition of sanctions may be separated.

that would ensure that complaints are actually handled seriously, in a manner that either corrects judges' behaviour or sanctions them for misbehaviour.

An emerging issue in the region concerns whether, and to what extent, ombudsmen may properly be involved in scrutinising judges' performance. Estonia, Slovakia and Slovenia have extended to ombudsmen the power to receive public complaints concerning judges and, in certain cases, have empowered them to initiate disciplinary proceedings. A number of critics, especially from the judiciary, argue that the power to initiate disciplinary prosecution of a judge violates judicial independence. It may be too early to assess whether this novel solution complies with the principle, or even whether it is effective in supplementing other mechanisms for public complaint.

Clearly, there a need for effective mechanisms to deal with public complaints against judges besides the appeal systems and systems for monitoring and periodic evaluation of judges' performance. In general, however, an ombudsman's office should be subject to the same tests and limitations as any other separate branch in its relations with the judiciary; this is especially the case if the ombudsman's office is in fact dependent on the legislature or executive, or if its independence is in any way limited.

b. The content of evaluation: As for the content of evaluation, meaningful criteria should include at least three elements: the quality of decision-making, the efficiency of case processing, and professionalism in conduct; in addition, measurement criteria should be selected to avoid encroaching on judges' independence. The challenge, in practice, is how to define and balance these elements, and how to select sources of data and information to use, so that evaluation serves to increase the opportunities and incentives for judges to develop their professional capacity.

These are the areas in which the systems employed in many of the candidate States present problems. Two candidate States (Czech Republic and Lithuania) have yet to introduce a system of periodic evaluation of judges' performance; in others (especially Bulgaria,[30] Estonia,[31] Latvia,[32] and Poland[33]) periodic evaluation systems exist, but require significant changes to improve evaluation criteria and procedure.

---

[30] The system was introduced in July of 2002.

[31] Estonia has introduced mandatory assessment for newly appointed judges at the end of their probationary period, but thereafter full judges' performance is not subject to periodic assessments after they are appointed.

[32] In Latvia performance evaluation is linked to the qualification system that determines judges' salaries. Although the law requires that promotion to a higher qualification class should be based on judges' knowledge and work experience, judges are promoted more or less automatically after completion of the minimum time in previous qualification class.

[33] In Poland evaluations are part of regular inspections by designated judges-inspectors and are supposed to be conducted every three years, although in practice this rule is not observed.

Several of the candidate States rely heavily on quantitative measurements of judges' efficiency,[34] analysing objective data such as numbers of cases received and disposed of, or length of proceedings. However, although it may provide incentives that decrease court delays, rigidly numerical measurements may not be reliable indicators of judicial performance; for example, a judge who completes ten highly complex cases in a month may in fact be working more efficiently than one who completes twenty simple cases.

More broadly, the incentives that a numerical system create for reducing delays may in fact lower the quality of adjudication; when not complemented by qualitative criteria, purely quantitative evaluation encourage judges to focus on completing cases quickly rather than deciding them well. This is especially true where sanctions attach to negative evaluations, as is the case in several candidate and member States.[35]

Where possible, evaluation should in the first instance be routinised and integrated into training rather than employed as an extraordinary disciplining mechanism. Judges should be given an opportunity to participate in the process of evaluation and get feedback, so that they see it as an opportunity for improvement and willingly participate.[36]

For all their shortcomings, attempts to introduce quantitative indicators into performance evaluation systems are a welcome improvement over essential standard-less or discretionary evaluation, and should be further encouraged and supported. More sophisticated measurement rubrics could take a variety of factors – such as the

---

[34] For example, the Judicial Council in Slovenia has introduced the *Criteria for Determining the Projected Amount of Judicial Work* that determines purely numerical norms for disposition of cases – 18 cases per month or 180 per year for district court judges. However, the *Criteria* do not take into consideration the complexity of cases and other specific circumstances, such as court location, space and human resources.

[35] In Slovenia, for example, the Judicial Council's decisions on periodic assessments by personnel councils can affect the career path of judges, such as promotions to higher courts and higher pay brackets; a negative assessment may result in removal from office by the Judicial Council. The Council's *Criteria for Determining the Projected Amount of Judicial Work*, while primarily intended as a tool to reduce court delays, are also used in the performance evaluation process; failure to achieve projected goals in caseload has a negative effect upon evaluation of judges' performance. Judicial and academic commentators have criticised the *Criteria* and its influence on judges' careers, arguing that the quantitative indicators for judicial work are not balanced by clear, qualitative evaluation criteria.

[36] At present, only Hungary and to a certain extent Slovenia involve individual judges in their own evaluation process.

complexity of court procedures – into account,[37] and could be counterbalanced by qualitative measurements, such as knowledge of laws, practical ability to apply them, and evidence of impartiality. The EU could play a useful role in coordinating efforts to develop common minimum standards or evaluation methodologies.

3. Training for a Professional Judiciary

Effective training for judicial candidates and judges is the most direct way to enhance their capacity for impartial, competent and efficient adjudication. Lack of adequate training may lead to poor performance and may even make judges vulnerable to influence. On the other hand, well-designed training not only increases judges' core adjudicative skills, it can also help make judges more responsive and accountable by reinforcing a proper understanding of the judge's role in society.

The importance of judicial training has been recognised by the European standard-setting instruments, which declare that States should ensure initial and continuing judicial training at State expense.[38] The European Charter on the Statute for Judges further provides that any authority responsible for ensuring the quality of training programmes should be independent from executive and legislative powers and draw at least half of its membership from among judges; it also indicates that judicial training should extend beyond technical legal training to include social and cultural knowledge.[39]

All the candidate States provide judicial training in one form or another, and increasingly, judges have substantial influence over planning and implementing judicial training.[40] In general, however, the level of public and political understanding of the

---

[37] In Slovakia, for example, the existing measurement system has been changed to a point system designed to account for the complexity of individual cases. Judges have to achieve a minimum standard of 1,000 points a month, which may be accumulated in different ways. The system does not seem to have particularly alleviated the serious problem of court delays, however, and it has been criticised as not having a rational relationship to the actual amount of work judges can or should undertake.

[38] Council of Europe Recommendation No. (94) 12 on the Independence, Efficiency and Role of Judges, adopted on 13 October 1994, Principle III, Art. 1.a; European Charter on the Statute for Judges, adopted 8-10 July 1998, DAJ/DOC (98) 23, Art. 2.3 and 4.4.

[39] European Charter on the Statute for Judges, Art. 2.3. and 4.4.

[40] There is a clear trend towards transfer of responsibility for judicial training from the executive to either independent entities or bodies within the judicial branch. Only Latvia, Poland and Romania still vest overall control for judicial training in the Ministries of Justice. The negative consequences of this model are perhaps best illustrated by the unilateral and dramatic reduction in 2001 of judicial training by the Polish Ministry of Justice.

role training plays is weak, resulting in a lack of adequate resources, limited institutional capacity, haphazard planning, and a narrow, technical scope for such training as does exist.

Stable and sufficient funding is perhaps the most decisive factor for ensuring a programme of sustained training. Inadequate funding – the most direct reflection of weak political commitment – makes strategic planning, institutionalisation, and professionalisation of judicial training very difficult. In all candidate States, financial support for judicial training is low, and is even decreasing in Estonia and Poland; the Bulgarian Government does not provide any support for its Magistrates Training Centre. Rather than relying on uncertain external sources, States should develop funding mechanisms such as multi-year block grants, or clear legislative commitments to prescribed funding levels, that are based on clear standards with a rational relationship to the intended scope of training.

Given the poor funding levels, it is unsurprising that institutional capacity to provide quality judicial training is also generally limited. Four countries – Hungary, Poland, Slovakia, and Slovenia – have no permanent judicial training institutions at all, while the institutions established in other States are poorly financed and staffed, and their future prospects (in some cases, even their survival) remain unclear.[41] Slovakia provides a cautionary example of a failed attempt to implement a training programme without secured and stable financing for the length of the project.

As a result, many States in effect rely on seminars organised and funded by NGOs or foreign donors as a complement to or even substitute for institutionalised training, even though such training is generally very limited in scope and *ad hoc*, and the funding itself often project-driven and of limited duration. Yet these seminars are usually not coordinated with judges' real work and often too basic and repetitive.

Generally, judicial training programmes are narrow and rarely include topics that would help judges to meet challenges related to the ongoing transition to democratic judiciaries. Typically, judicial training programmes in the candidate States teach judges about the main branches of substantive and procedural law, but do not incorporate

---

[41] In Bulgaria, Estonia, Latvia and Lithuania judicial training has been carried out by non-governmental judicial training centres. As foreign donors gradually reduce their financial support for the programs of these centres, States should either start providing finances to these establishments or incorporate them into State-run judicial training systems, or otherwise use experience accumulated in the centres so that their potential is not wasted. In some cases, the assistance of the EU might be crucial to ensure long-term sustainability of these establishments; EU contributions to institutional capacity-building might be a better long-term investment than funding for specific training programs.

topics affecting attitudinal and behavioural change. Such training only rarely addresses relevant non-judicial skills, such as case management techniques.

Although updating judges' knowledge of the substantive law is important, well-conceived and comprehensive training should also teach practical skills necessary to deal with the increasing complexity of cases and the court caseload. At a minimum, an effective judicial training programme should address topics and skills that will help ensure that judges are adequately trained to meet the challenges that administering an autonomous and professional branch entail, such as:

- understanding of the basic elements of a democratic system of government, including the proper role of courts and judges;

- appreciation for the importance of judicial ethics, and knowledge about how to apply specific ethical concepts in practice;

- knowledge of higher legal principles that guide law-making and law implementation in a democratic system;

- familiarity with modern interpretative techniques, legal reasoning and drafting;

- critical thinking skills;

- social and psychological knowledge and people skills; and

- knowledge of case management techniques and training for court presidents.

Other factors that might improve the output of training efforts – such as ensuring that training sessions are attended by judges doing related work, mandating attendance, or even ensuring that pay, promotion and evaluation systems do not incorporate implicit disincentives for judges to attend[42] – are generally absent, and should be considered.

C. INSTITUTIONAL CAPACITY OF THE JUDICIARY

Much of the attention paid to the judiciary has focused on the large-scale legal or constitutional framework, or on individual judges' adjudicative independence. Equally important in ensuring that judges enjoy a proper scope of authority, however, is the judiciary's collective administrative and managerial capacity, at both the national and

---

[42] Slovenia's *Criteria for Determining the Projected Amount of Judicial Work* seem to discourage participation in training: while the *Criteria* provide for reduction in workload for judges with administrative responsibilities, they do not make any accommodation for judges attending professional development seminars.

court levels. An autonomous judiciary will be better able to respond with flexibility to its own perceived needs than will one that is directed by an external authority. The organisational set-up of the judiciary, its operational standards and practices, and its level of managerial and administrative expertise have direct and indirect links to the independence, competence and efficiency of the judicial process.

1. Governance and Administration of the Judicial Branch

In the region as a whole, there is a clear trend towards transfer of governing, representative and administrative powers to bodies formed outside the executive branch and controlled by judges, who thereby undertake a collective responsibility for their conduct and role. However, there are still a number of States in which the executive retains an unduly intrusive level of involvement in judicial administration at the national level.

Although constitutional and legal guarantees for the separation of powers and judicial independence have long been recognised in Europe, and in the candidate States since the early 1990s,[43] only recently has the concept of the judiciary as a single, national entity gained wide currency, recognising that limits to judges' independence and professional capacity may come from more indirect sources, as well as from direct intervention, and that judges collectively require some broader measure of autonomy in order to develop their ability to provide society with effective and impartial adjudication of its disputes.[44]

Judges who feel that they are responsible for or can influence the administration of their own affairs are likely to have more incentives to act as equal, active participants in improving judicial performance. Institutional reform giving judges a meaningful role in organising court operations on the national level is a means to enhance judicial

---

[43] In the candidate States in particular, the legacy of the recent past has provided an additional impetus towards institutional reform. Under the previous regime judiciaries were of little relevance and low status, and were subordinated to and dependent on the executive for all their needs, including funding and administrative support. This legacy has made it more difficult for the political branches to recognise judiciaries as equal partners; the perception that the judiciary is a public sector that has to be guided, managed and supervised persists, and has partly prevented judges from developing a collective sense of themselves as a separate, independent and equal branch.

[44] *See, e.g.,* Judges' Charter in Europe, Art. 6 (declaring that administration of the judiciary must be carried out by a body representative of the judges and independent of any other authority). Indeed, when another branch is responsible for the judiciary, it will always have incentives and opportunities to make the judiciary a lower priority. *See EUMAP Reports 2001,* p. 24.

competence, impartiality and efficiency, provided judges are willing and able to develop a necessary expertise and sound and transparent operational practices.

Among the candidate States there are three basic models for governance and administration, which may be broadly termed independent, intermediate or power-sharing, and executive-centred. Budgeting matters will be considered separately, as in general across the region judges have very little real involvement in the budgeting process, which in turn limits their effective degree of autonomy under any of these models.

a. Independent model – Hungary and Lithuania: This model provides for autonomous governing and administrative bodies – commonly called Judicial Councils[45] – that assume all but political responsibilities for the system of justice. Such a system creates a framework with strong potential to improve judicial performance, but in turn requires an additional focus on developing an administrative capacity within the independent governing and administrative bodies, since they may no longer rely on expertise and support from the executive; more broadly, such newly autonomous institutions may have to confront a professional culture that commonly is reluctant to admit external expertise into the judiciary.[46] It is also important that institutionally independent judiciaries operate transparently; without specialised expertise and transparent procedures, judiciaries may become inefficient, unresponsive, unaccountable, and distrusted professional guilds.

Both Hungary and Lithuania have created largely self-governing and self-administering judiciaries. The Judicial Councils are policy-setting, representative and decision-making institutions. They approve draft budgets for courts, provide a regulatory framework for court operations, supervise court activities, decide on matters related to judicial selection and careers, and participate in disciplining judges. Independent national offices for court administration service the Councils; these offices assist the Councils through research, analysis and preparation of decisions and implementing Councils' decisions, and are responsible for the day-to-day operations of courts.

The Hungarian Judicial Council and Office have been operational since 1998, and appear to be efficient and fairly transparent institutions; they have adopted a number

---

[45]   *See, generally,* Wim Voermans, *Councils for the Judiciary in EU Countries,* (European commission/TAIEX, Tilburg University/Schoordijk Institute, 1999), *available at* <http://cadmos.carlbro.be/Library/Councils/Councils.html#_Toc459267097>, (accessed 21 June 2002).

[46]   *See, e.g.,* Giuseppe Di Federico, "Judicial Independence in Italy: A Critical Overview in a (Non-systematic) Comparative Perspective", in *Guidance for Promoting Judicial Independence and Impartiality* (United States Agency for International Development, Office of Democracy and Governance, Technical Publication series, January 2002), p. 93.

of standards to ensure competent and efficient court procedures, and publish annual reports on their activities. The Office in particular could benefit from developing clearer requirements for non-legal positions to ensure that competent professional managers and experts are employed. (The Lithuanian Office for National Court Administration has only recently started operations.)

The Hungarian experience also shows that the autonomy afforded a self-managing judiciary may be limited by the effects of the budgetary process, in which the judiciary's involvement is still nominal. Even though the National Judicial Council drafts a budget proposal, the executive has the right to draft a parallel proposal, which Parliament has in practice accepted as the basis for its deliberations instead of the Judicial Council's proposal. In these circumstances, it is not clear how much practical participation the judiciary actually enjoys, despite its formal rights.

The new Government has pledged to respect the budgetary powers of the National Judicial Council; however, reliance on the good will of changing Governments undermines the very idea of judicial self-governance and, in practical terms, leads to consistent under-funding of the judiciary, which has direct repercussions on judicial capacity.

b. Intermediate or power-sharing systems – Bulgaria, Estonia, Poland, Romania, Slovakia, and Slovenia: Although the precise form of judicial organisation in these States differs significantly, in all of them governing and administrative powers over the judiciary to a certain degree are shared between an autonomous Judicial Council and another body, usually in the executive.

These Judicial Councils do not have the same degree of governing authority as the Hungarian or Lithuanian models, but they generally have significant responsibility for or participation in personnel decisions such as judicial selection, promotion and discipline, which in principle should help to safeguard judges' independence. Increasingly, Councils also give their consent or issue advisory opinions on matters such as draft budgets and draft legal acts relevant to operations of the judiciary. In some cases, they may exercise certain standard-setting powers, such as determining norms for court workloads (Slovenia). However, the Ministries of Justice retain major or exclusive powers related to policy-making, the budget process and court administration. Sometimes Supreme Courts, as in Slovenia, perform certain representative and decision-making functions.

This model may well constitute an improvement in policy-making and administration over the executive-centred model, provided the Judicial Council is able effectively to counterbalance the Ministry of Justice in areas of joint decision-making. However, the practice to date in the candidate States suggests that there are major obstacles to full realisation of this model's potential for reform, including problems with the composition of Councils, control over their agenda, their administrative capacity, and clarification of the division of powers between the Ministry and the Council.

These obstacles are especially evident in Bulgaria and Romania. Bulgaria has created an institutional structure that, on paper, is quite close to the independent model, while Romania has followed the French model of a more limited Council that primarily participates in personnel decisions. However, in their practical operations, these councils' ability to act autonomously, or to protect the legitimate interests of the judiciary and promote its professional development, is quite limited.

One of the most important limits concerns the Council's composition. Councils in both States include prosecutors, and in Bulgaria investigators, as well as judges. The negative consequences of a mixed composition are best illustrated by the Bulgarian example. The conflicting interests of judges, prosecutors and investigators – and the bodies that elect them to the Council – have often limited the ability of the Council to provide consistent management; instead, different management rationales – arising from the different role investigators, prosecutors and judges play – have led to conflicting policies being imposed on the justice system. For example, as the Government is held politically responsible for successfully tackling crime, it has had a clear interest in establishing some control over investigation and prosecution in order to carry out consistent policies to combat crime. This had led three Governments to pass legislation replacing the Supreme Judicial Council before its constitutionally mandated term had expired. Such direct political intervention inevitably creates disincentives for Council members to take principled positions at odds with the interests of the Government in power, even if those interests might be detrimental to the professional development of the judiciary.

Romania represents a striking example of the need for Councils to control their own agenda or, at least, participate in shaping it. The Superior Council of Magistracy participates in decisions relating to judges' career paths, and can express opinions on draft laws and matters concerning courts' administration; however, the Council can act only upon the Minister of Justice's proposals. In effect, this Council appears to act as a rubber-stamp institution for important decisions taken elsewhere.

The ability of the Councils to efficiently fulfil their tasks also depends on their administrative capacity, which tends to be insufficient in all candidate States that follow a power-sharing model. The Ministries of Justice tend to continue to provide administrative support for Councils. The administrative capacity of Bulgaria's Supreme Judicial Council, for example, is clearly insufficient to handle its many formal responsibilities; in practice, the Council relies on the Ministry, which has a far larger staff, for administrative support and standard-setting. The Councils' administrative dependence on the Ministries, especially when coupled with the Ministries' control or significant influence over agendas and funding, and the lack of a precisely defined division of powers between them, may give the Ministries an opportunity to influence the administration of the judiciary to an extent beyond their legal mandate.

The often-indistinct division of responsibilities between the Council and the Ministry and the low administrative capacity of the Council contribute to regulatory deficiencies. To a certain degree, all candidate States lack sufficient standards in areas such as caseload norms (which provides the basis for determining the number of judges and court staff), budget preparation, distribution of allocated funds, technology and equipment, court space and facilities. In Slovenia, for example, the Supreme Court in coordination with the Ministry of Justice formulates the budget for the judiciary on the basis of courts' financial plans and presents it to Government, while the Judicial Council also provides its opinion on the proposed budget; however, the judiciary is rarely represented during the crucial stage when the State budget is deliberated within the executive, as the Ministry of Justice, being a member of the Government, has no formal responsibility to represent it.

c. The executive-centred model: the Czech Republic and Latvia: Under this model the judiciary is not treated as a separate entity, but rather as an agency subordinated to the Ministry of Justice. The Ministry develops and supervises the policy of the judicial system and exercises governing, representative and administrative powers over it, with the exception of the self-governing Supreme Courts.[47] Ministerial powers include drafting the budget for the judiciary, allocating funds, determining the numbers of judges and court personnel, selecting and disciplining judges, appointing and dismissing court presidents, and setting standards such as caseload norms. Typically, the Ministry also exercises broad monitoring powers with regard to the organisation and functioning of courts and judges. Court presidents function effectively as officers of the executive.

The executive-centred model not only violates the principle of judicial independence, it does little to promote efficiency in management and administration. It has not been successful in involving judges in improving their professional capacity, but rather has encouraged dependency and limited initiative.

Moreover, despite their extensive authority, these Ministries of Justice have not proven able to ensure courts' efficient operation. Their leadership has been unstable, with frequent changes of ministers[48] exposing the judiciary to shifting political priorities. Most importantly, the Ministries lack the expertise necessary to develop clear and

---

[47] Traditionally, Supreme Courts are self-managing institutions under all institutional models. In practice, although Supreme Courts are administratively autonomous from the court system, Supreme Court judges and especially Supreme Court presidents often speak on behalf of the whole judiciary.

[48] In Poland, for example, where the Ministry of Justice plays a major role in judicial administration, there have been five Ministers of Justice over the last 25 months.

rational standards that would assist in the modernisation of courts to support competent and efficient adjudication. In Latvia, for example the EU pre-accession advisor has noted that the Ministry's employees have insufficient professional capacity, caused by frequent staff changes and inexperience;[49] this has resulted in a lack of clear criteria in areas such as budgeting, numbers of judges and support staff, or norms for technology and equipment.

Both Latvia and the Czech republic should revise their existing models for governance and administration to provide judges with autonomous mechanisms to articulate and defend their interests. Regardless of which model is adopted, however, these judiciaries need more professional and transparent management.

d. Budgeting and infrastructure: Much of the progress that has been made towards administrative autonomy is limited, however, by restrictions on judges' participation in the budgetary process. Control over the judicial budget may function as a powerful economic tool that directly affects judicial capacity. While it is normal in a democracy for the legislature to exercise predominant control over budget decisions, input or participation from the judiciary helps ensure that the judges' legitimate interests are protected from indirect economic pressure. Judges are best positioned to make informed estimates about the investment needs of courts; in turn, judges who are at least partly responsible for budgetary decisions – or at least for allocation of budgets – are more likely, over time, to take responsibility for courts' administration, and in so doing develop their own ability to act autonomously and professionally.

Where, however, such control is completely insulated from judges' input or participation, legislatures tend to give judicial funding a lower priority; in turn, under-funding results in reduced investment, lower professional standards and outdated infrastructure. Under-funding can contribute to maintenance of a culture of administrative dependence in the judiciary, and over time, under-funding undermines judicial independence, making individual judges and court staff more vulnerable to economic corruption, and making courts as institutions more dependent on economic largesse from the political branches and less able to defend their legitimate interests.

In most of the candidate States, the courts have been chronically under-funded. In part, as noted, this has been a consequence of judges' minimal opportunity to participate in the budgetary process (except, to some degree, in Hungary[50] and Lithuania), as well as a lack of clear methodology or standards for determining budget allocations, and even, in those cases in which the courts do have some say, a

---

[49] Court System Reform of Latvia, Tiesu Namu Agentura, Riga, 2001, pp. 26, 30.

[50] *See* section II.C.1.a. of this report.

demonstrably low level of professionalism in preparing budget requests.[51] If courts are granted greater participation in the budget process, relevant officials – court presidents or court managers – should be trained in principles of budgeting and finance; at present, no State provides such training.

2. Court Administrative Capacity

Much day-to-day administration occurs at the court level; the increase in courts' relevance and the growing quantity and complexity of litigation require that court operations be modernised not only technologically, but also organisationally. The current general model employed throughout the candidate States – that of relying on untrained court presidents – is inadequate; steps should be taken to introduce or strengthen professional management skills into the courts.

In all candidate States court presidents perform important managerial functions, yet their managerial competence is limited; despite broad responsibilities for ensuring efficient court operations, court presidents receive no managerial education or training. There are no systems for post-appointment training for judges in managerial positions, and the occasional courses offered on topics relating to court management are not sufficient to enable court presidents to manage increasingly complex court operations.

In addition, in all candidate States, judges who are not in managerial positions are nonetheless frequently involved in court administration – such as supervision of registries, court archives, enforcement offices – technical tasks related to pre-trial and post-trial phases,[52] and simple, non-contentious legal acts such as registry entries. Judges overloaded with numerous administrative, technical and professional non-adjudicative tasks cannot deal adequately with their core adjudicative functions.

Courts across the region are therefore in need of more competent management and administrative support. As an interim measure, court presidents should receive special training in areas such as strategic planning, personnel management and case management as a priority. Even if they were adequately trained, however, judges performing managerial tasks necessarily have less time to devote to their core

---

[51] In Lithuania, for example, a State audit found that a district court had failed to follow mandatory budgeting procedures laid out in the statewide regulation on drafting budgets.

[52] Research conducted in Hungary shows that, on average, trial time occupies 27 percent of judges' time and writing judgements 15 percent, with the remainder devoted to administrative tasks such as management, statistics and dictation of trial records.

adjudicative work.[53] A more effective long-term solution would be to concentrate on professionalising court management by transferring certain management functions to non-judicial professionals operating under court presidents' overall supervision.

Courts should employ trained managers who know how to plan court operations, perform budgeting tasks, and manage court infrastructure and personnel. Bulgaria, Estonia, Poland and Slovenia have recently introduced new court administrative positions, such as managing directors or court secretaries. In the long run, this may improve court management, provided that judges are willing to transfer to these new professional officials meaningful and clearly delineated powers, and steps are taken to ensure that these positions are filled by individuals with relevant education and skills.[54]

Throughout the region the quantity and quality of court support staff is insufficient – again in part a function of chronic under-funding. Salaries are generally quite low – commonly lower than salaries of comparable administrative staff in other branches – and work conditions difficult, and there are few prospects for professional growth; the situation is especially troublesome in the Czech Republic,[55] Latvia, and Romania, making it difficult to hire and keep even junior court staff members, yet recent reforms have not addressed this problem. In all States consideration should be given to improving remuneration, training, and work conditions for court support staff.

Courts could also improve efficiency by employing trained junior legal and administrative staff for specific quasi-judicial and non-judicial tasks such as the non-contentious register and records or case management; junior staff positions with competencies similar to those established in Poland, or of *greffiers* or *Rechtspfleger*, could be considered. Such employees also should be given an opportunity to regularly upgrade their competence through on-going training. Such a system would free up judges to concentrate on their core adjudicative functions.

In addition to its deleterious effects on the judiciary's ability to develop professional administrative skills, insufficient funding directly creates a number of concrete problems that restrict courts' capacity to deliver quality judicial services. Physical court conditions in most candidate States need considerable improvement, especially in Latvia, Lithuania and Romania. Chronic lack of investment has resulted in shortages of space, poor facilities, and

---

[53] In Romania court presidents, who are usually experienced judges, reportedly devote 90 percent of their time to handling administrative matters, and consequently have little time for adjudication or for assisting less experienced judges.

[54] In Slovenia, court secretaries – who hold managerial positions in all but district courts – are lawyers, not trained managers.

[55] In the Czech Republic, salaries of court support staff range between 6,000 and 12,000 Czech crowns (€200 to 400), while the average income is now 16,000 Czech crowns (€540).

out-dated equipment. Only in Estonia and Slovenia are working conditions generally satisfactory, although in Slovenia some courts still lack sufficient space.

Modernisation is especially needed for record management, case-flow management, case statistics, and trial recording. In a number of States court documents are still processed manually, while trial recording is likewise still performed with dictaphones or by hand, which greatly increases the opportunities for error and corruption; Romania's archaic system of manually maintained case registers, and Lithuania's partial and handwritten trial recording system in particular need reform and modernisation. Automated document systems and real-time recording would increase administrative efficiency and enhance the courts' ability to provide professional judicial services.

Case backlogs in particular continue to plague consumers of court services in most candidate States. Case backlogs negatively affect the quality of judgements and damage public trust in courts. The problem is especially severe in Latvia,[56] Romania, Slovakia, and, according to anecdotal evidence, in Bulgaria;[57] the situation has stabilised or slightly improved in the Czech Republic, Estonia, and Slovenia.

Most of the infrastructure and administrative improvements discussed above would contribute directly to more efficient and speedier case resolution by allowing judges to concentrate more on adjudication, which in turn, would speed up court proceedings and decrease case backlogs. In addition, more concentrated effort is needed on legal reform, such as decriminalisation of certain offences, simplified procedural rules and alternative methods of dispute resolution; very few candidate States have comprehensive programmes in place to explore alternatives that reduce reliance on the courts.

---

[56] In Latvia, courts regularly disregard procedural requirements concerning time limits for hearing cases. In many courts the docket is so full that cases are scheduled several years in advance. The worst situation is in the Riga regional court, which is currently scheduling hearings for 2004; appeals in criminal cases are sometimes reviewed after the appellants have served their sentences and been released.

[57] Bulgaria does not have a reliable case tracking and information system.

D. RECOMMENDATIONS

Recommendations directed to individual States are included in the country reports. Here, only generally applicable recommendations and recommendations to the EU are noted.

1. To Candidate States

- Ensure that judicial reform aimed at consolidating the judiciary's independence and enhancing its professional capacity is made a political priority.

- In countries in which the executive retains control or influence over the administration of the judiciary or over judges' career paths, reduce or eliminate that influence so as to ensure judges' adjudicative independence. Consider the introduction of autonomous judicial administration.

- In countries in which the judiciary already has considerable autonomy, ensure that society's legitimate interest in accountable adjudication is protected by the introduction of transparent, non-controlling forms of input and scrutiny.

- Consider revising budget procedures to give courts greater input into the process, so as to ensure that courts' administrative autonomy can be meaningfully realised.

- Develop more objective, regularised, merit-based, and transparent procedures for administering judges' career paths.

- Consistent with the principles of judicial independence and accountability, take steps to develop systems for periodic evaluation of judicial performance that are transparent and based on balance of relevant quantitative and qualitative criteria. Consider integrating performance evaluation with training programs.

- Ensure that judges' training is financed in a stable and sustainable manner. Incorporate technical and managerial skills into training curricula.

- Introduce more professional management at the court level. Transfer managerial and administrative functions from judges to trained professionals under their supervision.

2. To the European Union

- Stress that the creation and maintenance of an independent, capable judiciary is a core value common to the Union and a continuing obligation of EU membership.

- Assist States in developing effective reforms by clarifying the content of values common to the Union with regard to an independent and functional judiciary, and consequently the minimal expressions of those values, in concrete policies, that continuing membership requires.

- Emphasise the importance of comprehensive rather than fragmentary judicial reform to address the lack of institutional independence and capacity in the judicial system.

- Drawing upon the experiences of other candidate and member States, provide technical assistance in the establishment of appropriate criteria and methods for selection to judicial office, promotion, and performance evaluation.

- Support efforts to ensure that judicial training has sufficient, stable, and sustainable funding. Support institutional consolidation of judicial training and facilitate exchange of judicial educators with training institutions in other EU candidate and member States in order to improve training in relevant judicial and management skills for judges and administrative skills for court managers and personnel.

- Consistent with the principles of judicial independence and accountability, take steps to develop systems for periodic evaluation of judicial performance that are transparent and based on balance of relevant quantitative and qualitative criteria. Consider integrating performance evaluation with training programs.

- Ensure that judges' training is financed in a stable and sustainable manner. Incorporate technical and managerial skills into training curricula.

- Provide technical support for programmes to reduce endemic court delays and backlogs.

Judicial Capacity in Bulgaria

Table of Contents

A. Introduction

Following the elections in June 2001, reform of the judiciary – including strengthening its independence and improving its performance – emerged for the first time as a central political concern. The new Government adopted several documents targeting deficiencies in the current system and in July 2002 Parliament approved amendments to the Judicial System Act as a first step in implementing reform.

It is now widely acknowledged that the many serious problems confronting the judiciary – such as lack of clear operational standards, opaque selection and promotion, and ineffective performance evaluation – require a comprehensive and committed solution. The envisaged reforms and the legislative amendments address a broad range of outstanding problems and provide a good basis for an overall reform effort. It is now essential that they be implemented in full and in a manner fully consistent with the principles of judicial independence and judicial capacity, if they are to improve the performance and independence of the judiciary.

Certain amendments, however – such as the amendments granting the Ministry of Justice an important role in the promotion procedure – would actually further jeopardise the position and professionalism of the judiciary, and should be reconsidered. Beyond that, the amendments fail to address a key issue: the need to reform the Supreme Judicial Council, the body that jointly governs judges, prosecutors and investigators, and in so doing unnecessarily limits judges' independence and their ability to improve the judiciary's professional capacity.

B. CURRENT DEVELOPMENTS AFFECTING JUDICIAL INDEPENDENCE AND CAPACITY

The Government has outlined a broad-ranging strategy to address the admitted need for comprehensive reform of the judiciary, and in July 2002 Parliament approved amendments to the Judicial System Act to enact the strategy. The amendments address a broad range of outstanding problems, but on many important issues they leave the actual standards to be developed by secondary legislation. Only if the legislative amendments are implemented in full and in a manner consistent with the principles of judicial independence and judicial capacity will they contribute to meaningful and much needed reform. In particular the increased involvement of the Ministry of Justice in promotion procedures should be reconsidered.

1. The Reform Proposals – Amendments to the Judicial System Act

In October 2001 the Government published a *Strategy Paper on the Reform of the Bulgarian Judicial System*,[1] outlining its priorities for reform of the judiciary as well as the prosecutorial and investigative services. The *Strategy Paper* was drafted in cooperation with the Supreme Judicial Council and in discussion with representatives of the judicial system. The high priority the new Government attached to judicial reform was clearly the result of the increased attention given the issue by the European Union.[2]

The *Strategy Paper* outlines a number of serious shortcomings in the functioning of the judiciary: inefficient court administration and case management; substantial delays in hearings and in delivering judgements; poor enforcement; lack of a clear distinction between the powers of the Supreme Judicial Council and the Ministry of Justice; a poor level of selection and training of the judges; lack of sufficient financial resources; and lack of a uniform information system that would allow tracking of individual cases from start to completion.

---

[1] Strategy Paper on the Reform of the Bulgarian Judicial System, Council of Ministers Decision no. 672 of 1 October 2001, *at* <http://www.mjeli.government.bg/strategiaus.htm> (in English) (hereafter, "Strategy Paper"), (accessed 25 September 2002).

[2] In its introductory part the Strategy Paper recognised the EU accession process and the political criteria of stability of institutions guaranteeing rule of law as a major impetus for the judicial reform, stating that "joining the EU requires the finalisation of the reform of the judiciary." *See* Strategy Paper, Preamble.

The *Strategy Paper* and a subsequent document, the *Implementation Program*,[3] outlined steps to be taken to counter those deficiencies; these would:

- introduce competitive selection of judges based on "uniform criteria for selection and appointment[;]"

- introduce standard evaluation of judges' performance prior to granting life tenure;

- introduce a system of workload monitoring and performance evaluation, and clear performance standards for promotion;

- adopt a Code of Ethics and improved disciplinary procedure;

- introduce continuing training for judges and support personnel and create a comprehensive training institution;

- improve case management and introduce a uniform information system;

- increase the Supreme Judicial Council's administrative capacity;

- streamline cooperation between the Ministry of Justice and the Supreme Judicial Council;

- introduce alternative dispute resolution mechanisms;

- improve access to justice; and

- introduce measures to improve the public image of the judiciary.

To give effect to the bulk of these proposals, Parliament approved a set of draft amendments to the Judicial System Act in July 2002.[4] The new amendments address issues of court management, initial appointment and subsequent promotion of judges, training and training infrastructure, performance evaluation, the relations between the Judicial Council and the Ministry of Justice, judicial ethics, and discipline; they also create a court security office, and introduce some anti-corruption measures.

In some important aspects the amendments to the Judicial System Act are only a first step laying down the ground rules for future regulation, which the Supreme Judicial Council will enact. This is the case with respect to the initial appointment of judges and performance evaluation, for example, for which the actual standards and procedures will be adopted only later in secondary regulations. This means that the

---

[3] Program on Implementing the Strategy Paper, *at* <http://www.mjeli.government.bg/program.htm.>, (accessed 25 September 2002).

[4] Judicial System Act, State Gazette, No. 59, 22 July 1994, last amended State Gazette no 74, 30 July 2002.

success of reform will depend, to a significant degree, on the actions of a constitutional body that itself is in need of reform in order to ensure the judiciary's independence and to increase its institutional and adjudicative capacity.

There are also certain problems with the amendments as adopted. For example, the amended Judicial System Act includes a procedure for promotion of judges that gives the Ministry of Justice powers over the process,[5] a step that unnecessarily introduces a threat to judicial independence.

Still, the impetus towards comprehensive reform is correct, because the problems identified in the *Strategy Paper* and partly addressed by the amendments to the Judicial System Act are serious. The reform proposals, particularly the amendments to the Act, need to be implemented fully and with a serious commitment to the principles of judicial independence and enhanced judicial capacity if they are to succeed in addressing those problems. The legislative amendments should also be followed by constitutional amendments addressing the current set-up of the Supreme Judicial Council.

C. PROFESSIONAL COMPETENCE OF JUDGES

The recent amendments to the Judicial System Act have improved the regulatory framework for selection and promotion; however, the amendments still must be effectively implemented in secondary legislation and actual practices. The selection process still lacks transparency and clarity, leaving undue discretion to decision-makers and undermining the credibility of the system; it is crucial that implementing regulations address these shortcomings if reform is to succeed. Likewise, the amendments lay the groundwork for improved performance evaluation and public complaint systems, but require comprehensive secondary implementing legislation to be truly effective; in addition, the increased role given to the Ministry in discipline ought to be examined. The training system requires long-term commitment, including stable funding sources and careful implementation of the proposed organisational transformation, building upon existing experience.

1. Selection and Promotion

Despite recent changes, the system for selection, appointment and promotion is still unsatisfactory; the process of identifying and nominating candidates lacks clear

---

[5] *See* Section D.1., "Governance and Administration of the Judicial Branch".

selection criteria and transparency and decision-making is unduly discretionary, which in turn undermines the credibility of the system.

While the amendments create the basis for the improvement of the selection and promotion system by introducing more open competition, this change is limited to the lowest level. At other levels the amendments reinforce the existing powers of court presidents; they also increase the influence the Ministry of Justice exercises over the promotion of judges, which unnecessarily puts judges' independence at risk. The amendments' real effectiveness will to a large extent depend on secondary regulations adopted by the Supreme Judicial Council, their proper implementation and the actual practices established.

The process of identifying, selecting and nominating candidates for judgeships is largely left to the discretion of court presidents. Candidates are identified and nominated by court presidents, and appointed by the Supreme Judicial Council.[6] Court presidents submit their proposal for appointment to the Supreme Judicial Council together with a statement describing the professional experience of that person. There are very few formal requirements: Bulgarian citizenship, a law degree, a clean criminal record, and a certain number of years of professional experience; candidates should also have "the required moral and professional qualities."[7]

It is not clear how court presidents identify eligible candidates or how their moral and professional qualities are assessed, but apparently personal contacts and preferences account for the major part of the decision-making process.[8] The procedure does not provide for input from relevant professional organisations of lawyers and judges. Given the limited information that the Council receives, it is largely bound by the nomination forwarded by the court president, who therefore exercises considerable influence over the process. The judiciary follows the career model, and promotion to a

---

[6] Judicial System Act, Art. 30.

[7] Judicial System Act, Art. 126 (4).

[8] If candidates address the Supreme Judicial Council directly, their request is referred to the president of the respective court for an opinion. As a practical result such candidates are not appointed.

higher-level court is treated as a new appointment, with the same potential for court presidents to influence the process.[9]

In recent years, on their own initiative, some courts have launched open competitions for initial appointment as a junior judge.[10] In the Sofia City Court, the first to adopt such a system, an examination committee appointed by the court president conducts a public competition consisting of written and oral examinations. On the written examination applicants analyse hypothetical cases addressing both civil and criminal law; applicants whose papers receive the best grades are invited for an interview with the committee. The interviews focus on legal issues, and ethical issues are barely raised.[11] The examination committee then submits a prioritised list of candidates to the court president, which he or she follows in nominating junior judges.[12]

Such open competitions are certainly a positive step, although as yet they are not administered in many courts. At present seven of the 27 regional courts have followed suit, running open competitions for junior judge vacancies.[13] The presidents of the respective courts decide the content and evaluation of such exams on an *ad hoc* basis, though they generally follow the model of the Sofia City Court. In such exams only the applicants' knowledge of the law is tested; there are no procedures for evaluating candidates' personal or ethical qualities. Even when an open competition is held, moreover, the Supreme Judicial Council does not receive information on the competition itself, but only on the person nominated for appointment. Finally, open

---

[9] Although there is no formal legal basis for the practice, the Supreme Judicial Council has normally required that proposals for promotion include statistical information as to the overall number of cases heard by the judge, the time within which judgements were delivered and the percentage of judgements overturned on appeal. This information is collected by the administrative personnel of the court from the case files. Because different types of cases require different amounts of work, and because judges are often specialised and hear only certain type of cases, a merely quantitative comparison of case statistics is not necessarily a good indication of performance.

[10] A junior judge is appointed to the regional court, where he or she sits in a panel of three judges. Junior judges participate in hearings and write judgements and generally exercise the full rights of a judge; however, as junior judges are just out of law school, they are considered trainees. After two years on the regional court, a junior judge is normally appointed to a district judgeship, where he or she sits and acts alone. This effectively extends the time before tenure is granted to five years.

[11] Candidates' professional records do not play a role, as all candidates have just completed law school.

[12] Interview with Dragomir Yordanov, Director of the Magistrates Training Centre, July 2002.

[13] Regional courts in Blagoevgrad, Burgas, Gabrovo, Plovdiv, Smolyan, Stara Zagora and Sofia run open competitions. Interview with Ignat Kolchev, President of the Smolyan District Court, July 2002.

competitions are only run for junior judges, who will be appointed to a regular judicial position in a district court just two years later without a competition.[14]

The amendments to the Judicial System Act require open competitions for the appointment of junior judges. For other judicial positions, court presidents are obliged to run an open competition only if there are no candidates for the vacancies among acting judges, junior judges, prosecutors and investigators.[15] The conditions and procedures for such competitions have not been outlined by the amendments, however; this responsibility has been delegated to the Supreme Judicial Council.[16]

The legislative amendments have also changed the procedure for promotion after the initial appointment. Appointment is still decided by the Supreme Judicial Council upon a proposal introduced by the relevant court president. Before submitting such a proposal however, the president must appoint a committee to evaluate the candidate.[17] Considering the method of composing the evaluation committee, there is little reason to suppose it will introduce any greater rigour or consistency into the promotion process. The amendments have adopted some general guidelines[18] as to the criteria on which the evaluation should be based, but have delegated the adoption of detailed procedures and criteria to the Council.[19]

In addition, the draft amendments unnecessarily increase the power of the Ministry of Justice to influence the promotion procedure. Any proposal for promotion to a higher court must to be submitted by that court's president to the Minister, who then submits it with an opinion within seven days to the Supreme Judicial Council;[20] the Minister may also directly nominate a judge to the Council for promotion on his own initiative.[21] The amendments also explicitly grant the Ministry the power to keep and maintain judges' personnel files, which may have an effect on promotion considerations;[22] until now, the Ministry has kept such files, though without an explicit legislative authorisation. These provisions, confirming and even expanding the Ministry's authority, will not contribute to either judges' adjudicative independence or their autonomous capacity to manage their affairs with efficiency.

---

[14] The Blagoevgrad Regional Court runs open competitions for every judicial vacancy, advertising them nation-wide.

[15] Judicial System Act, Art. 127a (1).

[16] Judicial System Act, Art. 127a (2).

[17] Judicial System Act, Art. 142 (4).

[18] *See also* Section C.2., "Evaluating and Regulating Performance".

[19] Judicial System Act, Art. 129 (4).

[20] Judicial System Act, Art. 30 (1).

[21] Judicial System Act, Art. 30 (6).

[22] Judicial System Act, Art. 35g.

2. Evaluating and Regulating Performance

The recent amendments to the Judicial System Act have laid the groundwork for improved performance evaluation and public complaint systems, which have been fragmented and ineffective. Comprehensive, periodic assessments based on clear qualitative and quantitative criteria, coupled with an effective public complaint system and greater public access to court documents, would assist judges in their professional development. It is essential that the amended Act be effectively implemented in secondary legislation and actual practices. In addition, the Act's provisions confirming and reinforcing the Ministry of Justice's role in discipline – though in part a response to the judiciary's failure effectively to police its own behaviour – raises concerns about the potential for executive interference with judges' independence and professional development.

At present, judicial performance is only monitored through an informal system of peer review – that is, mostly through appeal of judgements to higher courts. Court presidents may, in the course of their judicial duties, examine judgements of a lower court on appeal, or have informal discussions with other judges about the performance of their colleagues. Such informally-gathered information can be used by court presidents in the process of nominating judges for vacancies on higher courts.[23] However, such mechanisms do not efficiently communicate to judges how they might improve their performance, and are open to discretionary abuse.

The amendments to the Judicial System Act create the foundation for a proper evaluation system. The amendments require evaluation of judges before the end of their initial three years in office – that is, before they receive life tenure. An evaluation is also required when a judge is nominated for promotion to a higher court, while a judge may request an evaluation for the purpose of securing promotion in rank.

The amended Act provides that evaluation shall take into consideration the following factors: the court president's reference or recommendation, the overall number and complexity of cases heard, the extent to which timetables were observed, the quality of the judge's decisions, as well as the judge's motivation, discipline and observance of ethical rules.[24] A detailed procedure for the evaluation of judges is to be adopted by the Supreme Judicial Council.[25] Obviously, any such procedure needs to ensure that the salutary general provisions outlined in the amended Act are comprehensively implemented in a manner in keeping with their spirit, which seeks to ensure that

---

[23] *See* Section C.1., "Selection and Promotion".

[24] Judicial System Act, Art. 129 (3).

[25] Judicial System Act, Art. 129 (4).

judges have objective information in order to improve their own professionalism and properly evaluate that of other judges.

The existing discipline and complaint mechanisms do not function properly. Complaints may be addressed to the relevant court president or the Ministry of Justice, as either may initiate disciplinary procedures with a motion to the Supreme Judicial Council. Unless the Council finds the motion manifestly unfounded it appoints from among its members a disciplinary panel. The panel carries out an initial investigation, takes a statement from the judge under investigation and holds a hearing open to judges, prosecutors and investigators, but not to the public; the decision of the panel[26] is subject to judicial review.

A major deficiency of the system is the lack of public access to disciplinary proceedings and the resulting limited access to information arising from such proceedings. Even when judges are disciplined for breach of professional duties, such information does not become public. Publicity would increase the preventative effect and contribute to increased public trust in the system.

Public access to court files and judicial opinions is likewise limited; case files are available only to the parties and their legal representatives.[27] There is no systematic publication of judgements of the Supreme Court of Cassation or the Supreme Administrative Court, although judgements of the Supreme Administrative Court are generally available.[28] Judgements of trial and appeal courts are not published at all. This limits the possibilities for the public, including legal professionals, to have an impact on the quality of adjudication through public debate and critical commentary.

The amended Judicial System Act introduces certain changes that should improve the effectiveness of the complaint and discipline procedures. The amendments oblige judges to adopt ethical rules that would then be approved by the Supreme Judicial

---

[26] Judges can be disciplined for "breach of their professional duties" and for delays in performing their duties. Judicial System Act, Art. 168 (1). A judge can be reprimanded, reduced in rank or salary for a certain period of time, barred from promotion for a certain period of time, or transferred to another court. Judicial System Act, Art. 169 (1). As the majority of complaints relate to improper delays, a separate complaint mechanism has been introduced in civil cases. Parties to a dispute may lodge a complaint with a higher court concerning substantial delays in a lower court proceeding; the higher court may rule that the procedure below should be expedited. Civil Procedure Code, Art. 217 (a).

[27] Ministry of Justice Regulation no. 28 of 20 March 1995, Art. 33 (1).

[28] The Supreme Administrative Court has established a web page, and most of its judgements are also available through different private providers. The Supreme Court of Cassation publishes a Bulletin containing some of its judgements, but the selection published is clearly subjective.

Council;[29] breach of these rules would then constitute separate grounds on which a judge could be disciplined.[30] Several changes improve public access to information about the judiciary, which will encourage honest application of the rules. The amendments oblige the Supreme Judicial Council to publish all its decisions, including those related to disciplinary proceedings;[31] they also oblige judges to file annual declarations of their assets as an anti-corruption measure.

At the same time, as noted above, the amended Judicial Systems Act confirms certain powers of the Ministry of Justice related to discipline, which in turn raises serious concerns about judicial independence even as it highlights the clear need for more effective autonomous procedures.

The Ministry of Justice only acquired the power to submit a motion for disciplinary proceedings in 1998, in an attempt to overcome the reluctance of court presidents to discipline judges from their courts and to make better use of the findings of the Inspectorate office within the Ministry.[32] The Inspectorate has the power to investigate courts' case management and general administration, on the basis of which it drafts general reports. If the Inspectorate receives a specific complaint, it may examine the relevant case files and report on its findings of fact, but it does not express an opinion as to whether there was a breach of duty.[33] Since 1998, however, the Ministry has been able to make use of these findings to submit motions. The amended Act now expressly provides for the Ministry of Justice to report the findings of its Inspectorate concerning breaches of duty by individual judges to the Supreme Judicial Council,[34] which then may decide to open a formal disciplinary procedure.

Clearly, it is not desirable that the Ministry of Justice, as a branch of the executive, has such considerable powers both to propose disciplinary proceedings and to conduct what inevitably is the principal investigation. Restoration and confirmation of the executive's power to involve itself in judicial disciplining generally runs counter to the principle of judicial independence and does not encourage the growth of a professionalised judiciary. To the greatest degree possible, such responsibility should vest in truly independent bodies or internal bodies on which judges themselves have

---

[29] Judicial System Act, Art. 27 (1)(13).

[30] Judicial System Act, Art. 168 (1)(3).

[31] Judicial System Act, Art. 27 (1)(15).

[32] The constitutionality of this provision has been challenged, but the Constitutional Court ruled that, as the Minister of Justice only has the power to address the Council and has no decision-making powers, there is no violation of the independence of the judiciary. Constitutional Court Judgement no.1, case no. 34/98, 14 January 1999.

[33] Judicial System Act, Art. 35.

[34] Judicial System Act, Art. 35b (2).

considerable representation; the investigative powers of the Inspectorate, likewise, would be better vested in an independent body. The most logical candidate is the Supreme Judicial Council, which already has by law, and should have in practice, full autonomy in pursuing disciplinary proceedings.

Of course, once judges are given the means and the political support to operate such systems, they must demonstrate a sincere and sustained willingness to police themselves, or to cooperate with those independent bodies responsible for policing them, if resort to political control over judges' performance is to be avoided. To the extent that the judiciary failed to discipline its own membership in the period prior to 1998, some measure of residual political control may be appropriate until a comprehensive system of internal or independent discipline can be established that better ensures accountability.

3. Training for a Professional Judiciary

The further professionalisation of the judiciary requires a commitment to long-term, continuing training that has been lacking; this should include, in particular, stable, dedicated funding and clarification of the newly proposed training institution's legal status. In the process, the existing potential for judicial training should not be wasted, as already-established institutions have proven capable of organising and conducting relatively good training programmes.

In 1998, the Ministry of Justice and two professional organisations of judges and lawyers[35] created the Magistrates Training Centre as a non-governmental organisation to meet the needs of the judiciary for initial and continuing training. The Centre's articles of incorporation envision that in the long run the Centre would be converted into a public institution for judicial training.[36] The Centre has carried out a number of training events and developed a considerable corps of trainers, mostly judges. Since 1999 all newly-appointed judges attend an initial training programme at the Centre, consisting of nine training events over a total of 43 days.[37] Because of good cooperation from court presidents, in practice every newly appointed judge in recent years has successfully completed this initial training programme. The Centre also provides continuing training. However, the Government does not provide any funding for the

---

[35] The Association of Judges and the Alliance for Legal Interaction.

[36] Articles of Association of the Magistrates Training Centre (unpublished).

[37] This training program was laid down in a document approved by the Centre's board, "The Initial Training Program of the Magistrates Training Centre".

Centre, which is funded by a large number of foreign donors.[38] This financing is neither secure nor stable, and does not contribute to the long-term sustainability of judicial training.

The amendments to the Judicial System Act provide for the creation of a National Institute of Justice.[39] This Institute would be a separate legal entity, with four board members appointed by the Supreme Judicial Council and three by the Minister of Justice. The new Institute is to begin operations in 2003.

The amendments to the Judicial System Act also require every candidate selected for a junior judgeship to undergo initial training;[40] only after completing one year of training at the National Institute of Justice may they be appointed junior judges by the Supreme Judicial Council.[41] Individuals exceptionally appointed directly through open competitions to serve as full judges will not be required to attend this one-year training programme, but will instead attend a separate programme approved by the Council.[42]

However, even under the amended Act there is no obligation for continuing training of judges, although the National Institute of Justice will offer such training as well as training for court administrative staff. As it is not clear whether the new Institute will have sufficient funding from the Government, the amendments leave open the possibility for judicial training provided by other organisations approved by the Minister of Justice.[43] Apparently the existing Magistrates Training Centre will continue to provide such services while the Institute is being established.

It is not clear, however, how the experience accumulated by the Magistrates Training Centre is to be integrated into the new National Institute of Justice. It would be counterproductive to lose the potential of the Centre, as it is unlikely that the Government will be able to provide full funding for judicial training in the near future, and will remain dependent on foreign aid. This argues strongly for the full integration of the fundraising capabilities, good donor relations and substantive experience established by the existing Centre.

---

[38] Interview with Dragomir Yordanov, Director of the Magistrates Training Centre, July 2002.

[39] Judicial System Act, Art. 35e.

[40] Judicial System Act, Art. 35j (1) and (2).

[41] Judicial System Act, Art. 35j (4).

[42] Judicial System Act, Art. 35j (6).

[43] Judicial System Act, Art. 35e (6).

D. INSTITUTIONAL CAPACITY OF THE JUDICIAL BRANCH

The conflicting interests of the various groups represented in the Supreme Judicial Council and its weak administrative capacity limit its ability to support competent and efficient court operations, while at the same time the Ministry of Justice continues to exercise considerable power in practice. The legislative amendments have clarified the division of authority between the Council and the Ministry of Justice in certain respects. Many issues, however, have been left subject to joint decision-making and some amendments actually – and unnecessarily – increase the powers of the Ministry. Courts have little input into the budget process, further limiting their ability to improve their professional capacity. Court presidents have substantial managerial powers and responsibilities, but do not receive proper training. The recent introduction of court administrators is a welcome step, but will require implementing regulations that clearly delineate responsibilities of court presidents and court administrators. These new posts should be filled by individuals with relevant education and skills.

1. Governance and Administration of the Judicial Branch

The weak administrative capacity and conflicting interests of the various groups represented in the Supreme Judicial Council, the body governing the judiciary, limit its ability to support competent and efficient court operations. At the same time the Ministry of Justice continues to wield considerable power in practice, which creates risks for the judiciary's independence and limits its ability to develop truly effective, autonomous professional governance.

The Supreme Judicial Council has considerable governance powers over the judicial system, including the prosecutorial and investigative services.[44] The Council has authority over the appointment,[45] promotion, and dismissal of judges and over judicial immunity and discipline. It also has responsibility for a broad range of administrative determinations, such as fixing the number of judges and support personnel in each court and setting judges' remuneration. It also prepares the draft budget of the judicial system and allocates funding within the budget voted out of Parliament. The Council's consent is required before the Ministry of Justice may fix the seats and the territorial jurisdiction of the courts.

---

[44] Prosecutors and investigators have the same status as judges, Judicial System Act, Art. 10, 133–135.

[45] Only two judges – the Presidents of the Supreme Court of Cassation and the Supreme Administrative Court – are appointed by the State President, but even these are proposed by the Council. *See* Section C.1., "Selection and Promotion".

Considering the considerable formal powers the Supreme Judicial Council exercises over judges' professional careers, it is essential that the Council be sufficiently insulated from improper political and institutional pressures. Yet its composition limits the Council's effectiveness and even creates serious risks for judges' independence and their professionalism.

The Supreme Judicial Council's membership includes representatives of judges, prosecutors, and investigators, elected out of their own ranks, as well a number of members elected by Parliament.[46] The conflicting interests of judges, prosecutors and investigators – and the bodies that elect them to the Council – have often limited the ability of the Council to provide consistent management; instead, different management rationales – arising from the different role investigators, prosecutors and judges play – have led to conflicting policies being imposed on the justice system.

For example, as the Government is held politically responsible for successfully tackling crime, it has had a clear interest in establishing some control over investigation and prosecution in order to carry out consistent policies to combat crime. This had led three Governments – in 1992, 1996 and 1998 – to pass legislation replacing the Supreme Judicial Council before its constitutionally mandated five-year term had expired. Such direct political intervention inevitably creates disincentives for Council members to take principled positions at odds with the interests of the Government in power, even if those interests might be detrimental to the professional development of the judiciary.

Within the Supreme Judicial Council itself there are structural relationships that likewise jeopardise the judiciary's independence and professional autonomy. As the mixed-composition Council prepares a draft budget for the courts, the prosecution, and the investigative service and has considerable powers to redistribute funds, the differing interests of prosecutors, judges and investigators have led to factional voting on the Council. Over the years a clear pattern has been established, with judges and prosecutors opposing each other on the Council, and investigators changing sides depending on the political context. In addition, the fact that prosecutors who are party to the judicial proceedings also decide on issues of appointment, promotion and disciplining of judges through their representatives on the Council raises concerns about threats to the independence of the judiciary.

---

[46] The Supreme Judicial Council consists of twenty-five members. Parliament appoints eleven of the members, and the bodies comprising the judicial branch elect another eleven: judges elect six members, prosecutors three members, and investigators two members. The Presidents of the Supreme Court of Cassation and the Supreme Administrative Court, and the Prosecutor General, are members *ex officio*. Judicial System Act, Art. 16 (2).

Beyond the effects created by these conflicts of interest, the administrative capacity of the Supreme Judicial Council is insufficient to handle its many formal responsibilities.[47] In practice, the Council relies on the Ministry of Justice, which has a far larger staff, for administrative support. The Ministry collects and processes statistical information on the performance of the judiciary and provides it to the Council, and its Inspectorate is empowered to monitor judges' performance.[48] The Ministry also monitors implementation of the judiciary's budget allocation, has administrative authority for court buildings,[49] and retains some standard-setting powers with respect to court and case management.

Even the changes created by the amended Judicial System Act leave this system of dependence largely in place. For example, prior to the amendments the Minister had the power to adopt regulations on the administration of the courts;[50] this power is now exercised jointly,[51] but the Council's continued administrative reliance on the Ministry suggests that it is not likely to have a truly equal role. The Ministry and Council will also exercise joint control over regulations governing the activities of the National Institute of Justice[52] and the activities of lay judges.[53] The new amendments also authorise the Ministry to keep the personnel files of judges, and proposals for promotion will have to be submitted to the Supreme Judicial Council through the Minister.[54] In all, despite a lack of significant legal powers, the Ministry in fact remains in a position to influence the administration of the judiciary in a manner that contradicts the principle of judicial independence established in the Constitution.[55]

Proposals to increase the Ministry's powers – especially as long as the Council remains effectively handicapped – should be discouraged;[56] rather, alternatives that increase the autonomous administrative capability of the Council should be considered, and the Council's division of authority clarified so that judges, prosecutors, and investigators are separately administered.

---

[47] As of July 2002 the Supreme Judicial Council had 14 staff members.

[48] *See* Section C.2., "Evaluating and Regulating Performance".

[49] Judicial System Act, Art. 36a.

[50] Judicial System Act, Art. 188.

[51] Judicial System Act, Art. 188 (1) and (3).

[52] Judicial System Act, Art. 35e (7).

[53] Judicial System Act, Art. 51.

[54] *See* Section C.1., "Selection and Promotion".

[55] Const. Rep. Bulgaria, Art. 117 (2).

[56] *See also* Section B.1., "The Reform Proposals".

Budget Process: The Supreme Judicial Council and the courts have little practical input in the budgeting process, despite a constitutional provision guaranteeing judicial independence in financial matters.[57]

The judicial system has an autonomous budget, which is drafted by the Supreme Judicial Council and submitted together with a financial report on the previous year to Parliament for a vote;[58] the Council of Ministers may make reasoned objections to the draft budget proposal of the Supreme Judicial Council.[59] In practice, however, the Council of Ministers introduces its own parallel budget proposal for the judicial system, which Parliament then enacts. In practical terms the fact that the Supreme Judicial Council submits its budget has little value; its budget proposals are generally reduced dramatically,[60] which in turn limits the resources available to the courts to develop their professional capacity.

Many local courts also lack expertise in developing their budget proposals. In the absence of professional accountants, court presidents prepare budget proposals with the assistance of untrained administrative staff. Without special training, court presidents and support staff are not able either to prepare a long-term financial strategy or to correctly distribute allocated funds. A large percentage of courts' budgets go for salaries and benefits;[61] as courts have to finance the work of expert witnesses, *ex officio* lawyers and lay judges from their own budgets, often they have to overspend or cut other expenses to be able to proceed with hearings. As a result, often there is a shortage of funding by the end of a financial year.[62] Such financial conditions as a result make any long term budgeting and planning impossible, and therefore handicap efforts to develop the courts' capacity.

---

[57] Const. Rep. Bulgaria, Art. 117 (3).

[58] Judicial System Act, Art. 196 (2).

[59] Judicial System Act, Art. 196 (3).

[60] The Cabinet decreased the 2002 budget proposal of the Supreme Judicial Council from 208 million Lev (€107,195,538) to 106 million Lev (€54,627,039). After members of the Council lobbied the Prime Minister at a meeting, he increased the budget by 15 million Lev (€7,730,902), to a total of 122 million Lev (€62,878,010). Both budgets were submitted to Parliament, which voted for the Government version.

[61] For example, roughly 75 to 80 percent of the budget of the Smolyan District Court goes for salaries and benefits. Interview with Ignat Kolchev, President of the Smolyan District Court, July 2002.

[62] Thus, the Smolyan District Court has 109 Lev (€50) per month per judge for expert witnesses and lawyers for the year 2002. As this amount is sufficient roughly for one fee, the court is required to cut from other expenses to be able to proceed with hearings. Interview with Ignat Kolchev, President of the Smolyan District Court, July 2002.

2. Court Administrative Capacity

Court presidents have substantial administrative powers and responsibilities, but do not receive proper training. The recent introduction of court administrators may improve court management, provided that implementing regulations transfer meaningful and clearly delineated powers to these new administrators in a manner that follows the spirit of the legislative reform, and that these new positions are filled by individuals with relevant education and skills.

Court presidents have overall responsibility for the policy, procedures, and long-term development strategy of their respective courts. Court presidents are responsible for managing and representing their courts, for collecting statistical information, and for submitting regular reports to the Council on their courts' activities. Court presidents propose judges for appointment, and appoint and dismiss administrative staff. They distribute work among the judges and oversee the work of the administrative staff. They draft and administer the court budget, and convene and chair their courts' general meeting.[63] However, despite their considerable managerial responsibilities, most court presidents are ill-prepared.

The system of selection for court presidents does not ensure that individuals with managerial qualifications are placed in charge of courts. The Supreme Judicial Council appoints court presidents, but there are no criteria for their selection.[64] The amendments to the Judicial System Act increase the input of each court's general meeting in the appointment of the court president; they also limit each term in office to five years. Each general meeting elects a judge as its appointee, and the president of the responsible higher court is obliged to submit that candidate to the Supreme Judicial Council. However, the Council is not bound by the vote of the general meeting, but may also consider proposals made separately by the president of the higher court or the Minister of Justice.[65] In addition, all proposals (including that of the general meeting) must be submitted via the Minister of Justice, who in submitting it to the Supreme Judicial Council may attach a separate opinion.

In general, more experienced judges have been appointed as court presidents. However, there have been significant exceptions, and because of the dominant role played by court presidents in the process of selection and nomination, personal politics has also played a substantial role. The opening up of the nomination process is certainly a positive step, as is the requirement that every five years court presidents face re-election

---

[63] Judicial System Act, Art. 30, 56, 63, 79, 100.

[64] Judicial System Act, Art. 30.(1).

[65] Judicial System Act, Art. 30 (4) and (6).

or re-appointment. The increased role of the Ministry of Justice, however, raises concerns about the independence of the judiciary.

However they are selected and appointed, court presidents need proper managerial skills; at present, they are not trained for managerial work either upon assuming their responsibilities or on a continuing basis. Managerial training for court presidents should be an immediate priority.[66]

The introduction of court administrators and open competition for vacancies on the courts' staff[67] should improve the local management of the courts. Amendments to the Judicial System Act relieve court presidents of a number of responsibilities related to court and personnel management and pass them over to court administrators. The amendments still leave the ultimate responsibility with the court presidents, and provide that court administrators will "plan, organise and oversee the work of the court staff" and will be responsible for "the management of the administrative activities in the court," and for "the long-term planning, budget policy, finances, automation and equipment."[68] These new posts provide a clear opportunity to improve court management; however, implementing regulations should clearly delineate responsibilities of court presidents and court administrators, and these new positions should filled by individuals with relevant education and skills.

The courts suffer from a number of infrastructure problems, many related to insufficient funding. Courts have been under-funded for years and as a result, work conditions are in need of considerable improvements, including increased funding for hiring and training legal and technical court staff, as well as for professional court buildings and office equipment. Although the Government increased the budget of the justice system for 2002 by about 20 percent compared to the 2001 budget, this still does not overcome years of under-funding.

---

[66] The Magistrates Training Centre does not offer managerial training for court presidents, although it is developing a special module for newly appointed presidents that will include judicial administration, personal management, budgeting, and media relations. Interview with Dragomir Yordanov, Director of the Magistrates Training Centre, July 2002. Meanwhile, during the last two years the project sponsored by the United States Agency for International Development (USAID) offered training courses that allowed a certain number of court presidents to acquire basic managerial skills. Although a positive initiative, this pilot project involved only a very limited number of court presidents (approximately one in 15 of the total number of court presidents) and does not contribute to a permanent, State-sponsored solution to the need for training.

[67] Judicial System Act, Art. 188c.

[68] Judicial System Act, Art. 188c.

In addition, the often-indistinct division of responsibilities between the Council and the Ministry and low administrative capacity of the Council[69] contributes to concrete regulatory deficiencies. For example, the judiciary lacks clear caseload or case management standards, even though caseload is in turn the basis for determining the number of judges and court staff and the distribution of allocated funds, technology and equipment, and facilities. The resulting irrationality in resource allocation tends to make courts inefficient and lowers incentives to improve operating procedures.

The system of case management in particular lacks proper standards or support for judges in handling technical matters related to timely disposition of cases. An initiative supported by USAID has been developing a fully computerised case file management system, which is run at present as a pilot project in several courts;[70] these projects should be continued and expanded. Increased funding is also necessary to meet increased court caseloads; anecdotal evidence suggests that court delays are a serious problem, which is concealed by the lack of a uniform case tracking and information system that would allow courts to track cases from start to finish.

E. RECOMMENDATIONS

1. To the Bulgarian Government and Legislature

- Follow through on the new commitment to comprehensive judicial reform by ensuring that regulations implementing the recent amendments to the Judicial System Act are fully consistent with the principles of judicial independence and enhanced judicial capacity.

- Consider reforming the Supreme Judicial Council or creating a new constitutional-level governing institution responsible for judges and courts only, and provide it with sufficient resources and support staff to ensure professional governance and management of the judicial branch.

- Consistent with the principles of judicial independence and accountability, reconsider the proposed amendments increasing the Ministry of Justice's administrative authority over courts.

---

[69] *See* Section D.1., "Governance and Administration of the Judicial Branch".

[70] Interview with Ignat Kolchev, President of the Smolyan District Court, July 2002.

- Take further steps to clarify judicial selection criteria and to make the selection and promotion process more transparent so that it ensures meritorious selection and promotion of judges and minimises possibilities for bias.

- Through implementing legislation, create a rational and comprehensive system of performance evaluation and public complaint to support judges' professional development.

- Ensure that the new judicial training system is backed by a commitment to long-term, continuing training. Clarify the new National Institute of Justice's legal status. Ensure that it makes full use of the existing resources and experience of the Magistrates Training Centre and has stable and sufficient financial resources to support continuing training.

- In new regulations, clearly delineate the responsibilities of court presidents and court administrators. Ensure that persons appointed as court administrators possess relevant education and skills. Prioritise managerial training for court presidents.

- Continue and expand pilot projects and reforms aimed at improving case management.

- Increase funding to improve working conditions for legal and support staff, including office space and equipment.

2. To the European Union

- Continue to emphasise the importance of judicial reform so that efforts to improve the judiciary's independence and capacity remain on the reform agenda both during the present accession period and during Bulgaria's continuing membership.

- Encourage the Government and Parliament to seriously consider constitutional reform of the Supreme Judicial Council so that the Council or its successor can fairly represent and defend society's legitimate interests in an independent judiciary, without unnecessary conflicts of interests.

- Encourage the Government and Parliament to reconsider any expanded role for the Ministry of Justice in administering the judiciary.

- Continue support for judicial training programmes for judges while encouraging the establishment of a financially stable permanent institution that also provides continuing training.

- Emphasise the need to enhance the level of professionalism in court management and in the selection and training of court personnel.

Judicial Capacity
in the Czech Republic

Table of Contents

B. Current Developments Affecting
    Judicial Independence and Capacity 78

    1. The New Act on Courts and Judges
        and the Constitutional Court Decision 78

    2. Other Developments 79

C. Professional Competence of Judges 80

    1. Selection and Promotion 80

    2. Evaluating and Regulating Performance 82

    3. Training for a Professional Judiciary 85

D. Institutional Capacity of the Judicial Branch .. 87

    1. Governance and Administration
        of the Judicial Branch 87

    2. Court Administrative Capacity 89

E. Recommendations 91

    1. To the Czech Government and Legislature .. 91

    2. To the European Union 92

OPEN SOCIETY INSTITUTE 2002

A. INTRODUCTION

Judicial reform in the Czech Republic remains in a state of flux, following the Constitutional Court's recent invalidation of important parts of the new Act on Courts and Judges, and its suggestion that further changes may be necessary in order to create a truly independent judicial system that complies with constitutionally mandated principles about the separation of powers.

In abolishing the new Act, the Constitutional Court delivered a substantial blow to the political branches' flawed approach to judicial reform, making it clear that an executive-centred model for governance and administration of the judicial branch is inappropriate, and should be revised.

The Court's decision is itself a welcome corrective to a flawed piece of legislation that did little to address the core problems of the judiciary. Now, however, the courts are still in a difficult and uncertain position, and still require a comprehensive solution that will require Parliament to act again. Court administration is still heavily influenced by the Ministry of Justice, both directly and through its appointment power over court presidents, for example.

Although the previous Act was flawed, the evident willingness to engage in serious debate about judicial reform that the political branches demonstrated in passing the Act in the first place is itself an important and welcome change. Rather than abandoning efforts at reform, the Government and Parliament should return to the still-outstanding question of how to shape an independent, accountable and efficient judiciary.

B. CURRENT DEVELOPMENTS AFFECTING JUDICIAL INDEPENDENCE AND CAPACITY

The new Act on Courts and Judges created new judicial institutions and rules for selection, training and evaluation of judges; it also set priorities for improving judicial efficiency and administration. However, the Act perpetuated the Ministry of Justice's central role in administration of the judiciary, especially in training and evaluation. These and other provisions were recently invalidated by the Constitutional Court, which, in basing its decision on arguments about the separation of powers, has made clear that an executive-centred model for governing and administering the judiciary is harmful to the rule of law. These legal provisions will have to be revisited by the political branches in a manner consistent with the Court's ruling and with the principle of judicial independence.

1. The New Act on Courts and Judges and the Constitutional Court Decision

Following a long period in which little meaningful judicial reform was undertaken and the rejection of several far-reaching legislative proposals in 2000,[1] a new Act on Courts and Judges was adopted by the end of 2001 and came into force in April 2002.[2] The Act created new judicial institutions – such as a Judicial Academy for training and advisory judicial councils[3] – new rules for evaluating judges' professional competence and new procedures for the selecting judicial apprentices. However, these changes did not significantly affect the central role of the Ministry of Justice in governing and administering the judiciary.

In June 2002, in response to a complaint lodged by the State President,[4] the Constitutional Court invalidated numerous provisions of the Act on Courts and Judges

---

[1] *See* EU Accession Monitoring Program, *Monitoring the EU Accession Process: Judicial Independence* (Open Society Institute, Budapest, October 2001), pp. 120–121, available at <http://www.eumap.org.>, (accessed 26 September 2002).

[2] Act on Courts and Judges, No. 6/2002 Coll., *superseding* Act on Courts and Judges, No. 335/1991 Coll.

[3] Under the new Act, judicial councils are to be formed at all courts, except small district courts with less than eleven judges. These councils will act as advisory bodies to the court presidents. *See* Act on Courts and Judges, No. 6/2002 Coll., Sec. 46 (1) and (2). Councils will have three to five members serving five-year terms. Act on Courts and Judges, No. 6/2002 Coll., Sec. 46–59.

[4] Constitutional complaint of the State President, at <http://www.hrad.cz/kpr/us_soudci.html.>, (accessed 26 September 2002).

related to the Ministry of Justice's authority and administration of the courts.[5] In particular, the Court invalidated parts of the Act introducing (1) periodic evaluation by the Ministry of judges' professional competence; (2) a system of mandatory continuing education of judges within an institution controlled by the Ministry; and (3) a system of State court administration effectively making court presidents answerable to the Ministry.[6] Perhaps most importantly, among its main reasons for the invalidation of the provisions, the Constitutional Court cited violations of the principle of separation of powers and two closely connected principles, judicial independence and impartiality.

The central role of the Ministry of Justice in courts' administration and the extent of the Ministry's competencies were not specifically addressed in the State President's complaint and therefore could not be considered by the Constitutional Court. However, by basing its decision on arguments about the separation of powers, the Constitutional Court delivered a substantial blow to the essence of the political branches' preferred approach to judicial reform. The Court has made it clear that an executive-centred model for governing and administering the judiciary is inappropriate, and must be revised.

The Constitutional Court's decision includes several recommendations or guiding opinions suggesting that the current system of court administration is inconsistent with the need, in a democratic State based on the rule of law, to establish a truly independent and capable judiciary. Thus the Court has clearly indicated that judicial reform will have to continue, and that the political branches will have to revisit a number of other legal provisions of the Act on Courts and Judges.

2. Other Developments

Although the media reported allegations of corruption[7] in the company register,[8] the overall confidence of public in the judiciary has increased for the first time in recent

---

[5] Decision of the Constitutional Court of Czech Republic, 18 June 2002, no. Pl. ÚS 7/02, at <http://www.aspi.cz/cgi-bin/jus/aspi_lit_4?WVCNC+300+jus-2.>, (accessed 26 September 2002).

[6] Decision of the Constitutional Court of Czech Republic, 18 June 2002, no. Pl. ÚS 7/02, <http://www.aspi.cz/cgi-bin/jus/aspi_lit_4?WVCNC+300+jus-2.>, (accessed 26 September 2002).

[7] For a comprehensive discussion of corruption issues in the Czech Republic, including in its judiciary, *see* EU Accession Monitoring Program, *Monitoring the EU Accession Process: Corruption and Anti-Corruption Policy in the Czech Republic* (Open Society Institute, Budapest, October 2002), at <http://www.eumap.org>, (accessed 26 September 2002).

[8] *See, e.g.* "Ať investoři řeknou, koho museli uplatit" (Let the investors disclose whom they had to bribe), *Lidové noviny*, 25 March 2002.

years. In a recent poll, 40 percent of people responded that they trust judges, representing a seven percent increase and the highest level of trust ever reported.[9]

A new system of bailiffs operating as independent private officers will enforce civil court decisions.[10] This is expected to speed up the process of enforcement of civil court decisions, which in turn should ease the burden on courts and further improve public opinion about the justice system.

C. Professional Competence of Judges

Although the new Act on Courts and Judges reduces the power of the Ministry of Justice over selection, the Ministry retains a significant degree of discretion; at the same time, decentralisation has granted court presidents – who are appointed by the Ministry – considerable discretion over these decisions. It is important that supporting ministerial regulations further clarify and rationalise the selection procedure and ensure its transparency. The new Act also sought to introduce a new system of periodic evaluation of judges' professional competence that delegated significant authority to the Ministry of Justice and other bodies, and sought to mandate training of judges in a Ministry-controlled institution; the Constitutional Court held these provisions unconstitutional. The judiciary and political branches of Government now have to develop new models for periodic evaluation and training that comply with the Court's decisions and ensure that decisions about judges' career paths do not infringe their adjudicative and institutional independence, but rather encourage the judiciary's increased professionalisation.

1. Selection and Promotion

The new Act on Courts and Judges outlines the criteria and procedure for the selection and promotion of judges.[11] Both selection and promotion procedures are presently too vague and discretionary to ensure that judges are not subject to improper influences; in particular, the broad discretion exercised by officials beholden to the Ministry of Justice will have to be reconsidered in light of the recent Constitutional Court decision.

---

[9] *See* "IVVM: Výrazně vzrostla důvěra v armádu, policii, soudy i media" (CROP [Centre for Research of Public Opinion]: Trust in the army, police, courts and media has grown significantly"), 1 November 2001.

[10] Act on Bailiffs (Execution Officers) and Their Activities, No. 120/2001 Coll.

[11] Act on Courts and Judges, No. 6/2002 Coll., Sec. 60.

Although the Act reduces the power of the Ministry of Justice over selection, the Ministry retains a significant degree of discretion; at the same time, decentralisation has granted court presidents – who are appointed by the Ministry[12] – considerable discretion over these decisions. It is important that supporting ministerial regulations, which are expected by the end of 2002, further clarify and rationalise the selection procedure and ensure its transparency. Otherwise, the new procedure may simply transfer the locus of discretionary power without reducing the risks to judicial independence and professionalism that accompany its exercise.

The Act on Courts and Judges stipulates that qualified candidates for judicial office[13] have to complete a judicial apprenticeship and pass an examination. The selection process for apprenticeships has four phases: a psychological test; a structured interview in front of the Commission of the Judicial Academy; an admissions interview in front of a selection panel of the relevant regional court; and the final decision by the regional court president. In taking final decisions, the regional court president is not bound by the evaluations issued in the previous phases. This affords the president broad discretionary power, the abuse of which may be difficult to control.[14]

The apprenticeship lasts three years, which might reduce the likelihood of experienced legal professionals applying. At the discretion of the Minister of Justice, however, experience in other legal professions may be counted towards an apprenticeship, although in no case can an apprenticeship be reduced to less than one year. The criteria for reduction of the apprenticeship period should be clearly defined, as should the goals of the apprenticeship programme, so that it does not exclude the possibility for experienced legal professionals to join the bench.

Upon completion of the apprenticeship, candidates must also pass an examination.[15] The State President may then appoint judges upon their nomination by the Minister of Justice. There appears to be no guarantee of nomination or appointment for candidates who have otherwise completed all the required steps.

The promotion of judges to superior courts is also subject to only few, rather broadly formulated rules. The Minister of Justice decides on promotions following consultation

---

[12] *See* Section D.2., "Court Administrative Capacity".

[13] Qualification requirements include Czech citizenship, legal capacity, a degree in law, and legal knowledge and moral qualities that guarantee good performance; candidates must be at least 25.

[14] While it is clear that there is no possibility of appeal against the final decision of the regional court president, it is not clear whether a rejected candidate may reapply.

[15] The Minister of Justice may waive the judicial exam for legal professionals who have passed other exams such as those for prosecutors or notaries. The exam is also not required for candidates who have worked as judges of the Constitutional Court for more than two years.

with the president of the court to which the judge is to be promoted; for promotions to the Supreme Court, the consent of the Court's President is required. Promotion to the Supreme Court requires at least ten years of practice while promotion to the high and regional courts requires eight years of practice.[16] Beyond this, however the criteria for promotion are stipulated only very vaguely: the promoted judge must have sufficient professional knowledge and experience to guarantee the proper execution of his function. The criteria and procedure for promotion should be further defined.

In its recent decision, the Constitutional Court considered the control exercised by the Ministry of Justice over the appointment and the recall of court presidents and vice-presidents in the context of promotion, and invalidated the provisions allowing the Ministry to recall court presidents absent clear disciplinary grounds.[17] Although this decision does not directly speak to promotion procedures as such, it clearly suggests that efforts to make procedures more transparent and rational will also have to ensure that principles of independence are more rigorously respected.

2. Evaluating and Regulating Performance

The introduction of a system for periodic evaluations of judges' performance in the new Act on Courts and Judges[18] was, in itself, a welcome development. However, some of the criteria introduced were not sufficiently precise and their relevance to judges' functions was unclear, while the process as a whole lacked transparency. Coupled with the broad discretionary powers vested in the Ministry of Justice and court presidents, these shortcomings led the Constitutional Court to invalidate the newly-devised system. The judiciary and the political branches now face the challenge of developing a new performance evaluation system that takes into consideration the arguments put forth by the Constitutional Court.

The performance evaluation system as developed in the Act on Courts and Judges mandated assessment of district and regional court judges' professional competence after three years, and thereafter every five years; judges of higher courts and the Supreme Court were to be evaluated every five years.[19] Court presidents would perform the evaluations.[20] The president was obliged to write an initial evaluation report, to

---

[16] Act on Courts and Judges, No. 6/2002 Coll., Sec. 71 (2–3).

[17] *See* Section D.2., "Court Administrative Capacity".

[18] Act on Courts and Judges, No. 6/2002 Coll., Sec. 134 *ff.*

[19] Act on Courts and Judges, No. 6/2002 Coll., Sec. 134 (1–2).

[20] Act on Courts and Judges, No. 6/2002 Coll., Sec. 135. District court judges are evaluated by their respective regional court presidents.

which the opinion of the relevant judicial council about the judge's decision-making and a report by the Judicial Academy summarising and evaluating any training undertaken by the judge were to be attached.[21] The president's report, taking into consideration all these evaluation documents and judgements, was to rate the judge's professional competence as "excellent," "satisfactory" or "non-satisfactory."[22]

The performance criteria were to evaluate a judge's knowledge of laws and judicial decisions, ability to apply this knowledge in the judicial decision-making process, level of theoretical knowledge, and ability to participate in and organise the work of the judicial department, as well as publications and pedagogical activities.[23]

An unsatisfactory rating, if not reversed in the later proceedings, would lead to a judge's recall. If the judge were given an unsatisfactory rating, a series of re-evaluations could follow. First, a special panel (the president and two other judges) from the same court would re-evaluate the matter.[24] If this panel also found the judge's performance unsatisfactory – or if the president alone still did not agree with the other judges' positive assessment[25] – the president was entitled to file a motion to have the judge's competence examined by a permanent council that sits for this purpose.[26] Finally, the judge, the court president, or the Minister of Justice could appeal the council's decision to the Supreme Court,[27] which would issue a final decision.[28]

The Constitutional Court concluded that although the goals of the Act – namely increasing the level of judges' professional competence and facilitating the removal of truly incompetent judges – are worth pursuing, the system and procedure selected by the new Act on Courts and Judges are unacceptable methods for its achievement.

---

[21] Act on Courts and Judges, No. 6/2002 Coll., Sec. 136 (2).

[22] Act on Courts and Judges, No. 6/2002 Coll., Sec. 136 (2) and (3).

[23] Act on Courts and Judges, No. 6/2002 Coll., Sec. 136 (1).

[24] Act on Courts and Judges, No. 6/2002 Coll., Sec. 137 (1–2).

[25] While it might be possible, theoretically, for the other two panel members to find the judge unsatisfactory and for the president to disagree, in practice that would be unlikely, as in order for the panel to consider the matter at all, the president would have had to find the judge's performance unsatisfactory in his original report.

[26] Act on Courts and Judges, No. 6/2002 Coll., Sec. 147. The council was to be created by the Ministry of Justice; it would have had nine members, serving three-year terms. *See* Act on Courts and Judges, No. 6/2002 Coll, Sec. 138 and 139.

[27] Act on Courts and Judges, No. 6/2002 Coll., Sec. 153. The Minister of Justice could file a motion to examine judge's professional competence if he did not agree with the decision of the Council, since he would be a party in the proceedings in front of the Council. *See* Act on Courts and Judges, No. 6/2002 Coll, Sec. 145 (1)(b) and 153.

[28] Act on Courts and Judges, No. 6/2002 Coll., Sec. 154 *ff.*

Among the most troublesome characteristics of the system and procedure the Court particularly found:

- that the broad competencies of the Ministry of Justice, court presidents, evaluation councils, and the Judicial Academy in the evaluation procedure – together with the fact that the involvement of the judicial councils was limited to merely non-binding recommendations to the executive – would amount to granting the executive excessive influence over the judicial branch and would violate the principles of separation of powers and judicial independence;

- that the fact that evaluations – and the accompanying possibility of recall – would be carried out after judges received life tenure appointments would violate the requirements of legal certainty and the principle of life tenure, as well as the prohibition against recalling a judge except through disciplinary proceedings for a specific violation of judicial responsibilities;

- that the criteria for evaluation were too vague and were not directly connected to judges' adjudicative function and thus depended on extraneous and irrelevant factors (such as ability to organise the work of the judicial department or on pedagogical activity); and

- that because the meritorious proceedings of the Supreme Court rendering final decisions were to be closed, they would contradict the open-proceeding principle.[29]

The Constitutional Court made further specific suggestions concerning the kinds of evaluation and preparation that might be adequate, or even required, in a system respecting the professionalism and independence of judges. The Court indicated that in order to avoid a threat to legal certainty in general and not to place decisions already rendered by recalled judges into doubt, the bulk of evaluation and screening of judges' qualifications needs to be carried out in the period *preceding* appointment or immediately following it, and ought properly not extend beyond three to five years.

The decision of the Constitutional Court does not seem to exclude the possibility of developing a system of periodic performance evaluation throughout judges' careers. Such a system, however, would have to comply with the principles and arguments noted by the Court, and more broadly with the principles of judicial independence and accountability upon which the Court implicitly rested its decision.

---

[29] Decision of the Constitutional Court of Czech Republic from 18. June 2002, no. Pl. ÚS 7/02, at <http://www.aspi.cz/cgi-bin/jus/aspi_lit_4?WVCNC+300+jus-2.>, (accessed 26 September 2002).

There are additional avenues for indirect evaluation or review of judges' performance that can assist individual judges in developing their professional competence. Individuals and legal entities are entitled to file complaints if judges or other court personnel unjustifiably delay proceedings, demonstrate unsuitable behaviour, or otherwise disturb the dignity of a trial.[30] At the national level, the Ministry of Justice's Department of Complaints and Pardons deals with these complaints,[31] while at the court level, court presidents or other designated persons deal with them.[32] Clearly-elaborated complaint mechanisms can provide an *ad hoc* check on judges' behaviour, so long as they are crafted to avoid impinging on the legitimate core of adjudicative discretion essential to the judiciary's independence.

In addition, disciplinary proceedings have also been modified by the Act on Courts and Judges;[33] as noted above, new provisions for evaluation, if they contemplate sanctions for judges as the recently invalidated provisions did, will have to effect those sanctions through the disciplinary mechanism, and not outside it.

3. Training for a Professional Judiciary

Important changes to the system for training judges have also been invalidated by the recent Constitutional Court decision. The new Act on Courts and Judges attempted to integrate judicial training into a new institution controlled by the Ministry of Justice and introduced mandatory continuing training;[34] together, these provisions risked seriously infringing judges' independence by giving the executive coercive power over judges.

The Act on Courts and Judges created a Judicial Academy to replace the Ministry of Justice's Institute for Education. The new Academy is responsible for organising and conducting education of judicial apprentices and judges, as well as helping to evaluate candidates in the selection process.[35] The Academy is financed jointly out of PHARE

---

[30] Act on Courts and Judges, No. 6/2002 Coll., Sec. 164 *ff*.

[31] Act on Courts and Judges, No. 6/2002 Coll., Sec. 167.

[32] Act on Courts and Judges, No. 6/2002 Coll., Sec. 168–171.

[33] Disciplinary proceedings may be initiated upon motion only; they are limited by subjective and objective time limits (that is, proceedings must be initiated within two months after the petitioner learns about the wrong but at the latest within two years after its commission); and provide for a wide range of sanctions, such as reprimand, reduction of salary, or discharge from managerial function.

[34] Act on Courts and Judges, No. 6/2002 Coll., Sec. 129–133.

[35] Act on Courts and Judges, No. 6/2002 Coll., Sec. 129 (2).

funds[36] and the State budget. Although it appears to be able to provide a stable and well-funded institutional base for judicial training, certain of its operating principles raised risks to judicial independence, as well as limiting the judiciary's opportunities to develop a truly autonomous professional capacity.

In particular, the new system would have preserved the Ministry of Justice's control over judicial training. The Minister supervises operations of the Judicial Academy, and appoints both the President and the Board of the Academy; the Minister also then appoints the Academy's lecturers upon their nomination by the President of the Academy.[37]

Most problematic was the provision that serving judges be required to participate in educational activities at the Judicial Academy.[38] Although no specific sanction for intentional or unexcused absence from the obligatory education was stipulated, non-participation could lead to disciplinary sanctions. The Constitutional Court concluded that imposing sanctions on judges for failing to participate in educational activities at an institution staffed, organised and supervised by the executive branch would violate principles of separation of powers and judicial independence. It invalidated the requirement for mandatory training at the Academy and stipulated that the Academy may, with regard to the system of continuing education of judges, represent no more than "one of the alternative sources to be selected by individual judges."[39]

The judiciary and political branches now face the challenge of devising a system for judicial training that both complies with the decision of the Constitutional Court and ensures continuing professional development of all judges. This may require that the authority of the Ministry of Justice over judicial training is transferred to or shared with judges. At a minimum, judges should be more involved in decision-making on issues relevant to judicial training, such as the educational policy, methodology, curriculum development, and operations of the new Judicial Academy.

---

[36] PHARE CZ-00-07-05.

[37] Act on Courts and Judges, No. 6/2002 Coll., Sec. 130 (4).

[38] Act on Courts and Judges, No. 6/2002 Coll., Sec. 132.

[39] Decision of the Constitutional Court of the Czech Republic, 18 June 2002, no. Pl. ÚS 7/02, <http://www.aspi.cz/cgi-bin/jus/aspi_lit_4?WVCNC+300+jus-2.>, (accessed 26 September 2002).

D. INSTITUTIONAL CAPACITY OF THE JUDICIAL BRANCH

The Ministry of Justice continues to exercise primary responsibility for governance and administration of the judiciary, and also exercises indirect authority through its power to appoint court presidents. In addition to violating the principle of judicial independence, the Ministry's role impedes improvements of the judiciary's capacity. This executive-centred model should be revised – a view, moreover, suggested by the decision of the Constitutional Court. Whatever body is made responsible for court administration must have the capacity and the will to design and implement a comprehensive, well-funded system that will protect judges' necessary independence and promote their professionalism and accountability. At the same time, court presidents' administrative responsibilities should be reduced by introducing professional managers and increasing the number and quality of support staff.

1. Governance and Administration of the Judicial Branch

The Ministry of Justice continues to exercise primary responsibility for governance and administration of the judiciary. In addition to being questionable in the context of a modern understanding of the principle of judicial independence, this model limits the development of administrative capacity within the judiciary and, indirectly, impedes the enhancement of judicial capacity. Judges who do not comprise a separate and self-governing branch will have fewer incentives or means to act as equal participants in improving judicial competence and efficiency; consistent with the recent decision of the Constitutional Court, the current executive-centred model should be revisited and revised.

The Ministry of Justice is the main representative, policy-making and administrative body responsible for the operation of the judiciary.[40] Generally, the Ministry and its specialised departments, acting in a managerial and supervisory capacity, are responsible for creating conditions that ensure the proper functioning of courts and meet their organisational, financial, educational, and personnel needs.[41] To a large extent the Ministry itself determines what those needs are and decides how to satisfy them; it is the Ministry that drafts the budget for the judicial sector (with input from regional and other courts), allocates funding, and determines the numbers of judges and personnel and the caseload norms at each court.

---

[40] Act on Courts and Judges, No. 6/2002 Coll., Sec. 119 (1).

[41] Act on Courts and Judges, No. 6/2002 Coll., Sec. 118 (1).

The breadth of the Ministry of Justice's powers over individual judges is, however, best illustrated by its power temporarily to transfer a judge to another court without that judge's consent. District court judges may be temporarily transferred for up to one year to a neighbouring district court without their consent, if such a transfer represents the sole possibility to ensure the proper functioning of the judiciary in that court.[42] Likewise, the Ministry may involuntarily transfer a judge in the event a court reorganisation is enacted by law, and such a transfer represents the sole possibility to ensure the proper functioning of the judiciary.[43] Although there are occasions when efficiency recommends the re-allocation of judges, vesting such a power in the executive creates risks to judges' independence without gaining any discernible advantage over alternative models that would vest the power in an autonomous body.

Apart from the risk to judges' independence that the Ministry's continuing authority represents, the quality of the Ministry's support for court operations has been criticised. For instance, the standards for judges' workload are unduly simplistic, with norms set quantitatively, without reference to the complexity of cases; and training for technical court staff has not been organised. Whatever body is responsible for court administration must have the capacity and the will to design and implement a comprehensive, well-funded system that will protect judges' necessary independence and promote their professionalism and accountability.

The Constitutional Court's decision indicates that the current model for the governance and administration of the judicial branch needs revision. Although the Court stated that it is not entitled to decide the model for the State administration of courts and that such power belongs to the legislative branch, it recommended that Parliament respect separation of powers in deciding on the new model. The Court specifically noted that the current model, in which the Ministry of Justice is the central body of court administration and the judiciary does not have its own representative body at an equivalent level, does not sufficiently "exclude the possibility of executive influence over the judicial branch (for example by allocation of budgetary resources and the control of its use)."[44] This appears to indicate the need to establish a national body, either controlled by judges or with meaningful participation of judges, to manage the judicial branch.

---

[42] Act on Courts and Judges, No. 6/2002 Coll., Sec. 69.

[43] Act on Courts and Judges, No. 6/2002 Coll., Sec. 72.

[44] Decision of the Constitutional Court of the Czech Republic, 18 June 2002, no. Pl. ÚS 7/02, <http://www.aspi.cz/cgi-bin/jus/aspi_lit_4?WVCNC+300+jus-2.>, (accessed 26 September 2002).

2. Court Administrative Capacity

The Ministry of Justice also continues to exercise unnecessarily broad indirect authority over court administration though its power to appoint court presidents, whose dual role as judges and administrators subject to the executive raises serious concerns about the separation of powers. The Ministry's influence should be restricted by confirming the court presidents' autonomy – a view consistent with the recent Constitutional Court decision – while at the same time court presidents' administrative responsibilities should be reduced by introducing professional managers and increasing the number and quality of support staff.

In the system of inter-court administration a principle of strict subordination applies; district court presidents are subordinated to regional court presidents, who in turn are subordinated to the Minister of Justice.[45] The Minister has the power to appoint court presidents and vice-presidents,[46] whom he selects from among judges of each court. Experience in management is not a requirement of appointment, and to date no special training for judges in managerial positions has been provided on a systematic basis. The Act on Courts and Judges further allowed the Minister of Justice to recall these and other functionaries if they do not "perform their responsibilities properly."[47]

Accordingly, court presidents, in addition to being judges, are treated as agents of the Ministry of Justice in particular courts. The Constitutional Court concluded that the principle of separation of powers bars an interpretation of the constitutional principle of incompatibility[48] as allowing judges to be involved in bodies beholden to the executive or legislative branch.[49] In particular, the Court held that the provision allowing the Ministry of Justice to recall court presidents was too vague and violated the principles of legal certainty and judicial independence. The Court also noted that the functions of court presidents are part of the judicial career path, and thus they should be recallable only for reasons stipulated by law and only through disciplinary proceedings – that is, through a court decision subject to review.[50]

---

[45] Act on Courts and Judges, No. 6/2002 Coll., Sec. 121.

[46] With the exception of the President and the Vice Presidents of the Supreme Court, who are appointed by the State President. *See* Act on Courts and Judges, No. 6/2002 Coll., Sec.102 (1)

[47] Act on Courts and Judges, No. 6/2002 Coll., Sec. 106 (1).

[48] CONST. CZECH REP., Art. 82 (3).

[49] In the same vein, the Constitutional Court stated that temporary placement of judges at the Ministry of Justice, or their membership in consulting bodies of the Ministry, other bodies of the executive or either chambers of the Parliament, violate the incompatibility principle.

[50] Decision of the Constitutional Court of the Czech Republic, 18 June 2002, no. Pl. ÚS 7/02, at <http://www.aspi.cz/cgi-bin/jus/aspi_lit_4?WVCNC+300+jus-2.>, (accessed 26 September 2002). *See* Section C.1., "Selection and Promotion".

At the same time, the Court, declaring its wish to leave Parliament sufficient space for the development and adoption of the new model of State administration of courts, suspended enforcement of this part of the decision until 1 July 2003.[51]

In addition to the risks to independence that the present system creates, court presidents' lack of professional management expertise seriously limits courts' ability to professionalise and improve their efficiency. Introduction of professional management in the courts could be a long-lasting solution for the improvement of court administration; in the interim, special managerial courses to impart managerial skills to court presidents and vice-presidents should be introduced.

Under the new Act, the judicial councils that are to be formed at all courts will act as advisory bodies to the court presidents. Although they may enhance collegiality in the decision-making process, the councils have no decision-making or regulatory powers and thus cannot provide a check over the managerial powers exercised by court presidents and the Ministry, nor will they increase the administrative capacity of the courts since they are not competent to give advice on managerial or administrative matters.

The material conditions of the judiciary have improved with the implementation of an investment programme adopted by the Ministry of Justice and covering the period from 1999 to 2003.[52] Although court delays persist, overall the judiciary functions fairly efficiently; the number of incoming cases and the length of court proceedings have stabilised. Recent measures to reduce workload, such as decriminalisation of certain offences and introduction of alternative methods for case resolution, may further contribute to improvement. Efforts to decrease the length of court proceedings should continue. However, at least one major cause of delays – the lack of qualified court support staff – still needs to be addressed.

Judges are now burdened with administrative and technical tasks that could easily be performed by qualified court support staff. However, little has been done either to hire more staff or to improve the professional qualifications of those currently employed. The low wages received by staff members (significantly under the average income)[53] make it difficult to hire and keep even junior court staff members. Recent reforms have made no provision for addressing this problem, however. Consideration should be given to

---

[51] Decision of the Constitutional Court of Czech Republic, 18 June 2002, no. Pl. ÚS 7/02, at <http://www.aspi.cz/cgi-bin/jus/aspi_lit_4?WVCNC+300+jus-2.>, (accessed 26 September 2002).

[52] See <http://portal.justice.cz.>, (accessed 26 September 2002).

[53] The salaries of court support staff range between 6,000 and 12,000 Czech crowns (€200 to 400), while the average income in the Czech Republic is now 16,000 Czech crowns (€540). See Czech Statistic Office, <http://www.czso.cz>, (accessed 26 September 2002), and interviews with employees of the Ministry of Justice, 20 May 2002.

improving the remuneration, training and work conditions of support staff, so as to improve their level of professionalism and to free up judges for core adjudicative work.

E. RECOMMENDATIONS

1. To the Czech Government and Legislature

- Continue the present political commitment to developing meaningful proposals that will respond to the still outstanding question of how to shape an independent, accountable and efficient judiciary.

- Take immediate and comprehensive steps to amend the Act on Courts and Judges in compliance with the Constitutional Court's decision of 18 June 2002. In particular:

- revise the existing executive-centred model of State administration of courts to introduce a truly autonomous institution to administer the judicial branch;

- consistent with the principles of judicial independence and accountability, develop a new system for periodic evaluation of judicial performance that is transparent and based on relevant criteria;

- devise a system for continuing judicial training that ensures the professional development of all judges and involves the judiciary in decisions about the design and operation of training, including the new Judicial Academy.

- Through timely subsequent legislation, clarify the criteria and procedure for selection and promotion of judges to prevent possible abuse of broad discretionary powers by the Ministry of Justice or court presidents; consider limiting or removing the Ministry's discretionary powers altogether.

- Reduce the broad authority the Ministry of Justice exercises – either directly, or indirectly through court presidents – over court administration.

- Consider introducing professional management into the courts; in the interim, introduce special managerial courses without delay to improve the managerial skills of court presidents and vice-presidents.

- Continue to take steps to address the causes of court delays, including increasing the number and quality of support staff.

2. To the European Union

- Emphasise the need for continued institutional reforms so as to ensure true respect for the principles of separation of powers and judicial independence as a condition for enhanced judicial capacity.

- Facilitate the transfer of expert advice from other EU candidate and member States with experience in creating models of judicial administration, selection, promotion, performance evaluation and judicial training systems that enhance judicial capacity while respecting the principles of judicial independence and accountability.

Judicial Capacity in Estonia

Table of Contents

OPEN SOCIETY INSTITUTE 2002

A. INTRODUCTION

Estonia has made significant progress in establishing and supporting an independent and capable judiciary. The courts are increasingly staffed with capable, trained professionals, who are supported with continuing education. Ongoing reform of judicial and administrative structures is given priority on the political agenda.

The new Courts Act, adopted in June 2002, potentially represents a major step forward in strengthening the judicial system. The Act introduces significant legislative changes that have yet to be implemented. Effective implementation of the Act, in particular of the provisions relating to the new Council for Court Administration, is essential for the consolidation of judicial independence and further improvement of the judiciary's adjudicative and administrative capacity.

In particular, further progress is needed to integrate the judiciary into the budget process, to clarify judges' selection process, to develop a comprehensive system for performance evaluation based on clear standards, to ensure stable funding and efficient use of existing training potential, and to enlarge the corps of support staff.

B. CURRENT DEVELOPMENTS AFFECTING JUDICIAL CAPACITY AND INDEPENDENCE

The new Courts Act introduces measures that, if effectively implemented, will both increase judges' independence and give them greater means and incentive to develop their professional competence. The most notable change is a creation of the Council for Court Administration, an autonomous body with predominant responsibility for judicial representation. The new legislation, however, does not integrate judges into the budget process sufficiently.

1. Courts Act

The Parliament adopted the new Courts Act in June 2002.[1] The new Courts Act contains changes which, if effectively implemented, will positively affect both the judiciary's independence and its professional capacity. The new legal provisions have not yet been tested in practice, and realisation of their potential will depend in large part upon their effective implementation. Among the changes the Act introduces, it:

- creates a Council for Court Administration with a majority of its membership drawn from the ranks of judges, and confers on it significant regulatory and administrative decision-making powers;[2]

- reduces the number of district courts from 22 to 20 and creates larger courts to enable specialisation of judges and more balanced caseloads;

- limits the tenure of court presidents to one term as a measure to make court presidents more independent from the executive;

- strengthens the managerial role of court managing directors, including granting them the power to appoint staff members, while increasing the responsibility of court presidents for the delivery of competent judicial services, in order to professionalise court administration;

- transfers the authority to initiate disciplinary proceedings against judges from the Minister of Justice to the Legal Chancellor (who functions as an

---

[1] Courts Act, *adopted* 19 June 2002 *and published* 19 July 2002 in the Official Gazette, Part I (hereafter, RTI), 2002, 64, 390.

[2] *See* Section D.1., "Governance and Administration of the Judicial Branch", below.

Ombudsman), and lower court presidents,[3] in order to eliminate political involvement in disciplining judges;

- transfers overall responsibility for training from the Ministry of Justice to a new Council for Judicial Training, and transfers budgetary responsibility for training from the Ministry to the Supreme Court, in order to strengthen judicial training;[4]

- raises the salary of judges to a level comparable to that of other State officials and high-level civil servants, in order to attract qualified candidates for judicial service and to enhance the economic independence of judges.[5]

All of these changes will depend on effective implementation, however, and on judges having the means to effect change. The new Act will not significantly increase the low integration of judges into the budget process. Without significant input into Parliament's deliberations on the budget process, and control of allocations, the judiciary's ability to realise the potential for improvements afforded by the new Act will be unnecessarily limited.

2. Judicial Review Act

The Judicial Review Act,[6] passed in March 2002, expands Supreme Court jurisdiction. In addition to the review of legislation, from 1 July 2002 the Supreme Court can review resolutions of Parliament and the State President, including decisions relating to appointments.[7] Although it principally affects the courts' substantive jurisdiction, this Act, because it necessarily also relates to acts of other branches that affect the judiciary, should also increase judges' collective ability to defend their interests against incursion by the other branches.

Collectively, these changes broaden the public's access to effective justice and increase the scope for needed internal reform of the courts. An increase in the number of

---

[3] The Chief Justice of the Supreme Court already has the power to initiate disciplinary proceedings against judges on that court.

[4] *See also* Section C.3., "Training for a Professional Judiciary", below.

[5] Judges' compensation will be a multiple of the average salary, ranging from four times for district court judges to six times for the Chief Justice of the Supreme Court. Court presidents will receive an additional 15 percent of the main compensation; presidents of courts consisting of 15 or more judges will receive an additional 25 percent.

[6] Judicial Review Act, RTI, 2002, 174, <https://www.riigiteataja.ee/ert/act.jsp?id=27828.>, (accessed 26 September 2002).

[7] Judicial Review Act, Art. 2.

Supreme Court Justice positions from 17 to 19 is also planned to help cope with the increased workload the legislative modifications will bring;[8] similar increases in management personnel should also be considered.

C. Professional Competence of Judges

The processes for selection, promotion, and evaluation of judges are not subject to sufficiently clear or standardised procedures. The new Courts Act may make the problem worse by mandating periodic evaluation of probationary judges without clarifying standards, a change that will not necessarily increase professional responsibility and may even threaten judges' independence. Moreover, recent changes have failed to extend performance evaluation to tenured judges. Qualified training facilities exist, but discretionary Government funding decisions have failed to utilise that potential effectively. Effective implementation of the relevant provisions of new Courts Act could bring significant improvements.

1. Selection and Promotion

The selection system, including promotion to higher courts, is generally well balanced; it includes significant representation from the judiciary as well as the political branches. However, certain shortcomings in the selection process – particularly the lack of clear standards – still need to be addressed. Greater rigour in the examination process and inclusiveness in selecting examiners are especially needed in light of the fact that the new Courts Act increases the Judicial Examination Commission's powers.

The Supreme Court sitting *en banc* proposes a single candidate for each district and regional court post to the State President, who then makes final appointment; the President may only refuse an appointment if it would violate a law or harm State interests.[9] The Chief Justice of the Supreme Court proposes candidates for posts on the Supreme Court to the Parliament, which makes a final decision.

The criteria for selection and promotion of judges need to be further defined and standardised. The criteria include general minimal requirements, such as Estonian citizenship, a law degree from an accredited university, ability to use the Estonian

---

[8] Courts Act, Art. 25 (3).

[9] Act on State President's Office, Art. 19 (4), RTI 2001, 43, 240 *as amended by* RTI 2002, 29, 174 <http://www.riigiteataja.ee/ert/act.jsp?id=27017.>, (accessed 26 September 2002).

language,[10] and undefined qualitative measures, including high moral standards and the capabilities and personal characteristics necessary for judicial office.[11] As no interpretation of these quite vague qualitative criteria has been developed, officials are left with unnecessarily broad discretion in selecting and promoting candidates, which undermines the credibility of the system.

The other basic conditions for a judicial appointment are an examination before the Judicial Examination Commission[12] and – under the new Courts Act – a mandatory two-year apprenticeship.[13] The oral part of the examination – an interview that constitutes an important part of the overall evaluation – is not sufficiently standardised, and members of the Commission do not receive training on how to conduct interviews.

The apprenticeship is mandatory for all new judges; only former judges and licensed advocates or prosecutors with at least two years' current service at the time of appointment may be exempted from obligatory apprenticeship.[14] On the basis of interviews, the Judicial Examination Commission nominates judicial apprentices for appointment and proposes a work programme for each apprentice to the Minister of Justice.[15]

---

[10] *See* EU Accession Monitoring Program, *Monitoring the European Union Accession Process: Minority Protection in Estonia* (Open Society Institute, Budapest, October 2001), and EU Accession Monitoring Program, *Monitoring the European Union Accession Process: Minority Protection, Volume I – An Assessment of Selected Policies in Candidate States* (Open Society Institute, Budapest, November 2002) (chapter on Estonia), available at <http://www.eumap.org,>, (accessed 26 September 2002), with reference to the status of the native Russian-speakers who constitute a significant portion of Estonia's population

[11] Courts Act, Art. 47.

[12] Courts Act, Art. 50-1. Under new Courts Act the Judicial Examination Commission includes representatives appointed by various bodies, but with a majority appointed by judges. The Commission consists of two trial district judges, two regional court judges and two Supreme Court judges elected by the General Assembly of judges, a legal scholar appointed by the University of Tartu Faculty of Law Council, a representative of the Ministry of Justice appointed by the Minister, an advocate appointed by the Bar Association, and a State prosecutor appointed by the Prosecutor General. Courts Act, Art. 69 (2).

[13] Courts Act, Art. 50.

[14] Courts Act, Art. 50.

[15] Courts Act Art. 62 (3).

2. Evaluating and Regulating Performance

Estonia is in need of a standardised and more inclusive evaluation system for gauging judges' performance to assist them in their professional development and facilitate clear decision-making for promotion. The new Courts Act mandates periodic evaluations only for probationary judges,[16] not for tenured judges. Moreover, no criteria for making the evaluations exist.

Unless these evaluations are conducted according to standardised criteria and supported by guidelines for handling poor performance, they are not likely to have a positive impact on judges' professionalism and capacity, and could even jeopardise judges' adjudicative independence. Subject to the requirements of judicial independence and accountability, Estonia should develop a system for evaluating judges systematically throughout their careers on the basis of clearly defined criteria and transparent procedures.

A certain measure of informal control over judicial performance is ensured by broad public access to court operations and judgements. All court judgements (except judgements that are not pronounced publicly to protect the legitimate interests of minors, spouses or victims) are available on the Internet. Electronic databases are equipped with search engines.[17] However, the system for handling public complaints against judges is less well developed: court presidents and the Ministry of Justice handle complaints, and the only clear requirement guiding their work is that they should investigate and provide an answer.[18] Clearer and more elaborated procedures could provide a useful check on judges' performance and professionalism.

---

[16] Courts Act, Art. 100 (2). Before the recent changes to the Act, during their initial three-year probationary period judges were evaluated by the Judicial Examination Commission at the discretionary request of any official entitled to initiate disciplinary proceedings against a judge.

[17] Available at <http://eoigus.just.ee/kola/>, (accessed 26 September 2002) (judgements of district courts); <http://www.tarturk.just.ee/>, (accessed 26 September 2002) (judgements of Tartu Regional Court); <http://www.nc.ee/lahendid/>, (accessed 26 September 2002) (judgements of the Supreme Court). At present, district court judgements can only be searched by the date of trial, number of the case and name of the judge; other databases have full text search capabilities.

[18] Reply to Complaints Act, Art. 3 (2), RTI 1994, 51, 857 *as amended by* RTI 2001, 58, 354. <http://www.riigiteataja.ee/ert/act.jsp?id=22292.>, (accessed 26 September 2002).

3. Training for a Professional Judiciary

Despite substantial efforts, existing structures for and expertise in judicial training are not utilised satisfactorily; changes made by the new Courts Act should create possibilities for more effective funding and planning if properly implemented.

The Ministry of Justice, which has been responsible for judicial training, has developed a *Strategy for Training Judges and Prosecutors for the Years 2001–2004*.[19] The Ministry mainly funds training organised by it or conducted by the Estonian Law Centre, which was founded several years ago by the Government, the Supreme Court and Tartu University. However, the commitment of the Government and Parliament to judicial training appears to be decreasing; the funds dedicated to the training of judges and prosecutors decreased from 4.344 million Estonian kroons (€277,631.49) in 1999 to 2.5 million Estonian kroons (€170,000) in 2002.[20]

Just as importantly, the practical division of training responsibilities between the Ministry of Justice and the Estonian Law Centre has led to a gradual decrease in utilisation of the Centre's potential. The Centre has good infrastructure – classrooms, equipment, and library – and has accumulated the experience and expertise necessary to provide qualified training. However, the Government's contribution to the Centre's budget is steadily decreasing; almost all the decline in funding for training noted above has come through cuts in the Government contribution to the Centre's budget, which has dropped from two million kroons (€127,822) in 1997 to 0.5 million kroons (€31,955) in 2002.[21] Accordingly, in the Spring semester of 2002 the Centre was able to offer only 132 hours of training, compared to 803 training hours offered by the Ministry of Justice itself.[22] This is a wasted opportunity to take advantage of demonstrably high quality training.

The new Courts Act envisions a transfer of overall responsibility for judicial training from the Ministry of Justice to a new Council for Judicial Training.[23] The Council will be composed of two district court judges, two regional court judges, two Supreme Court judges, and one representative each from the Ministry of Justice, the Prosecutor's Office and the University of Tartu. The Act also transfers budgetary responsibility for training

---

[19] Strategy for Training of Judges and Prosecutors for the Years 2001–2004, *adopted on* 20 February 2001; <http://www.just.ee/index.php3?cath=2232.>, (accessed 26 September 2002).

[20] State Budget for 2002, Official Gazette, RTI, 01.01.2002, 8;
see <http://www.riigiteataja.ee/ert/act.jsp?id=27571>, (accessed 26 September 2002),
State Budget for 1999, Official Gazette, RTI 1999, 3, 49; see <http://www.riigiteataja.ee/>,
(accessed 26 September 2002).

[21] Interview with Aavo Kaine, Managing Director of the Estonian Law Centre, 24 April 2002.

[22] Interview with Aavo Kaine, Managing Director of the Estonian Law Centre, 24 April 2002.

[23] Courts Act, Art. 44 (1).

from the Ministry to the Supreme Court.[24] This is widely perceived as a positive step towards reversing the decline in funding, and may also encourage fuller utilisation of existing potential. It is projected that judicial training will be carried out on the basis of yearly training programmes developed by the Council. The Council will also be able to make certain training programmes compulsory for judges. However, as these changes have not yet been tested in practice, it is too early to assess their merit.

D. INSTITUTIONAL CAPACITY OF THE JUDICIARY

The new Courts Act increases the judiciary's authority over its own affairs, although it does not increase judges' participation in the budget process and the Ministry of Justice retains major responsibility for administration of the judicial system. Similarly, the Act increases the role of court managers, allowing judges to focus more effectively on their core adjudicative functions. It is important that court managers are professionally trained for their increased responsibilities.

1. Governance and Administration of the Judicial Branch

Through its Courts Department, the Ministry of Justice maintains primary responsibility for policy, planning, and administration of the judicial branch. However, under the new Courts Act although the powers of the new Council for Court Administration[25] are mostly advisory, the Minister is required to seek the Council's consent for a number of important policy and administrative decisions.

Provided it is effectively implemented, this arrangement may provide a needed improvement in governance and administration of the judicial branch. Until now, for example, the Ministry has failed to develop standard norms for caseloads, which produces inefficiencies in planning for other areas such as court technology and equipment; the new system has the potential to remedy such problems if implemented comprehensively and with full political and bureaucratic support.

The new Council for Court Administration consists of:

- the Chief Justice of the Supreme Court, as the Council's President *ex officio;*

- five judges elected by the General Assembly of judges;

---

[24] Courts Act, Art. 44 (5).

[25] Courts Act, Art. 40.

- two Members of Parliament;

- a licensed advocate appointed by the Bar Association;

- the Prosecutor General (or an appointee); and

- the Legal Chancellor (or an appointee).

The Minister of Justice participates in the meetings of the Council but without the right to vote. The Minister or the Chief Justice of the Supreme Court convenes meetings of the Council; the official convening the meeting decides its agenda.

The Council for Court Administration has both advisory and consensual powers. The Minister of Justice must seek the consent of the Council in order to:

- determine the territorial jurisdiction and location of courts;

- determine the number of judges in district and regional courts;

- appoint and remove court presidents;

- adopt court rules;

- determine the number of judicial apprentices and appoint apprentices;

- decide on additional payments to judges who consent to reappointment to a different court in the interests of delivery of justice.[26]

In addition, The Council's consent is required for determining the number of lay assessors, and for court presidents and court administrative directors to determine the structure of their courts.[27]

The Council for Court Administration is entitled to render non-binding opinions concerning candidates for vacant Supreme Court Judge's positions; any decrease in the number of courts or judges; release of judges on health grounds; release of judges after non-judicial service for the Ministry of Justice or the Supreme Court when there are no vacant judicial positions; and release of judges due to incompatibility of continued judicial service with other engagements.[28]

The creation of the Council for Court Administration therefore represents an important step towards limiting the unnecessarily broad influence of the Ministry of Justice over the judiciary's administration. However, the new requirements for joint decision-making with the Ministry combined with a lack of administrative capacity (the Council will not have an

---

[26] Courts Act, Art. 41 (1).

[27] Courts Act, Art. 41 (1).

[28] Courts Act, Art. 41 (3).

independent budget or support staff, but rather will be serviced by the staff of the Ministry) may hinder the independent and efficient work of the Council.

The lack of independent budgetary authority in particular threatens to undercut the otherwise positive developments initiated by the new Courts Act. The Ministry of Justice retains primary responsibility for district and regional court budgets, and there are neither objective criteria nor guarantees of funding levels to guide the Ministry in this process. Furthermore, there is no dedicated chapter for courts in the State budget; the chapter allocated to the Ministry of Justice includes a separate budget line for district and regional courts.

Court managing directors plan and prepare budgets that, after approval by the court president, are submitted to the Ministry of Justice and then to the Ministry of Finance for approval or revision.[29] After submission, court officials do not have the opportunity to make further comment. Allowing for greater participation by court presidents or managing directors in the budget process would help ensure that courts' legitimate infrastructure needs are met.

One significant development is a new provision in the Courts Act that entitles the Council for Court Administration to adopt principles for drawing up and changing court budgets.[30] The Ministry of Justice is obliged to take the adopted principles into account in determining the court budgets,[31] although it is not clear how they will limit the Ministry's scope of discretion.

The new Courts Act also provides that the Chief Justice shall deliver an annual report to Parliament on the state of affairs in the judicial system.[32] As the reports will be publicly available, they may encourage a certain measure of public scrutiny of operations of the judicial system and provide an opportunity for public feedback about courts' performance and their legitimate organisational needs.

2. Court Administrative Capacity

Court presidents, assisted by managing directors, administer day-to-day court operations and supervise their courts' performance and efficiency. Court presidents have extensive managerial responsibilities, yet the procedures for their selection and appointment by the

---

[29] State Budget Act, Articles 11-15, RTI 1999, 55, 584 *as amended by* RT I 2000, 55, 360; see <https://www.riigiteataja.ee/ert/act.jsp?id=22451.>, (accessed 26 September 2002).

[30] Courts Act, Art. 41 (2).

[31] Courts Act, Art. 43 (1).

[32] Courts Act, Art. 27 (3).

Ministry of Justice are insufficiently clear or regularised. Specialised training courses for court presidents began only this year. There have been no special courses for managing directors, although the need for courses has been discussed and it is planned that such courses will be offered in the near future.[33]

The new Courts Act does support the professionalisation of court management by increasing the responsibilities of the managing directors. However, the Act does not ensure that managing directors have sufficient qualifications or that they regularly upgrade their competence through training; the Act only requires that managing directors have a higher degree.[34]

Although the caseload has stabilised and even slightly decreased since 2000, the significant increase in caseloads since the middle of the 1990s – including an over 50 percent increase in criminal case filings since 1995, for example[35] – requires a concomitant increase in the number of qualified and trained support staff, especially professional legal staff, which has not occurred. This would further relieve judges of peripheral technical burdens, such as case preparation, and allow them to focus more effectively on substantive matters related to their core adjudicative responsibilities.

The length of court proceedings has been widely criticised, but the situation currently is not severe.[36] Working conditions in courts are generally good, and courts generally have sufficient equipment and facilities. Under the new Courts Act, the structure of support and administrative staff in a given court is no longer determined by the Ministry of Justice, but by the relevant court presidents and managing directors.[37] As before, however, the court presidents' and managing directors' scope of decision remains limited by budgetary processes outside their discretion or control, in which the Ministry retains influence.

---

[33] Interview with Aavo Kaine, Managing Director of the Estonian Law Centre, 24 April 2002.

[34] Courts Act, Art. 125 (5).

[35] See <http://www.just.ee/files/statistika/Statistical%20Report%202001.html>, (accessed 26 September 2002).

[36] The average length of a criminal case is three months and 21 days, and in the most overburdened court just over 14 months. For civil cases the average length is nearly five months, and nearly 13 months in the most overburdened court. Several cases have taken more than a year to be tried, most often due to delays caused by some parties or witnesses being missing. <http://www.just.ee/files/statistika/Statistical%20Report%202001.html.>, (accessed 26 September 2002).

[37] Courts Act, Art. 9 (4), 18 (4), 22 (7). Court presidents are responsible for those staff involved in the delivery of justice, while managing directors are responsible for other support and administrative staff.

E. RECOMMENDATIONS

1. To the Estonian Government and Legislature

- Ensure effective implementation of the new Courts Act in subsequent regulations and practice. In particular, provide the new Council for Court Administration with the means necessary so that it may function effectively.

- Improve judicial selection and promotion procedures by: further clarifying eligibility criteria; providing specialised training for members of the Judicial Examination Commission; and including representatives of legal professions or associations and other non-governmental organisations in the process.

- Fully fund and unify judicial training initiatives, utilising the expertise already developed by the Estonian Law Centre.

- Establish clear criteria and mechanisms for the evaluation of performance throughout judges' careers in order to support their professional development and facilitate clear decision-making for promotion.

- Improve the budgeting process by developing objective criteria for budget preparation and by including judges more broadly in budget deliberations and allocation decisions.

- Increase staffing levels of court personnel, in particular legal court staff; transfer more daily management responsibility to managing directors under the control of court presidents. Ensure that the professional qualifications of managing directors are relevant and adequate.

2. To the European Union

- Assist in the ongoing reform of judicial branch management by utilising the recent experiences of reforms in other EU candidate and member States to develop clear implementing regulations and efficient practices expressive of European values and the interests of the Union.

- Encourage development of a comprehensive judicial training programme and cooperate both in the funding and operation of unified judicial training mechanisms.

- Emphasise the importance of the periodic evaluations of judicial performance for enhancing the competence of judges.

Judicial Capacity in Hungary

Table of Contents

A. INTRODUCTION

The independence of the judiciary as a separate branch is well established in Hungary. Generally, the structures of judicial self-government and self-administration function efficiently. A recent ruling by the Constitutional Court concerning the mandatory establishment of appellate instances has helped ensure that basic questions about the organisation of the judiciary are protected from politics.

At the same time the continued involvement of the executive in the budgeting process for the judiciary has resulted in consistent under-funding and has effectively weakened its independence and capacity. Certain areas of operations should be made more transparent and professional management should be introduced into the courts, freeing up judges to focus on their core adjudicative work and thus helping address case delays.

More broadly, the very success the judiciary has had in asserting extensive institutional autonomy makes it imperative that it continue to develop specialised expertise in public administration and enhance the transparency of its operations, in order to increase judges' professionalism and to avoid creating an insular and unaccountable institution that lacks public trust and support.

B. CURRENT DEVELOPMENTS AFFECTING JUDICIAL INDEPENDENCE AND CAPACITY

In an important ruling, the Constitutional Court declared that the failure to establish appellate courts violated an express provision of the Constitution; the ruling ensured that basic questions about the organisation of the judiciary are protected from politics and will increase the caseload capacity of the judiciary. Legislative measures have also been introduced to increase the transparency of court operations and the public accountability of individual judges.

1. Constitutional Court Ruling on the Creation of Appellate Courts

In an important ruling in late 2001, the Constitutional Court declared that a politically controversial decision not to establish a system of appellate courts violated an express provision of the Constitution[1] and ordered their establishment by the end of 2002.[2]

The Court's ruling further refined and strengthened the separation of powers and ensured that basic questions about the organisation of the judiciary are protected from politics, thus increasing the stability upon which the development of a professional judiciary relies. In addition, the creation of the appellate instance will increase the capacity of the judicial system to deal with increasing caseloads.[3]

2. Other Developments

An amendment to the Act on the Legal Status and Remuneration of Judges makes it mandatory for judges to submit disclosure declarations concerning their property, just

---

[1] CONST. REP. HUNGARY, Act XX/1949, Art. 45(1f). *See also* EU Accession Monitoring Program, *Monitoring the EU Accession Process: Judicial Independence in Hungary*, (Open Society Institute, Budapest, October 2001), available at: <http://www.eumap.org>, (accessed 26 September 2002). (Corrigendum: The Report, at footnote 5 (p. 192), wrongly quotes the Constitution; it should read: "In the Republic of Hungary justice is administered by the Supreme Court, appeals *courts...*" [emphasis added]).

[2] Decision of the Constitutional Court No. 49/2001 of 22 November 2001.

[3] *See* Section D.2., "Court Administrative Capacity".

as civil servants are required to do.[4] This amendment may help ensure the professionalism and accountability of judges and limit corruption in public life.[5]

At the beginning of 2002 a system of predefined case distribution was introduced.[6] The system of case distribution is determined by court presidents, taking into account the types of incoming cases, the size of the court divisions (civil, criminal, labour, and administrative), and judges' specialisation inside each division; maintaining a balanced caseload among each court's judges is also a factor.[7] The distribution of cases is made public on posters in the court buildings. This provision significantly enhances the transparency of the courts and court proceedings. It is too early, however, to assess the effectiveness of this innovation.

C. PROFESSIONAL COMPETENCE OF JUDGES

The procedures for selecting and promoting judges would benefit from clearer and more standardised criteria; the present lack of transparency and the broad discretion afforded officials involved in the process encourage arbitrariness and even abuse, and may discourage the development of a professional corps of judges. Hungary has a good system for evaluating judges' performance; however, the system affords legal professionals and other individuals outside the judiciary only limited input. The general public's limited opportunity to monitor the quality of adjudication contributes to public distrust of courts. Although Hungary has a fairly efficient training system, its capacity and level of financial support are not sufficient to develop necessary training programmes in management skills, and political support for the creation of a separate institute for judicial training is lacking.

1. Selection and Promotion

The procedures for selecting and promoting judges would benefit from increased transparency and further elaboration of the applicable criteria. The present lack of

---

[4] Act on Legal Status and Remuneration of Judges, LXVII/1997, Art. 10 (4a).

[5] For a comprehensive discussion of corruption in Hungary, including in its judiciary, see EU Accession Monitoring Program, *Monitoring the EU Accession Process: Corruption and Anti-Corruption Policy in Hungary* (Open Society Institute, Budapest, October 2002), available at <http://www.eumap.org.>.

[6] Act on Organisation and Administration of Courts, LXVI/1997, Art.11, *as amended by* Act CV/2001, Art. 16 (1).

[7] Interview with János Zanathy, head of the Office of the National Judicial Council, May 2002.

transparency and the broad discretion afforded bodies and officials involved in the process encourage arbitrariness and even abuse, and may discourage the development of a professional corps of judges.

Under present rules, an eligible candidate[8] may submit an application for a judgeship after having worked at least one year as a court secretary or in another law-related occupation that requires an examination in law or public administration.[9] Candidates also have to pass a medical and psychological test.[10] As these constitute the only basis for admittance to the profession, the formal eligibility requirements and psychological examination should be complemented by more specific and transparent rules that would guide decision-making in the process.

Judicial vacancies are commonly announced in the Court Bulletin (Bírósági Közlöny), the monthly publication of the National Judicial Council.[11] The Bulletin is only distributed to courts, which limits its usefulness in ensuring that the broadest possible range of qualified individuals can apply; moreover, regulations do not stipulate the timeframe for advertising or accepting applications for vacant positions. Although no cases of abuse have been reported, this lack of legal regulation creates an opportunity for tampering; it would be preferable to give announcements a broader distribution, and to stipulate timeframes and procedures for them.

The relevant judicial council screens applications and makes non-binding recommendations to the presidents of courts with vacancies. The presidents select their preferred candidates on the basis of these recommendations (and a personal interview, if they decide to have one),[12] and forward them to the National Judicial Council for nominations. The State President makes the final appointment upon the nomination of the National Council.[13] It is unclear on what basis, besides formal eligibility requirements and medical examination, the judicial councils, court presidents and the National Council select candidates. In addition, there are no provisions for input from or scrutiny by external experts or relevant professional groups. This lack of transparency should be

---

[8] Eligibility requirements include Hungarian citizenship, a clean criminal record, eligibility to vote, a university law degree, and a successful legal examination. *See* Act on the Legal Status and Remuneration of Judges, LXVII/1997, Art. 3 (1).

[9] Such as a judge of the Constitutional Court, public prosecutor, notary public, and attorney. *See* Act on Legal Status and Remuneration of Judges, LXVII/1997, Art. 3 (1).

[10] *See* Ministry of Justice and the Ministry of Health Joint Decree No. 1/1999, 18 January 1999, *as amended by* Decree No. 5/2002, 29 March 2002.

[11] For an explanation of the Council, *see* Section D.1., "Governance and Administration of the Judicial Branch".

[12] Act on the Legal Status and Remuneration of Judges, LXVII/1997, Art. 8.

[13] Act on the Legal Status and Remuneration of Judges, LXVII/1997, Art. 2 (2).

remedied by clearer selection criteria and a more public deliberative process. Officials involved in the process would also benefit from specialised training. In particular, the decisive and unchecked role of individual court presidents should be mitigated, as it unnecessarily allows opportunities for arbitrariness and undermines the credibility of the whole selection system.

The powers of court presidents are even greater concerning promotion of serving judges to higher instance courts. In such cases, court presidents are simply entitled to select judges to fill vacant positions.[14] Even more than is the case with initial selection, the procedure is opaque; indeed, it is even less clear what criteria serve as a basis for court presidents' decisions as serving judges obviously have already met formal eligibility requirements and undergone medical and psychological examinations. Here again, the broad discretionary power of court presidents ought to be limited or balanced, perhaps by a multi-step or reviewed process.

Although lawyers from outside the judiciary are entitled to apply for judgeships, the judges who control the system prefer young law graduates for initial appointments and their fellow judges for promotions. This unnecessarily narrows the pool of qualified candidates and encourages the creation and consolidation of an insular and hierarchical professional corporation. A greater openness to experienced external candidates would go some way to mitigating this evident tendency.

2. Evaluating and Regulating Performance

Hungary has developed a balanced and detailed system for evaluating judges' performance. However, this system is insulated from input from legal professionals or other interested individuals and bodies outside the judiciary. The general public's limited opportunity to monitor the quality of adjudication contributes to public distrust of courts, including doubts about judges' professional aptitude.

The evaluation system provides for three mandatory assessments. A judge's performance is reviewed at the end of his initial three-year appointment and then again six years and twelve years after receiving a life appointment.[15] In addition, a judge's work can be subjected to extraordinary assessment upon the motion of the court president.[16] In addition, judges themselves may request an extraordinary evaluation.[17]

---

[14] Act on the Legal Status and Remuneration of Judges, LXVII/1997, Art. 8 (2).

[15] Act on the Legal Status and Remuneration of Judges, LXVII/1997, Art. 11.

[16] Regional court presidents may request review of both regional and district court judges beneath them.

[17] Act on the Legal Status and Remuneration of Judges, LXVII/1997, Art. 49.

The criteria and procedure for evaluation are established by the National Judicial Council, and are the same for both periodic and extraordinary evaluations.[18] A judge appointed by the president of the relevant court conducts a comprehensive two-month qualitative and quantitative examination of the judge's work that also takes into account the opinion of the court president.

The examination procedure includes review of cases and trial observation. At least fifty completed cases must be examined; the majority of the cases are selected randomly, but the judge being examined may recommend five cases for evaluation, and the regional court hearing appeals from that judge's district court may recommend additional cases. The judge's professional conduct is evaluated by observing trials in progress. In addition to the legal quality of decisions and the judge's manner of conducting trials, evaluation criteria include criteria that are not clearly defined, such as treatment of trial participants.

Evaluation may result in one of three grades: excellent, satisfactory, or unsatisfactory.[19] A judge whose performance is found unsatisfactory may challenge the determination in the Labour Court; appeal is to the Supreme Court.

This evaluation procedure is effectively confined to a few officials and does not allow any broader participation from judges or other legal professionals; results of the examination may not be made public.[20] More broadly, there are only limited opportunities for the public to review court decisions, as access to case files is limited and court judgements are made public only exceptionally; this unnecessarily limits the opportunity for public commentary to provide informal feedback to the judiciary about its professional performance.

3. Training for a Professional Judiciary

Although Hungary has developed a fairly effective system for judicial training, the capacity of the existing organisational framework and level of financial support do not allow for its expansion and refinement to include managerial and judicial skills. Political support for the planned creation of a separate institute for judicial training is lacking.

---

[18] Decree of the National Judicial Council No. 5/1998, Bulletin of the National Judicial Council No. 3, 1998.

[19] Act on the Legal Status and Remuneration of Judges, LXVII/1997, Art. 53.

[20] Act No LXIII of 1992 on Protection of Personal Data and Disclosure of Data of Public Interest.

Training is centralised within the National Judicial Council.[21] The Personnel and Education Division in the Office of the Council[22] develops and coordinates specific training programmes that are carried out at various locations. Training programmes generally concentrate on analysis of new laws and familiarisation with the legal norms of the European Union; training in judicial and managerial skills is insufficient.

The National Judicial Council has concluded that the current organisational framework has reached capacity,[23] and further expansion of training into areas such as management, administration, and interpretative skills would require setting up a separate, dedicated training institute.[24] Current plans call for a Judicial Training Institute to be organised as a division of the Office of the Council; the Institute's curricula would include both initial and continuing training of judges, as well as training of court personnel. Implementation of this large-scale project – originally slated to begin in September 2003 – would require financial support from the political branches, which has not materialised. The executive and the legislature should reconsider their posture towards supporting the institutionalisation of training through the establishment of the Institute.

D. INSTITUTIONAL CAPACITY OF THE JUDICIAL BRANCH

Problems persist in the budget process; although the judiciary now has the right to draft its own budget proposal, the executive routinely submits a parallel proposal, which in practice Parliament accepts. This practice has resulted in consistent under-funding of the judiciary. The present system relies on serving judges to manage and administer the courts; introducing professional management would free up judges – who are not trained for management in any event – to focus on their core adjudicative work and thus help address case delays. More broadly, developing the judiciary's professionalism will help minimise the risk of its becoming an insular and unaccountable institution.

---

[21] Act on the Organisation and Administration of Courts, LXVI/1997, Art. 39 (h).

[22] For an explanation of the Office, *see* Section D.1., "Governance and Administration of the Judicial Branch".

[23] The Personnel and Education Division has ten employees to plan and organise the training of 2,556 judges (as of beginning of 2002) and numerous court staff.

[24] Recommendation of the National Judicial Council No. 3, 2001.

1. Governance and Administration of the Judicial Branch

Although problems with the courts' budgetary authority persist, the 1997 judicial reform has created a largely self-governing and self-administering judicial branch that functions satisfactorily. Indeed, it is the judiciary's very success in establishing its institutional independence that makes its professionalisation and increased transparency matters of current importance, in order to minimise the risk that the courts, though independent, might become an insular, unaccountable, socially unresponsive and distrusted institution.

Although the Ministry of Justice retains certain policy-setting powers – such as the right to propose bills regulating the court system – management of the courts is the sole responsibility of the National Judicial Council.[25] The powers of the Council are broad and include legal representation of the judiciary, nomination of judicial appointees, determination of promotions and other personnel matters, responsibility for drafting the courts' budget proposal and control over implementation of adopted budget for the judiciary, initiation of bills related to the work of the courts, and power to regulate and supervise court operations.[26]

The National Judicial Council consists of 15 members: nine judges elected by secret ballot of the judges conference, the President of the Supreme Court (*ex officio* president of the National Judicial council), the Minister of Justice, the Attorney General, the President of the Hungarian Chamber of Attorneys, and representatives of Parliament's Constitutional and Judiciary Committee and Budgetary and Financial Committee.[27] The non-judicial membership in the Council appears to be the only direct channel through which representatives from the political branches and professional groups of lawyers have a direct input on administration of the judicial system.

The National Judicial Council meets at least once a month. The body in charge of day-to-day operations of courts on a national level is the Office of the Council. The Office prepares sessions of the Council and is responsible for implementing its recommendations and regulations. The Office appears to be an efficient and fairly transparent institution. It conducts analyses of courts operations and has proposed clear standards to support efficient court procedures. In particular, it analyses the distribution of ongoing cases and designs plans for processing case backlogs. Every year the Office publishes a detailed report on its work. However, given the legal requirement that the head of the Office be a judge[28] and the fact that many of its

---

[25] Act on the Organisation and Administration of Courts, LXVI/1997, Art. 34.

[26] Act on the Organisation and Administration of Courts, LXVI/1997, Art. 39.

[27] Act on the Organisation and Administration of Courts, LXVI/1997, Art. 35.

[28] Act on the Organisation and Administration of Courts. LXVI/1997. Art. 56 (1).

leading officers are judges who have no specialised managerial training, it would be advisable to ensure that they have professional managers or experts assisting them.

Certain problems do persist, however, particularly in the budget process. Even though the judiciary now may draft its own budget proposal, the executive retains the right to draft a parallel proposal. In practice, each year the Government has submitted its parallel, lower budget proposal, which Parliament has accepted as its basis instead of the National Judicial Council's proposal, even though the law expressly provides that the part of the budget pertaining to the court system should be elaborated by the Council.[29] Reportedly, the Government has failed even to provide an itemised explanation for discrepancies between the two proposals, even though this is required by law.

This practice has contributed to the consistent under-funding of the judiciary – the current budget approved by Parliament is fully 40 percent lower than the request submitted by the Council[30] – and should be redressed. An insufficient budget limits the possibility to increase the numbers of judges and court staff in proportion to the growing caseload[31] and restricts improvements in work conditions.[32]

The present Government has pledged to respect the budgetary powers of the National Judicial Council. The Minister of Justice has declared that the basis for the Parliamentary deliberations on the budgetary chapter for the judiciary will be the version proposed by the National Judicial Council, and that the Government will not draft a separate budget proposal.[33] This proposal – which appears to accord with the

---

[29] Act on the Organisation and Administration of Courts, LXVI/1997, Art. 39 (b).

[30] The budgetary proposals (in Hungarian Forints) for the last three years:

	2000 (HUF)	2001 (HUF)	2002 (HUF)
Council Proposal	44,122,300 (€179,760)	59,167,100 (€241,060)	57,420,300 (€233,940)
Government Proposal	34,243,500 (€139,510)	35,586,200 (€144,990)	36,130,400 (€147,200)
Parliament's Budget	34,081,600 (€138,850)	36,348,800 (€148,100)	37,636,500 (€153,338)

Note: Euro amounts are calculated with rate available on 9 October 2002.

[31] For example, following the transfer of jurisdiction over misdemeanour cases to the regular courts, the National Judicial Council in its 2002 budget proposal requested an additional 120 judges and 180 court employees; the final budget, however, only allowed the appointment of an additional 40 judges and 40 employees. Interview with János Zanathy, head of the Office of the National Judicial Council, May 2002.

[32] For example, the introduction of a witness protection system placed additional burdens on courts to ensure compliance with a number of clearly defined physical criteria; the budgetary chapter on the courts does not include the financing necessary to meet these conditions.

[33] Interview with Péter Bárándy, Minister of Justice, Népszabadság, 6 June 2002.

law's requirements as well as respect the principles of judicial independence – should be followed during the Parliament's deliberations.

2. Court Administrative Capacity

The autonomous judicial administration relies on serving judges to manage and administer the courts. Introducing professional management would be especially advisable since it would free up judges to focus on their core adjudicative functions and thus help address case delays; in any event, the judges responsible are not well trained to handle court administration.

Ensuring and controlling the day-to-day operation of particular courts is the task of the court executives – that is, the court president and vice-president, the head and deputy head of the college, the president of the council, the division head and deputy division head.[34] All these offices are filled by serving judges for six-year terms; these judges must divide their time between adjudication and managerial or administrative concerns, for which they receive no special training.

Court presidents in particular have especially broad powers that include responsibility to ensure material conditions for court operations, hire and manage court personnel, oversee financial operations, and implement regulations of the National Judicial Council.[35] In spite of this, there are no requirements that court presidents have prior training in management techniques or that they receive post-appointment training. Occasional courses organised by the Office of the National Judicial Council on topics relating to court management are not sufficient to enable court presidents to manage increasingly complex court operations. There is consequently a need for more specialised training in managerial skills for court presidents and other executives. The introduction of professional management in the courts could be a long-term solution for the improvement of court administration.

The National Judicial Council and its Office regularly analyse case traffic and the workload of judges, and take measures to decrease delays in processing cases. However, the problem of case delays persists and is partly caused by insufficient budget allocations; shortage of staff in a number of courts is a particularly serious problem.

Between 1990 and 2001 the number of cases received increased by 200 percent,[36] and it is expected that the number of cases will increase even more in coming years –

---

[34] Act on the Organisation and Administration of Courts, LXVI/1997, Art. 62.

[35] Act on the Organisation and Administration of Courts, LXVI/1997, Chapter V.

[36] 2001 Report to the National Judicial Council, Court Bulletin No. 3, 2002.

perhaps up to four times – due to the extension of the courts' jurisdiction to include review of misdemeanour cases.[37] Nonetheless, the courts received less than half of the funding they requested from the Government for new personnel and technical assets in order to respond to the expected increase in caseload.[38]

Certain legal measures are available to decrease the length of proceedings, such as limited possibilities for mediation,[39] and the National Judicial Council's power to order extraordinary or expedited proceedings in any ongoing court case.[40] In addition, judges have to fill out monthly reports with the detailed causes of case postponements.[41]

However, further improvements will require increases in support staff. Currently, there are only two support staff allocated for each judge; in addition, a number of these positions are not filled.[42] By one estimate, on average, trial time occupies 27 percent of judges' time and writing judgements 15 percent, with the remainder devoted to administrative tasks such as management, statistics and dictation of trial records.[43] These tasks could be performed by trained legal and support staff, freeing up judges to concentrate on competent and timely disposition of cases.

---

[37] Preliminary estimates made by the Office of the National Judicial Council suggest in particular that the transfer to the courts after January 2002 of jurisdiction for reviewing rulings by administrative authorities in misdemeanour cases will add an additional 30 to 40 thousand cases annually to the courts' docket. Interview with János Zanathy, head of the Office of the National Judicial Council, May 2002.

[38] 2001 Report to the National Judicial Council, Court Bulletin No. 3, 2002; *also* interview with János Zanathy, head of the Office of the National Judicial Council, May 2002.

[39] *Report to the National Judiciary Council on the assessment of judicial data provided during 2001,* Bírósági Közlöny no. 2002/3.

[40] Act on the Organisation and Administration of Courts, Art. 41 (1a).

[41] The Decree of the National Judicial Council requires that judges fill out a monthly reports with detailed causes of the postponement of court proceedings. Reports are submitted to the appeal court and to the National Judicial Council.

[42] 2001 Report to the National Judicial Council, Court Bulletin No. 3, 2002.

[43] Ágnes Kövér, *Costs relations of the operation of the criminal justice system. Elaboration of a practical model of calculation,* Kriminológiai Tanulmányok, 2002, p. 84.

E. RECOMMENDATIONS

1. To the Hungarian Courts, Government and Legislature

- Ensure that the basis for parliamentary debate on the judicial branch's budget is the draft proposed by the National Judicial Council.

- Further define criteria for selection and promotion of judges and make those processes, as well as performance evaluation, more transparent; allow for increased input or scrutiny from external experts of the deliberative process.

- Provide necessary support for the establishment of the planned Institute for Judicial Training.

- Introduce professional management in the courts as a priority. As an interim measure, increase specialised training for court presidents and other executives.

- Take necessary measures to increase the number of auxiliary judiciary personnel and ensure their continuing professional training.

2. To the European Union

- Ensure that relevant EU institutions and officials develop direct channels of communication with the autonomous governing and administrative organs of the judiciary, to effectively assist in formulating policy and developing assistance plans.

- Emphasise the importance of professionalising the management of an independent judiciary to ensure its efficiency and accountability to society.

- Emphasise the necessity to establish the Institute for Judicial Training as a means to further increase the competence and efficiency of courts, and provide technical support by facilitating communication with similar institutions in other EU candidate and member States.

Judicial Capacity in Latvia

Table of Contents

A. INTRODUCTION

Latvia lacks a comprehensive approach to modernising and strengthening its judicial branch. Reform has been piecemeal and has failed to address the serious shortcomings of the judicial system, in large part because there has not been sufficient and serious political commitment to real reform.

The problems confronting the judiciary are systemic and broad ranging. Courts are generally not well respected; they are perceived as inefficient at best, and at worst, unskilled and corrupt.[1] The administrative capacity of the judicial branch as a whole is quite low; management professionalisation, adequate professional and support staff and appropriate facilities are necessary to deal with endemic court delays. Indeed, one local NGO has reported that the principal human rights problem in Latvia is a significant backlog in the courts, resulting in excessive pre-trial detention.[2]

Efforts to address these issues have been only partial at best and have lacked any timeline for implementation. Judicial reform has proceeded, when it has, in an *ad hoc* manner in response to specific problems, and as a result it has failed to establish effective systems for selecting, training, evaluating, and administering judges. The problems that plague the judiciary's operations are largely a result of consistent under-funding, which in turn reflects a lack of political commitment.

Recently proposed amendments to the laws governing the judiciary promise some improvement, but there does not yet seem to be sufficient political will to ensure that the amendments can be effectively implemented; at present the amendments even include elements that will likely do nothing to improve the judiciary's position. The amendments will help only if they are systematically implemented in a manner consonant with the higher and more pressing goal of creating a truly independent and capable judiciary.

---

[1] For a detailed evaluation of corruption in Latvia, including in its judiciary, *see* EU Accession Monitoring Program, *Monitoring the EU Accession Process: Corruption and Anti-Corruption Policy in Latvia* (Open Society Institute, Budapest, October 2002), available at <http:www.eumap.org.>, (accessed 26 September 2002).

[2] "Human Rights in Latvia in 2001", report by the Latvian Centre for Human Rights and Ethnic Studies, accessible at <http://www.politika.lv/index.php?id=102691&lang+lv>, (accessed 26 September 2002).

B. CURRENT DEVELOPMENTS AFFECTING JUDICIAL CAPACITY AND INDEPENDENCE

Two major changes to the organisation of the judiciary have been proposed: amendments to the Law on the Judiciary, and a framework paper on creating a separate judicial administration. While both proposals contain promising elements, the political establishment has yet to commit to either in a way that would lead to systemic change. Furthermore, the framework paper currently includes proposals that would do nothing to redress the judiciary's insufficient level of institutional independence.

1. Proposed Amendments to Act on Judicial Power

In early 2002, the Ministry of Justice proposed a package of amendments to the Act on the Judiciary aimed primarily at tackling lengthy court delays and backlogs; currently the amendments are being deliberated in Parliament.[3] The amendments contain provisions allowing individual judges to work on several cases at one time, creating a standardised case allocation and allowing for cases and judges (with their consent) to be transferred to relieve overburdened areas.

The amendments, however, specify no timeline for legislative action and have not generated significant discussion among the public or professional legal community. Although potentially a positive development, these amendments alone will not do enough to address the systemic problems that plague the judiciary. They will have to be supported by a political commitment to effect systemic changes, such as increased funding and improved administrative capacity for the judiciary on both the national and court level.

2. Creation of a Judicial Administration

Concerns expressed by the European Union regarding insufficient *de facto* independence of the judiciary[4] led the Ministry of Justice to propose the creation of a

---

[3] Draft amendments to the Act on Judicial Power (first reading), *adopted* 6 June 2002. *See* <http://www.saeima.lv>, (accessed 6 August 2002).

[4] 2001 Regular Report on Latvia's Progress Towards Accession, 13 October 2001, Section B, 1.1. available at <http://www.eumap.org>.

judicial administration,[5] with the idea of enhancing the representation of the judiciary vis-à-vis the other branches of power and consolidating the judiciary's control over its own affairs, including its finances.

The Ministry of Justice's proposal contains three possibilities, including an independent courts agency, a semi-autonomous body under the supervision of the Ministry, or a regular unit within the Ministry itself. Only the first alternative would actually redress the problem of the judiciary's insufficient independence and would create conditions for the development of administrative capacity within the judiciary. However, no proposal has been formally drafted into a concrete legislative proposal and there is no timeline for submission to Parliament.

C. PROFESSIONAL COMPETENCE OF JUDGES

The system for selecting and promoting judges requires thorough reform. A lack of defined criteria, transparent procedures and professionalism in selection and promotion raises serious concerns about the soundness of the present system. Combined with the lack of substantive performance evaluation and low investment in judicial training, these factors threaten the professional competence of judges.

1. Selection and Promotion

The lack of defined decision-making criteria, insufficient procedural transparency, and limited input from relevant professional groups all raise serious questions about the objectivity of the system of selection and promotion and its potential to create a truly professional corps of judges.

The Ministry of Justice is responsible for the initial selection of district and regional court judges.[6] Both the Ministry itself and presidents of courts in which an opening exists may solicit individuals to submit an application. Once identified, candidates

---

[5] Tiesu administrācijas koncepcija (Draft Framework Paper on Court Administration), 20 December 2001, available at <http://www.politika.lv/index.php?id=102382&lang=lv.>, (accessed 26 September 2002).

[6] Act on Judicial Power, 15 December 1992 (with subsequent amendments), Official Gazette (Zinotajs), 14 January 1993. Candidates for the Supreme Court are selected and nominated by the President of the Supreme Court. *See* Act on Judicial Power, Art. 59.

eligible for appointment to a district court[7] complete a short apprenticeship.[8] The criteria upon which candidates are evaluated and chosen for apprenticeship are opaque, and the value of the short practical training periods is particularly doubtful.

Apprenticeships are awarded on the basis of informal interviews with the President of the Supreme Court or the Under-secretary of State at the Ministry of Justice, although there is no legal requirement to do so. There are no clear criteria for selection of candidates for interviews or for apprenticeships, nor does there appear to be any verification of candidates' qualifications. Representatives from judicial associations, professional groups and academia do not participate in the apprentice selection process.

The specific duration of an apprenticeship, which is organised according to an individual programme prepared by the Ministry of Justice, depends on the relevant experience of the apprentice and may span from one to five months with a possibility of extension for a sixth month.[9] It is questionable whether such short practical training – as little as one month – is sufficient to verify the suitability of a candidate for the profession and prepare him for a judgeship.

Likewise, the subsequent stages in the selection procedure are not sufficiently standardised or transparent. Following the apprenticeship, the court president evaluates the apprentice. There are no clear guidelines or uniform evaluation criteria to assist court presidents in evaluating apprentices, even though a single court president's negative opinion prevents a candidate from participating further in the selection process.[10]

After receiving a positive opinion, a candidate must then complete a judicial examination before the Judicial Qualifications Board.[11] The examination, prepared by the Courts' Department of the Ministry of Justice, is inadequate, consisting only of an oral interview testing the candidate's legal knowledge. There is no written component, assessment of legal reasoning or writing skills, or psychological assessment to determine

---

[7] Eligibility requirements for a judgeship in the district court are Latvian citizenship, 25 years of age, legal education and two years experience in legal field. All candidates have also to be "fair lawyers," although the meaning of this term has not been specified. *See* Act on Judicial Power, Art. 52 (1).

[8] Act on Judicial Power, Art. 52 (5). Apprenticeships are not required for candidates to regional courts and the Supreme Court.

[9] Ministry of Justice Regulation on Procedure of In-Service Training of Judicial Candidates, Art. 8, *adopted* 2 September1999.

[10] Ministry of Justice Regulation on Procedure of In-Service Training of Judicial Candidates, Art. 9, *adopted* 2 September1999.

[11] Act on Judicial Power, Art. 52, and Regulation of the Ministry of Justice on Procedure of In-Service Training of Judicial Candidates, Art. 9, *adopted* 2 September1999.

the candidate's suitability for a judicial post, nor do there appear to be any grading criteria or procedures. In addition, the Board consists exclusively of judges who have received no additional training to prepare them for evaluating the suitability of judicial applicants.[12] Finally, the Board does not bind the Minister, who therefore has an unnecessarily broad discretion in making nominations to the Parliament.

At the end of this process, district court judges are initially appointed by the Parliament for a probationary term of three years, at the end of which the Minister of Justice, with a non-binding opinion of the Judicial Qualifications Board, may recommend that Parliament appoint the judge for an unlimited term or for an additional two-year probationary term. If Parliament appoints the judge to an additional two-year term, then, after the expiration of the term, Parliament – again acting on the recommendation of the Minister of Justice – may confirm the judge for an unlimited term.[13]

The Minister of Justice, having considered the non-binding opinion of the Judicial Qualifications Board, may choose not to nominate a judge for either an unlimited or an additional term if the work of a judge is unsatisfactory.[14] However, it is not clear which criteria are used to determine that a judge's work is unsatisfactory, affording the Minister and the Qualifications Board an unnecessarily broad discretion that harms both the basic independence of new judges and hinders their professional development.

Promotions to regional courts and the Supreme Court are treated as new appointments. Accordingly, the Minister of Justice and the President of the Supreme Court make nominations to the Parliament on the basis of an opinion by the Judicial Qualifications Board.[15] The criteria used by the Judicial Qualifications Board in making its recommendation to the Ministry of Justice or the President of the Supreme Court are undefined.[16]

---

[12] The Judicial Qualifications Board is composed of ten judges: two from the Supreme Court Senate, one each from the chambers for civil and criminal cases, and six elected by the Conference of Judges of Latvia to represent the regional, district and land registry courts. *See* Act on Judicial Power, Art. 93.

[13] Act on Judicial Power, Art. 60 (1-2).

[14] Act on Judicial Power, Art. 60 (3).

[15] Act on Judicial Power, Art. 57, 59.

[16] Apart from the concerns noted about risks to judicial independence, the usefulness of the selection system for initial appointments is vitiated by the fact that no apprenticeship or qualification exam is required for initial appointment to regional courts or the Supreme Court, for which there are no clearly defined criteria beyond basic eligibility requirements that do not differ significantly save in requiring a certain number of years of professional experience.

The draft amendments to the Act on Judicial Power do not address the numerous deficiencies in the selection process.[17] They would only increase the minimum age for a judgeship from 25 to 28 and the minimum legal experience requirement from two years to three.[18]

2. Evaluating and Regulating Performance

There is not at present a coherent system for analysing judges' performance. There are no practical criteria for evaluating and rewarding highly competent judges or guiding the professional development of judges who require additional assistance. A substantive system of evaluation would assist judges in improving their professional skills.

The primary method of performance control is the qualification system that determines judicial salaries. There are six qualification categories for judges, with the Judicial Qualifications Board deciding on placement within each category. Each qualification category carries a pay raise.[19] Judges are automatically reviewed for promotion to a higher qualification category based on time served.[20] Although the law requires that the Board take into account judges' knowledge and work experience,[21] the Board promotes judges more or less automatically once they have completed the minimum time in service requirement.[22] This timeserving approach does not encourage professional development.

In deciding to grant a promotion to a higher qualification category, the Judicial Qualifications Board reviews a judge's personnel file.[23] It may also rely on references

---

[17] The President of the Supreme Court, an active player in the selection process, acknowledged that "the present system for the selection of judges is formalistic. It does not facilitate the most professional lawyers' becoming judges." Diena, 8 March 2002.

[18] Draft amendments to the Act on Judicial Power (first reading), *adopted* 6 June 2002. *See* <http://www.saeima.lv.>, (accessed 26 September 2002).

[19] Act on Judicial Power, Art. 98 and 120.

[20] When a judge becomes eligible for promotion the Minister of Justice must make a recommendation on assignment to the next class within two months of eligibility. *See* Statute on the Judicial Qualifications Board and the Procedure for the Certification of Judges, Part 4, *adopted* 23 April 1999.

[21] Act on Judicial Power, Art. 98.

[22] Interview with Ivars Bickovics, President of Latvian Judges Association and Head of the Criminal Chamber at the Supreme Court, 21 May 2002.

[23] Personal files are maintained by the Personnel Department of the Ministry of Justice and include results of appeals against judgements of a given judge, his or her disciplinary record and complaints against him or her, and records of participation in continued legal education.

from the State Secretary of the Ministry of Justice and the president of the court on which the judge has served. Information from the Ministry's Courts Department may also be utilised, although this tends be general statistical information. In any event, reliance upon these sources is discretionary, as there are no formal assessment requirements or defined criteria by which to evaluate judicial performance. Judges are not interviewed by the Judicial Qualifications Board during the procedure of promotion in qualification, and they are not provided any written assessment or feedback in this process,[24] which is largely opaque both to judges and to the public.

The opportunities for members of the legal professions and the public to act as a check on the quality of judges' work are limited, as few judicial opinions are published and available. Access to court files is quite limited; while judgements must be pronounced publicly, files are only accessible by parties to the case.[25] While the public and media can usually obtain information regarding case scheduling by telephone or in person, in most courts this information is not routinely posted in public areas, in the media or on the Internet. Often court administrative staff will not provide information or will request the reason for which information has been requested[26] frequently, the ability of the public and media to get information depends on the attitude of the court president or chancellor. Creating uniform guidelines for courts to regularly publish and post court dockets, and making court files available for review for the public and media would enhance judicial performance control as well as public trust in the courts.

The public has only limited possibilities to file complaints. While complaints can lead to disciplinary proceedings, court presidents are only obliged to ensure that replies to complaints are given in due time and that the person who examines the submission and prepares the answer does not have a personal interest in the results.[27]

---

[24] Interview with Ivars Bickovics, President of Latvian Judges Association and Head of the Criminal Chamber at the Supreme Court, 21 May 2002.

[25] Code of Criminal Procedure, Art. 95, 97, 100, 102, 103. Code of Civil Procedure, Art. 74.

[26] Diāna Kurpniece and Laura Lazdāne, Research Paper "Informācijas pieejamība valsts un pašvaldību iestādēs". ("Access to Information in State and Local Governmental Institutions"), Pētījums. Sabiedrība par atklātību – Delna, Riga, 2000, available at <http://www.delna.lv.>, (accessed 26 September 2002).

[27] Act on Procedure for the Review of Submissions, Complaints and Proposals in State and Local Governmental Institutions, 27 October 1994, *Official Gazette* (Latvijas Vēstnesis), 5 November 1994.

3. Training for a Professional Judiciary

While a training centre exists to organise and conduct judicial training, political commitment to the continued education of judges appears to be weak. There is minimal State funding for the training of judges and no long-term strategy either to ensure the sustainability and expansion of the centre and its training programmes or to develop an alternative long-term solution.

The Ministry of Justice is legally responsible for training judges.[28] In practice, judicial training is conducted by the Judicial Training Centre, a non-profit organisation established in 1995 by the Latvian Judges' Association and several international organisations.[29] Initially, the Centre was funded jointly by the Ministry and its founders; however, the Centre was supposed to move toward complete local governance and funding over time, and in 1999, a number of co-founders either withdrew or decreased their support.[30] As a result, the Centre has had insufficient operational funds. Although in 2000 the Ministry concluded an agreement that delegates the organisation and implementation of training to the Centre and slightly increased its share of funding for the Centre, the long-term prospects of this structure remain unclear.[31]

In 2000 and 2001, the Judicial Training Centre was allocated 40,000 Ls (€71,000). In 2002, Government funding was increased to 60,000 Ls (€107,000).[32] The limited and uncertain financing restricts training mostly to periodic seminars on new substantive and procedural laws. There are no special courses for judges assuming positions in governance or administrative structures, court presidents, or chairs of court divisions, nor are there specific courses to prepare judges for promotion to a higher court.[33]

The Judicial Training Centre continues to receive in-kind donations and a certain amount of funding from its founders and other international organisations for its operations and special programmes. Although beneficial, this supplementary training

---

[28] Act on Judicial Power, Art. 107.

[29] Founders include the American Bar Association – Central and East European Law Initiative, the United Nations Development Program and the Soros Foundation – Latvia. Information Leaflet of the Latvia Judicial Training Centre. March 2001.

[30] Transparency of Courts Information, Report of the EU PHARE technical assistance project "Prevention of Corruption Within Court System", 26 March 2002, available at: <http://www.policy.lv/index.php?id=100640&lang=en.>, (accessed 26 September 2002).

[31] The agreement is valid until the end of 2004.

[32] Information provided by Roberts Rusis, Director of Latvian Judicial Training Centre, April 2002.

[33] 'Prevention of Corruption in the Court System' (EU PHARE technical assistance project), *Transparency of Courts Information*, 26 March 2002, available at <http://www.policy.lv/index.php?id=102337&lang=en.>, (accessed 26 September 2002).

does not contribute to a long-term consolidation of judicial training, and the State should itself do more to meet that need.

The Judicial Training Centre offers the opportunity and structure to provide quality judicial training; due to foreign donors, there are sufficient training facilities equipped with all necessary and modern equipment, and the staff has sufficient managerial expertise. However, no long-term plan exists to ensure the sustainability and expansion of the Centre, in large part because future State funding is completely unpredictable. Also, it is not clear whether the newly proposed court administration, if established, would take over the functions of the Centre; the draft Framework Paper on Court Administration does not address this issue.[34]

D. INSTITUTIONAL CAPACITY OF THE JUDICIARY

The Ministry of Justice retains an unnecessarily large concentration of supervisory functions over the courts, threatening their independence and preventing the development of administrative capacity within the judiciary – and even then the Ministry's capacity to carry out these functions with sufficient professionalism is insufficient. At the court level, court presidents also lack professional management skills. Whatever body administers the judiciary needs to develop more professional capacity, ensure better work conditions in particular courts, and address the inefficient processes that distract judges from their core work.

1. Governance and Administration of the Judicial Branch

So long as the Ministry of Justice continues to exercise its current high concentration of authority over the daily operations of courts, the judiciary will never develop the administrative expertise required to ensure its autonomy and competence. To the degree that it does retain such authority, however, the Ministry – or whatever body ultimately exercises administrative control over the courts – needs to develop more professional administrative capacity.

Overall policy-making and administration of courts of the first two instances are some of the main functions of the Ministry of Justice.[35] The Ministry represents the judiciary in its

---

[34] Tiesu administrācijas koncepcija (Draft Framework Paper on Court Administration), 20 December 2001, available at <http://www.politika.lv/index.php?id=102382&lang=lv.>, (accessed 26 September 2002). *See* Section B.2., "Creation of a Judicial Administration".

[35] The Supreme Court manages itself autonomously.

relations with other branches, identifies priorities, prepares budget and distributes allocated funds, collects data on court activities, prepares organisational standards, supervises the work of the courts and provides the courts with the necessary materials.[36] Concentration of so many regulatory, administrative, information-gathering, and supervisory functions in the Ministry makes courts dependent on it for almost all their needs.[37]

The Ministry of Justice administers regional and district courts through a special Department of Courts and through the court presidents, who are responsible for day-to-day administration. Among other powers, the Ministry of Justice is entitled to carry out inspections of the district and regional courts, using either Ministry employees or judges from the Supreme Court and regional courts. In practice, however, judges are not normally involved in inspections, which are conducted entirely by Ministry employees. Such inspections, combined with the Ministry's other broad powers, even though they are not directed at judges' core decision-making, often serve as a tool to restrain judges and, in effect, to subordinate them to the Ministry. The organisational dependence and subordination of the court system to the Ministry in turn creates conditions for the executive improperly to influence judges and especially court presidents, and does not allow the development of independent managerial capacity.

Furthermore, the Ministry of Justice does not appear capable of providing strategic leadership and sufficient administrative support for court operations. Due to the traditional weakness of the Ministry's position in the system of governance, it has not managed to build support for substantial judicial reform. The Ministry has not developed specific standards to govern its administrative decisions on matters such as the numbers of judges and support staff in courts, norms for caseload, provision of technology and equipment, and court space and facilities.

In addition, despite having sole responsibility for preparing the judiciary's budget and allocating its funds,[38] the Ministry has not developed clear criteria for reviewing budget requests or the distribution of allocated funds. This creates a situation in which personal relationships of district and regional court presidents and the Ministry of Justice may in large part influence budget allocations to particular courts. In turn, the lack of standards

---

[36] Act on Judicial Power, Art. 108.

[37] See EU Accession Monitoring Program, *Monitoring the EU Accession Process: Judicial Independence* (Open Society Institute, Budapest, October 2001), p. 239.

[38] At no stage of the budgeting process do district and regional courts have input as to their budget allocation.

contributes to the judiciary's continued under-funding.[39] Insufficient funding has resulted in poor staffing and facilities, as well as long case delays and backlogs.

In response to the recommendations of international institutions, in particular by the European Union, to further develop and strengthen the judiciary, the Ministry of Justice has prepared a *Framework Paper on Court Administration*.[40] This document mentions a possibility to transfer administrative responsibility from the Ministry to an autonomous State institution. However, deliberations on the new framework have been quite slow:[41] after it was presented at a meeting of State Secretaries in December 2001, in August 2002 the Framework Paper was accepted by the Committee of the Cabinet of Ministers, the stage proceeding review in the Cabinet.

2. Court Administrative Capacity

At the court level, administrators lack professional and managerial capacity. Training for court presidents, who carry overall management responsibility, should be an immediate priority, although a long-term solution would be to concentrate on professionalising court management.

Court presidents manage and control courts operations; deputy court presidents and court chancellors assist them. Court presidents and deputy presidents oversee case allocation and management; legal training for lay judges and court personnel; court schedules; the compilation of court statistics; and the execution of court decisions. Despite significant management and personnel responsibilities, relevant education, training or experience is not a prerequisite for appointment. The Ministry of Justice appoints presidents of district courts, and Parliament appoints presidents of regional courts and the President of the Supreme Court from among the judges of those courts.[42] Although the Judicial Qualifications Board gives its opinion on candidates for

---

[39] There has been an increase in budgetary allotments for the judiciary in 2002, although funding levels remain low. In 2001 court funding was 7,316,892 Lats (about €13,193,000) representing approximately .50 percent of the overall State budget. The 2002 budget is 10,417,924 Lats (about €18,785,000), which accounts for .60 percent of the State budget. *See* Act on State Budget for 2002, *Official Gazette* (Latvijas Vēstnesis), 19 December 2001.

[40] Draft Framework Paper on Court Administration, 20 December 2001, available at <http://www.politika.lv/index.php?id=102382&lang=lv.>, (accessed 25 September 2002).

[41] *See* Section B.2., "Creation of a Judicial Administration".

[42] Act on Judicial Power, Art. 33, 40–41, 50.

president at the district and regional level,[43] there are no clear standards to assess their managerial capabilities.

There are no specialised courses for judges newly assigned to management positions, nor are these officials provided with appropriate training after their appointment. Court presidents and their deputies need training in areas such as strategic planning, personnel management and case management if they are to modernise and increase the efficiency of court operations. In addition, certain management functions should be transferred to non-judicial management professionals operating under court presidents' overall supervision.

Difficulties in court management are compounded by a shortage of qualified support and professional staff,[44] and as a consequence judges are overburdened with technical matters, such as preparation of inquiries and sending court documents. The process of case preparation for trial in particular requires further improvement, and would benefit from the involvement of dedicated non-judicial professionals, freeing judges to focus more effectively on their core adjudicative functions.

Public access to information about court operations is insufficient; the results and conclusions of periodic inspections and audits carried out by the Ministry of Justice in district and regional courts are not publicly available. Public criticism, comments and suggestions might be a useful resource to aid in improving court administration.

Lack of resources for personnel, premises and equipment have resulted in poor facilities,[45] insufficient and out-dated equipment,[46] insufficient and poorly trained court staff,[47] and poor legal research resources.[48] Poor work conditions contribute to severe case delays and backlogs. Courts regularly disregard procedural requirements

---

[43] Act on Judicial Power, Art. 33 (1), 40 (1), 50 (1).

[44] Interview with Ivars Bickovics, President of Latvian Judges Association and Head of the Criminal Chamber at the Supreme Court, 21 May 2002.

[45] *Many court buildings do not meet basic requirements for operation. There are not enough offices for judges and court staff, courtrooms for hearings, and storage rooms.*

[46] In many courts, technical equipment such as printers, copying machines and safes are in short supply and of poor quality. There are no tape recorders or stenographic machines in courtrooms for recording court hearings. Instead, court secretaries record trial minutes by hand, which reduces the efficiency of proceedings, makes appellate procedures more time-consuming and allows for the potential of abuse.

[47] The shortage of professional and technical staff appears primarily to be a consequence of low staff salaries and resulting high turnover. Salaries for court staff average about 100 Lats per month (about €180), which is two-thirds the average national salary. The lack of space to accommodate court staff contributes to high turnover as well. No training for court staff has been planned in 2002 to date.

[48] Most courts, including the Supreme Court, have no law library. An electronic database of legislation, international legal instruments and judgements exists but is not available to all courts.

concerning time limits for hearing cases. In many courts the docket is so congested that cases are scheduled several years in advance. The worst situation is in the Riga regional court, which is currently scheduling hearings for 2004; appeals in criminal cases are sometimes reviewed after the appellants have served their sentences and been released.[49]

Several attempts are underway to address case delays and backlogs. Amendments to the Act on Criminal Procedure, adopted in February 2001, reduced the number of criminal cases for which regional courts had first instance review.[50] The amendments also allowed for transfer of criminal cases among district courts to speed review.[51] Other incremental efforts, including temporary assignment of retired judges and increasing the number of judges in the Riga regional court, where backlogs are particularly acute,[52] may produce some improvements.

However, although these measures may contribute to a decrease in backlogs, they are insufficient to reverse the systemic problem of court delays. There is no comprehensive national plan to address delays that would include new approaches such as alternative methods of dispute resolution. This tends to distract politicians, State officials and judges from other important structural reforms and reduce public support for the judiciary. A working group has been created to prepare the overall reform of the criminal procedure. However, no date for completion of its work has been announced. The proposed amendments to the Act on Judicial Power would also streamline the case allocation system, although they do not clarify what the criteria for case distribution would be.[53]

E. RECOMMENDATIONS

1. To the Latvian Government and Legislature

- Acknowledge the pressing importance of immediate, serious and sustained political commitment to comprehensive judicial reform.

- Develop comprehensive reforms aimed at reorganisation and modernisation of the judiciary, in particular by increasing its institutional autonomy and funding.

---

[49] "Kas notiek Latvijā" (What is going on in Latvia), 29 May 2002.

[50] Amendments to the Act on Criminal Procedure, *adopted* 15 February 2001, *Official Gazette* (Latvijas Vēstnesis), 6 March 2001.

[51] Amendments to the Act on Criminal Procedure, *adopted* 15 February 2001, *Official Gazette* (Latvijas Vēstnesis), 6 March 2001.

[52] "Kas notiek Latvijā" (What is going on in Latvia), 29 May 2002.

[53] *See* Section B.1., "Proposed Amendments to the Law on Judicial Power".

- Ensure that reforms already undertaken or proposed do not actually harm judicial independence or decrease the judiciary's administrative capacity.

- Establish a rational system for judicial selection and promotion, including clear-criteria for decision-making and transparent procedures.

- Develop a meaningful evaluation system based on clear and rational criteria and a transparent process for measuring judicial performance rather than on time served in office.

- Ensure consistent funding and institutional sustainability of judicial training. Prioritise training for court managers and court staff.

- Intensify efforts to decrease court delays, and consider pilot projects such alternative dispute resolution mechanisms.

2. To the European Union

- Emphasise the importance of comprehensive rather than fragmentary judicial reform to address numerous problems related to a lack of institutional independence and capacity of the judicial system.

- Assist Latvia in developing an effective reform programme by clarifying the values common to the Union and essential for membership with regard to an independent and functioning judiciary, and consequently the minimal expressions of those values, in concrete policies, that continuing membership requires.

- Drawing upon the experiences of other candidate and member States, provide technical assistance to Latvia in the establishment of appropriate criteria and methods for selection to judicial office, promotion, and performance evaluation.

- Support institutional consolidation of judicial training and facilitate exchange of judicial educators with training institutions in other EU candidate and member States in order to improve training in relevant judicial and management skills for judges and administrative skills for court managers and personnel.

- Provide technical support for devising effective means to reduce endemic court delays and backlogs.

Judicial Capacity in Lithuania

Table of Contents

A. INTRODUCTION

Lithuania has taken a decisive step towards ensuring judicial independence; new institutions of judicial self-governance enjoy broad powers that can ensure adequate representation of the judiciary's interests and needs.

This greater institutional autonomy makes it imperative that the judiciary also ensure its accountability, in part by acquiring specialised expertise in public administration, and enhance the transparency of its operations. Early signs suggest the system may be tending towards insularity and resistance to administrative professionalisation; as implementation of comprehensive institutional reform is undertaken, it is important that the new framework is used to enhance judicial capacity rather than to create an unaccountable and poorly managed judiciary.

Secondary legislation and implementing regulations should ensure that the new Council of Courts and National Court Administration are capable of efficiently governing and administering the judiciary. In particular, it may be necessary to increase managerial professionalisation on the national level and introduce professional management personnel in courts.

Certain specific areas require attention. The system for selection and promotion of judges needs to be made more objective, merit-based, and transparent. There is no system of evaluation; consideration should be given to developing a system of periodic assessment of judges' performance consistent with the requirements of the principle of judicial independence and accountability. Training still needs to be placed on a stable and sustainable footing; at the same time, it ought to be broadened to address the sort of administrative and managerial skills that a self-governing judiciary requires.

B. CURRENT DEVELOPMENTS AFFECTING JUDICIAL INDEPENDENCE AND CAPACITY

In 2002, Lithuania passed a package of new laws that substantially improved the basic regulatory and institutional framework, giving the courts substantial and comprehensive institutional and administrative autonomy. Greater institutional autonomy, itself quite a welcome development, makes it imperative that the judiciary acquire specialised expertise in public administration, as well as enhanced transparency in its operations. Lack of management expertise may undermine support for the very idea of a judiciary capable of efficient self-government.

1. The New Courts Act and Law on Court Administration

The Constitutional Ruling of 21 December 1999, which declared several provisions of the Courts Act unconstitutional,[1] prompted an effort comprehensively to review and revise the relationship between the executive and judiciary. As a result, in early 2002, two major new laws were promulgated: the Courts Act[2] and National Court Administration Act.[3]

The new Laws substantially strengthen the institutional independence of the judicial branch. They create a Council of Courts and a National Court Administration. The Council, with elected representatives of judges forming a majority of its members,[4] is responsible for a broad range of matters, such as determining personnel issues, developing budgets, and setting administrative standards and supervising their implementation.[5] The Administration has responsibility for day-to-day administration

---

[1] Ruling of the Constitutional Court of 21 December 1999, Official Gazette 109, 1999. *See also* EU Accession Monitoring Program, *Monitoring the EU Accession Process: Judicial Independence in Lithuania* (Open Society Institute, Budapest, October 2001), pp. 273–274, available at <http://www.eumap.org>, (accessed 25 September 2002).

[2] Courts Act, No. IX-732/2002, Official Gazette 17, 20 February 2002.

[3] National Court Administration Act, No. IX-787/2002, Official Gazette 31, 27 March 2002.

[4] 15 of the Council's 24 members are judges elected by various bodies, and several more are judges who are members *ex officio*. 14 members are judges elected by the General Meeting of Judges and one member is a judge elected by the largest professional association of judges. Nine *ex officio* members are the presidents of the Supreme Court, the High Administrative Court, the Court of Appeal, as well as a representative of the State President, a representative of the Chairman of the Parliament, the chairmen of the parliamentary legal and budget committees, and the Ministers of Justice and Finance. Courts Act, Art. 119.

[5] Courts Act, Art. 120. *See* Section D.1., "Governance and Administration of the Judicial Branch".

of the court system on a national level, for implementing the Council's decisions, and for supporting the Council through research and analysis.[6]

The new Courts Act also mandates creation of a number of new bodies with responsibility for specific administrative and regulatory activities.[7] This process is underway; at the first meeting of the Council of Courts in June 2002, the Court of Honour of Judges was formed and members of the Commission of Judges' Ethics and Discipline were appointed, while members of the Judicial Examination Commission were nominated.[8] In its first sitting, the Council also confirmed a number of regulations and procedures governing the work of these bodies as well as selection and promotion procedures.[9] The combination of broad policy-setting, supervisory and administrative powers gives the new institutions of judicial self-government substantial and comprehensive authority that will ensure more adequate representation of the interests and needs of the judiciary.

Still, it is too early to assess whether or not these broad institutional reforms – so important for the judiciary's independence – will increase judicial capacity as well. Practical implementation of the new Laws is essential to ensure that they realise their potential for creating an independent, accountable, and capable judiciary. Indeed, greater institutional autonomy, itself quite a welcome development, makes it imperative that the judiciary also acquire specialised expertise in public administration, as well as enhanced transparency in its operations if the new institutional arrangements are to lead to increased capacity and greater public trust in courts. Lack of management expertise and a closed institutional culture may undermine support for the very idea of a judiciary capable of efficient self-government.

2. Other Developments

A July 2001 ruling of the Constitutional Court ensured judges' economic security by forbidding political manipulation of salaries.[10] This ruling declared that provisions of the Law on Remuneration for Work of State Politicians, Judges and State Officials that

---

[6] Courts Act, Art. 125; National Court Administration Act, Art. 2. *See* Section D.1., "Governance and Administration of the Judicial Branch".

[7] *See* Section D.1., "Governance and Administration of the Judicial Branch".

[8] Information provided by Virgilijus Valančius, President of the Lithuanian Judges' Association, 25 June 2002.

[9] *See* Section C.1., "Selection and Promotion".

[10] Ruling of the Constitutional Court of 12 July 2001, State Gazette 62, 18 July 2001; State Gazette 86, 10 October 2001. *See* <http://www.lrkt.lt/doc_links/20011.htm>, (accessed 25 September 2002).

would have allowed reductions in judges' remuneration violated the principle of the rule of law embodied in the Constitution.

C. PROFESSIONAL COMPETENCE OF JUDGES

The new legal provisions for selection and promotion of judges are still not sufficiently transparent or standardised; without further elaboration of the implementing regulations, too much discretion may be vested in the Council of Courts and court presidents. There is still no system of evaluation; consideration should be given to developing a system of periodic assessment of judges' performance, consistent with the requirements of the principles of judicial independence and accountability, that will reward competent judges and guide the professional development of judges who require additional assistance. The institutional setting for judicial training still needs to be established in a way that ensures judges are prepared to manage their own affairs effectively, and that the Ministry of Justice does not exercise improper coercive authority over judges; in particular, stable and sustained funding needs to be secured to ensure the new training framework can function effectively.

1. Selection and Promotion

The new legal provisions for selection and promotion of judges – both the Courts Act and the implementing regulations adopted by the Council of Courts – unnecessarily narrow the pool of qualified candidates and leave procedural gaps that limit transparency and may give undue discretion to decision-makers, in turn potentially undermining the credibility of the system.

The new Courts Act creates a career system for selection and promotion, in which almost all candidates enter at the lowest level. An exception is made for one professional group – legal educators – who may join the bench at any level and without taking the requisite judicial examination.[11]

Under the new system, individuals who comply with the legal requirements[12] and pass an examination are included on the list of candidates for vacancies in district courts, according to rules established by the Council of Courts. The list of candidates for vacancies of judges of district courts, managed by the National Court Administration,

---

[11] Courts Act, Art. 51.

[12] Requirements include a university law degree, at least five years' legal work experience, impeccable reputation, and presentation of a health certificate. *See* Courts Act, Art.51–52.

is then presented to the State President and the Council of Courts.[13] The new Courts Act and implementing regulations promulgated by the Council of Courts[14] do not make clear in what order candidates should be included on the list or how candidates will be selected from it for appointment by the State President. This procedural gap affords undue discretion to the National Court Administration and the Council of Courts, and undermines confidence in the objectivity of the system.

Under the new Courts Act, a person seeking promotion to a higher court is included in a Register of Persons Seeking Promotion in Judicial Office maintained by the National Court Administration.[15] As with initial selection, regulations determining the order of enrolment on the promotion register fail to provide sufficient detail;[16] the regulations only restate that the National Court Administration transmits data on persons included in the register to the State President and the Council of Courts.[17]

The system of promotion is open only to serving judges, and individuals holding a Ph.D. in law with the requisite number of years of pedagogical experience;[18] effectively, therefore, professionals with considerable legal experience may only apply to the district court. The rationale behind granting an exception only to legal academics seems questionable, as legal practitioners may have no less legal knowledge and more relevant experience than academic lawyers; experienced legal professionals should have the same opportunity to apply to both entry level and higher courts that legal academics have under the current system.

It is arguable whether the new system will be effective in selecting and promoting the best available candidates. Moreover, a rigid career system, which allows only one narrow exception, may discourage applications by experienced and qualified lawyers, in turn contributing to the creation of a hierarchical and insular institutional culture unfavourable to further professionalisation.

---

[13] Courts Act, Art. 55.

[14] Procedure for the Inclusion on the List of Candidates for Vacancies in District Courts, adopted by Council of Courts, 17 June 2002, No. 9.

[15] Courts Act, Art. 65.

[16] Procedure for the Inclusion in the Register of Persons Seeking Promotion in Judicial Office, adopted by Council of Courts, 17 June 2002, No. 10.

[17] Courts Act, Art. 65 and Procedure for the Inclusion in the Register of Persons Seeking Promotion in Judicial Office, Art.15.

[18] Five for a regional court, ten for appeals, and fifteen for the Supreme Court. Courts Act, Art. 66–68.

2. Evaluating and Regulating Performance

There is no system of performance evaluation; in addition, the existing public complaint procedure is not applicable to courts. The only control mechanism for judges' performance is through the ordinary appeal procedure.[19] Over time, this may further harm public trust in the judiciary, which is already tarnished.[20] Consistent with the principles of judicial independence and accountability, consideration should be given to developing a system of periodic assessment of judges' performance to guide the professional development of judges who require additional assistance and to ensure that promotions are based on merit.

Although the new Courts Act does not explicitly provide for a complaint mechanism, in practice individuals have been filing complaints against judges with court presidents or the Council of Courts, either of which may initiate disciplinary proceedings.[21] A disciplinary action may be instituted against a judge in the Judges' Disciplinary Court: 1) for an action which discredits the judicial office; 2) for commission of an administrative offence; 3) for non-compliance with the limitations on the work and political activities of judges.[22] Whether the new disciplinary system will contribute to enhanced judicial performance remains unclear, as the system has not been tested yet.

One avenue for informal public scrutiny and commentary could be through the National Court Administration's obligation to publish decisions, judgements, rulings and orders by regional administrative courts, regional courts and the Court of Appeals in cases that involve the public interest.[23] It is unclear, however, how the public interest

---

[19] Interview with Aldona Juljana Kudinskiene, Head of the Department of Organisation of Operations of Courts of the Department of Courts, Vilnius, 15 April 2002.

[20] Recent opinion polls suggest that about 44 percent of the population distrust the courts, and only about 17 percent express trust in the judicial system. See Lietuvos Rytas, 20 July 2002. Courts are often criticised by the media for poor performance and lack of public control. See, e.g., "Sign of the Times", Lietuvos Rytas, 9 August 2001, commenting on the then draft Courts Act: "It seems that authors of the draft Law [on Courts] have never heard of any rulings of discredited judges. . . . The new law has no mentioning of a possibility to increase judges' personal responsibility, make the control of rulings more strict and strengthen the judges' corps. . . .If the law is adopted, the clan of lawyers will become more closed and less controlled. The opinion of society regarding courts would have even less impact."

[21] Courts Act, Art. 84.

[22] An act discrediting the office of a judge is understood as an act incompatible with the requirements of the Judge's Code of Conduct and which undermines the authority of the court. Any misconduct in office – negligent performance of any specific duty or omission to act without a good cause is also be recognised as an act discrediting the office. See Courts Act, Art. 83 (3).

[23] Courts Act, Art. 39 (3).

will be determined; obviously, the least discretionary definition possible should be employed, both to ensure public access and to limit the incentives for the Administration to employ the advertising value of publication selectively for improper purposes. Decisions and orders of the Supreme Court will be published in the Bulletin of the Supreme Court and on its web site.[24]

3. Training for a Professional Judiciary

The institutional setting for judicial training still needs to be established in a way that ensures judges are prepared both to adjudicate well and to manage their own affairs effectively. In the process, existing experience in organising judicial training should not be wasted.

The Courts Act establishes introductory training and compulsory continuing training.[25] Newly appointed district court judges must complete at least one month of training prior to assuming office. Thereafter, training is required: at least once every five years; or when laws substantially change; or whenever judges are promoted, appointed or transferred from courts of general competence to a specialised court or *vice versa*; or when they change their specialisation; or as needed,[26] although this last condition has not been clarified.

The Ministry of Justice retains significant responsibility for the organisation of training. The Council of Courts and the Ministry jointly organise the curricula and methodology; the Ministry approves judges' training programmes, rules of evaluation, yearly training plans and schedules, and funding for training, with the consent of the Council.[27] Since training is mandatory, care should be taken that any sanctions for non-compliance or unsatisfactory performance, if they involve discretionary determinations by the Ministry, do not improperly infringe upon judges' core adjudicative independence. In addition, training should focus not only on substantive legal issues, but also on judicial skills and effective self-management.

It is not clear which institution will actually provide the training; the future role of the Lithuanian Judicial Training Centre, a non-governmental organisation established in 1997 by the Ministry of Justice, the Lithuanian Judges' Association, the Supreme

---

[24] Courts Act, Art. 39 (5).

[25] Courts Act, Art. 92.

[26] Courts Act, Art. 92.

[27] Courts Act, Art. 93.

Court and a group of donor organisations,[28] is unclear. The Centre has conducted continuing training of judges and has developed considerable expertise. However, during the five years of its operation little has been done to assure the Centre a stable source of income to finance its operations; after the planned withdrawal of foreign assistance by the end of 2002, the only source of income to sustain the Centre will be the State budget, but a proposal to integrate the Centre into the new system –thus ensuring its financial sustainability – was rejected.[29] Alternative ways to integrate the Centre's expertise into the new training system should be considered soon, before it is forced to cease operations and its expertise is lost.

D. Institutional Capacity of the Judicial Branch

The level of administrative professionalisation of the new institutions of the judicial branch and courts will to a large extent determine whether the reforms succeed in increasing judicial capacity and accountability. Early signs suggest the system may be tending towards insularity and resistance to professionalisation. The newly autonomous judiciary still lacks expertise in public administration and budgeting. Despite having broad managerial powers, court presidents lack management training; it may be necessary to introduce professional management personnel into the judicial system to take full advantage of the ongoing institutional reform. The new judicial institutions should also open their operations to public scrutiny.

1. Governance and Administration of the Judicial Branch

The new Courts Act and the National Court Administration Act have created independent institutions entrusted with broad authority over district, regional and appellate courts. The level of administrative capacity of these institutions will to a large extent determine whether reform will result in increased judicial capacity or will create a closed, inefficient and unaccountable guild. It is imperative that the judiciary develop in its ranks specialised

---

[28] United Nations Development Programme (UNDP), the American Bar Association/Central and Eastern Europe Law Initiative (ABA/CEELI), and the Open Society Fund - Lithuania. The additional founding contributors were the United States Agency for International Development (USAID), the EU PHARE Programme, and the Government of Finland. The Articles of Association of the Lithuanian Judicial Training Centre were signed on 29 May 1997.

[29] An earlier draft of the Courts Act provided that the Centre, as part of the structure of the National Court Administration, would be instrumental in organisation of judicial training. Explanatory Note No.IXP-729/2001 on Draft Law on Amendment of the Courts Act and Related Draft Laws, 31 May 2001, para. 12.
See <http://www3.lrs.lt/cgi-bin/preps2?Condition1=136185&Condition2>, (accessed 25 September 2002).

expertise in public administration and open its operations to public scrutiny. Although only a few implementing regulations have been developed so far, some already show signs of a system tending towards insularity and resistance to professionalisation.

The new Council of Courts has broad policy-setting and decision-making responsibilities. In particular, the Council:

- approves the draft budgets of courts and the National Court Administration and submits them to the Government;

- represents the courts on budgetary matters before the Government and other State institutions;

- approves the framework for administration of the courts;

- supervises the activities of the National Court Administration and receives its reports;

- advises the State President on matters related to judicial selection and career path;

- appoints the members and chairperson of the Judicial Examination Commission;

- appoints the members of the Commission on Ethics and Discipline and approves its chairperson;

- appoints the members of the Court of Honour of Judges;

- approves the Regulations on Administration in Courts;

- approves the standard structures for district, regional, and administrative regional courts, as well as standard staffing lists and descriptions of duties; and

- approves court investment programmes.[30]

The new National Court Administration assists the Council of Courts through providing research and analysis, implementing the Council's decisions, and exercising responsibility for the day-to-day operations of courts. In particular, the Administration:

- provides technical assistance to other self-governing institutions of the judiciary;

- organises centralised procurement of goods and services to courts;

- prepares a consolidated report on budgetary expenditures of the Administration and district, regional and regional administrative courts;

- analyses courts' activities and submits proposals pertaining to working conditions in the courts; and

- collects and analyses statistics.[31]

---

[30] Courts Act, Art. 120.

[31] Courts Act, Art. 125 and National Court Administration Act, Art. 2.

The efficiency of these new institutions will to a large extent depend on the competence of the staff that will prepare and implement decisions of the Council. For example, specialised knowledge is essential to develop national standards concerning the number of judges and support staff needed in the courts, standard caseload norms, standard record systems and methods for determining training needs – all areas for which standards are yet to be prepared and implemented. Yet the only criteria for appointment as head of the National Court Administration are a university law degree and at least five years of legal experience – requirements that might be indicative of an institutional culture that is not disposed to open itself to specialisation. Moreover, the appointment and dismissal procedure appears undemocratic and neglects collegiality in decision-making. The State President appoints and dismisses the head of the National Court Administration upon the suggestion of the President of the Supreme Court,[32] who is neither obligated to consult with nor answerable to any State institution or official.

The budgetary process has been improved, although courts appear to lack sufficient expertise in drafting their budgets. Each court (and the National Court Administration for its operations) prepares its own budget, which is then submitted to the Council of Courts for approval, and then to the Government[33] and through it to Parliament. During the preparation and adoption of the annual Law on the State Budget, the courts (with the exception of the Supreme Court, the Court of Appeal and the High Administrative Court) will be represented by the National Court Administration.[34] There are no clear methods for determining the amount of funding for different court levels or spending in each court; in particular, there seems not to be any correlation between budget allotments and caseload. In addition, courts lack expertise in budget preparation; for example, an audit of the Visaginas district court showed that in preparing its budget request for 2000, the court had failed to follow mandatory budgeting procedures laid out in the *Requirements of the Interim Method Pertaining to Programmatic Formation of the State Budget of the Republic of Lithuania*.[35]

---

[32] National Court Administration Act, Art. 3 (2).

[33] Courts Act, Art. 127.

[34] Courts Act, Art. 127.

[35] Decision of Utena Control Department of the State Auditor *Concerning Results of Audits of Economic Financial Activities of Visaginas District Court*, No.19, 15 June 2001. *See* <http://www.litlex.lt/portal/start.asp?act=disk&fwd=komentarai.asp?dskID=1523&view=1>, (accessed 14 April 2002). *See also "Requirements of Interim Method Pertaining to Programmatic Formation of State Budget of the Republic of Lithuania"*, approved by Ministry of Finance Order No.102, Official Gazette 41, 2 May 1998. *See* <http://www3.lrs.lt/cgi-bin/preps2?Condition1=55052&-Condition2=>, (accessed 14 April 2002).

2. Court Administrative Capacity

Despite having broad managerial powers, court presidents are neither professional managers, nor are they trained in such matters; it may be necessary to introduce professional management principles and personnel into the judiciary system to take full advantage of the ongoing institutional reform.

Court presidents have broad managerial responsibilities. They distribute judges into departments, define judges' specialisations, employ and dismiss court personnel, approve court staff's descriptions of responsibilities, and are responsible for ensuring adequate work conditions for judges and court staff, including providing necessary equipment and technology.[36] Despite these broad responsibilities, the only requirement to be appointed a court president is that the candidate be a judge of that court;[37] court presidents receive no training either before or after their appointments.[38] As an interim measure, consideration ought to be given to developing management-oriented training for court presidents; in the long term, it may be advisable to introduce non-judicial professional management staff under the supervision of court presidents.

The new national court administration also faces immediate challenges in enhancing the capacity of courts to deal with increasing workloads and deteriorating work conditions. If not dealt with effectively and soon, these problems will only further hinder the effective operations of courts.

High caseloads result in constant time pressure that affects the quality of trials and court decisions and ultimately engenders public dissatisfaction with the work of the courts. Judges at the district level have the biggest workload; the average caseload per judge in district courts has increased by 38.75 percent during the last five years, from 40.48 cases per month in 1997 to 56.17 per month in 2001.[39] There have been no specific measures to improve the ability of courts to deal with the increased caseload, such as introduction of alternative dispute resolution methods.

---

[36] Courts Act, Art. 103.

[37] Presidents of district and regional courts are appointed by the State President upon the advice of the Council of Courts. Both the State President and the Parliament must approve appointment of the Presidents of the Appeal Court and the Supreme Court. *See* Courts Act, part VIII.

[38] The Judicial Training Centre has occasionally organised seminars for court presidents on topics such as public administration, legal requirements related to public services, ethics, communication and cooperation skills. Information provided by Asta Buitkute, Director of the Judicial Training Centre, Vilnius, 16 April 2002.

[39] Interview with Dainius Radzevicius, Public Relation Officer, Department of Courts, Vilnius, 5 April 2002 and Aldona Juljana Kudinskiene, Head of the Department of Organisation of Operations of Courts of the Department of Courts, Vilnius, 15 April 2002.

Physical conditions in many courts are also unsatisfactory, a product of long-term under-investment; there is a pressing need in many courts to redress this situation, as many judges work in court buildings that are in emergency conditions.[40] At the First District Court of Vilnius, there are only three courtrooms available for approximately 38 judges.[41] Lack of space affects adversely not only judges, but other participants in trial. Finally, the efficient functioning of courts is still hampered by the lack of necessary technical equipment, such as computers, typewriters, copying machines and computerised legislation databases. Modernisation is especially needed in case of trial recording; there is a requirement that only significant moments of a trial are to be recorded, allowing ample opportunity for inaccuracy and abuse. Full recording would not be practical at present, as court proceedings are recorded in handwriting.

E. RECOMMENDATIONS

1. To the Lithuanian Courts, Government and Legislature

- Ensure effective implementation of the judiciary's new institutional structure by introducing modern public administration methods, procedures and specialised management expertise.

- Ensure that, in exercising their independence and autonomy, the courts and their administration remain properly accountable to society and its political representatives.

- Ensure that the basic legislative framework's reform agenda is further clarified and reinforced by the implementing regulations that the Council of Courts adopts.

- In particular, implementing regulations should further specify the system for selection and promotion of judges to ensure that the process is transparent and does not allow for undue discretion. Consider enlargement of the pool of qualified candidates by extending the possibility for experienced legal professionals to join the bench under conditions similar to those afforded to legal educators.

- Through legislation or implementing regulations, and consistent with the requirements of judicial independence and accountability, develop a system of

---

[40] *See, e.g.,* "The Neglected Courts – a Misery for Judges and Citizens", Lietuvos Rytas, 7 November 2001.

[41] Information provided by the National Court Administration, 22 July 2002.

periodic evaluation to assist judges in their professional development and ensure that promotion is based on merit.

- Implement a system of judicial training that focuses on judicial and managerial skills training as well as substantive law, and that integrates the existing expertise and potential of the Lithuanian Judicial Training Centre.

- Ensure that any sanctions attached to mandatory training, if they involve discretionary determinations by the Ministry of Justice, do not improperly infringe upon judges' core adjudicative independence.

- Consider introducing professional management into the courts, subject to judicial oversight. As an interim measure, develop and implement programmes for the continuing training of court presidents in management, as well as programmes for court staff in aspects of court administration such as case management and budget preparation.

- Develop and implement a national plan to improve work conditions in courts and to tackle court delays; in particular, consider the introduction of alternative dispute resolution mechanisms.

2. To the European Union

- Ensure that EU bodies and officials develop direct channels of communication, not only with the executive and legislature, but with the autonomous administrative organs of the judiciary, to effectively assist in formulating policy and developing assistance plans.

- Emphasise the need for professionalisation in the judiciary's new policy-making and administrative institutions.

- Facilitate exchange with other EU candidate and member States that have similar institutional structures, so that the newly created institutions of judicial self-government may acquire the experience necessary to develop methods and procedures that will enhance judicial capacity.

- Encourage the introduction of a system for periodic evaluations of judicial performance; assist in the development of relevant criteria and procedures for such a system by drawing upon the experiences of other EU candidate and member States.

Judicial Capacity in Poland

Table of Contents

A. INTRODUCTION

Poland has made important progress in judicial reform in the past year. Two new Acts on Ordinary Courts and on the National Council of the Judiciary have introduced new procedures and professional staff posts that – if properly implemented – could enhance courts' ability to manage themselves professionally and autonomously.

However, reform efforts should be pursued more vigorously. Although a trend toward granting the courts more autonomy is observable, reform has proceeded piecemeal, and there have been reversals. Last year, for example, the Ministry of Justice imposed sweeping austerity measures that not only limited efforts to professionalise the judiciary, but also demonstrated the risks to the judiciary's autonomy that exist when the executive retains fiscal or administrative supervision over courts. The judiciary faces a number of problems caused primarily by delays in comprehensive institutional reforms that are necessary for its modernisation and enhanced capacity.

Most broadly, the judiciary continues to rely on the Ministry of Justice for administrative support, which unnecessarily introduces opportunities for indirect interference with adjudication and contradicts the principle of judicial capacity that courts should have a meaningful institutional role in organising their work. Whatever body has the authority to administer the courts system – whether an autonomous judicial institution or the Ministry – needs to be more transparent and to develop more regularised and inclusive procedures.

In particular, procedures for admittance to apprenticeships – the main avenue to appointment – need clearer criteria and enhanced transparency. Monitoring of judges' performance is unsystematic and opaque; consistent with the requirements of judicial independence, new legislation should establish a rational system for periodic evaluation. Likewise, there is no comprehensive system for judicial training; if the Ministry of Justice retains the authority to manage training, it should develop a clear and coherent conceptual framework that includes training in management techniques. In the longer term, more managerial tasks should be transferred to professional staff, leaving judges free to focus on adjudication.

B. CURRENT DEVELOPMENTS AFFECTING JUDICIAL INDEPENDENCE AND CAPACITY

Two new acts – the Act on Ordinary Courts and the Act on the National Council of the Judiciary – have introduced new procedures for selection, budgeting, and remuneration, as well as new posts that – if properly implemented – could enhance courts' ability to manage themselves professionally and autonomously. Last year, however, the Ministry of Justice imposed sweeping austerity measures that have reduced resources available for maintaining and developing the judiciary; not only does this limit efforts to professionalise the judiciary in a direct sense, it also demonstrates the risks to courts' autonomy that exist when the executive retains fiscal or administrative supervision of the judiciary.

1. New Legislative Initiatives

In October 2001 new legislation strengthening the independence, accountability and capacity of the judiciary came into force. The new Acts on Ordinary Courts[1] and on the National Council of the Judiciary[2] introduced new procedures for selection,[3] the budgetary process,[4] disciplinary procedures,[5] and remuneration of judges,[6] as well as new posts of court director in appellate and regional courts, financial coordinator in district courts, and the post of legal assistant.[7]

If supported by implementing regulations that reflect the intent of the reforms, the new Acts may enhance the courts' ability to manage themselves professionally and autonomously, and may ease widespread concerns about the unsatisfactory state of

---

[1] Act on Ordinary Courts, 27 July 2001, Journal of Laws [J.L.] 2001, No. 98, item 1070.

[2] Act on National Council of the Judiciary, 27 July 2001, J.L. 2001, No. 100, item 1082.

[3] *See* Section C.1., "Selection and Promotion".

[4] *See* Section D.1., "Governance and Administration of the Judicial Branch".

[5] Appellate courts now function as disciplinary courts of the first instance, and the Supreme Court as a second instance disciplinary court; before this change all cases were dealt with by the Supreme Court. As a rule, disciplinary hearings are now held in public. *See* Act on Ordinary Courts, Art. 107–133.

[6] The system of remuneration links pay rises to seniority. *See* Act on Ordinary Courts, Art. 91 (3–4,7).

[7] *See* Section D.2., "Court Administrative Capacity".

affairs in the judiciary, which in the public perception is corrupt, inefficient and unaccountable.[8]

In addition, in October 2001 the courts took over jurisdiction for minor offences that previously were handled by quasi-judicial misdemeanour boards. It is estimated that this will cause a ten percent increase in the number of cases filed, putting additional strains on court caseloads and the organisational infrastructure.[9]

2. Austerity Measures Imposed by the Ministry of Justice

In June 2001 the Ministry of Justice introduced a series of dramatic austerity measures that include bans on expenditures for training, examinations, conferences, business travel, vehicle maintenance, purchase, and maintenance of premises (beyond the necessary minimum).[10] The severity of these cuts suggests the difficulties courts face in securing the funding necessary for stable operations. Moreover, the Ministry's ability to order such sweeping reductions – regardless of the economic need – is a demonstration of the risks to courts' autonomy that remain when the executive retains fiscal or administrative supervision of the judiciary. Such risks should be minimised by ensuring that the courts have sufficient, stable funding that is reasonably insulated from discretionary political interference.

C. PROFESSIONAL COMPETENCE OF JUDGES

The procedures for admittance to an apprenticeship – the main avenue to appointment to the bench – need clearer criteria and enhanced transparency; ways to encourage more experienced legal professionals to join the judiciary should also be explored. The procedure

---

[8] Aleksander Checko, "Sąd nad sędziami" ("Judgement over judges"), *Polityka*, No. 26/2001, which also notes that, according to the Centre for Public Opinion Research, only 5.3 percent of Poles consider judgements of courts just and appropriate. For a comprehensive discussion of corruption in Poland, including in its judiciary, *see* EU Accession Monitoring Program, *Monitoring the EU Accession Process: Corruption and Anti-Corruption Policy in Poland* (Open Society Institute, Budapest, October 2002), available at <http://www.eumap.org.>, (accessed 25 September 2002).

[9] H.F. "Wykroczenia wkrótce w sądach" (Misdemeanours soon in courts), *Rzeczpospolita*, 16 May 2001.

[10] "Temida tightens her belt", Internet Journal of Polish Press Agency, 17 September 2001.

*for monitoring judicial performance is unsystematic and opaque, and does not aid judges' professional development; consistent with the requirements of judicial independence, new legislation or regulations should establish an efficient system for periodic evaluation of judicial performance. There is no comprehensive system for judicial training; most training is **ad hoc** and narrow in scope, and the limited amount of State-sponsored training has been dramatically reduced. So long as the Ministry of Justice retains authority for judicial training, it should develop a clear and coherent conceptual framework – including funding and training priorities – and take immediate practical steps to improve coordination of existing efforts.*

1 . Selection and Promotion

Poland has taken steps to improve procedures for selecting judges. For example, written tests for apprenticeships are now developed centrally by the Ministry of Justice and administered the same day throughout the country. However, the procedure for admittance to an apprenticeship – the main avenue to appointment to the bench – needs clearer, standardised criteria and enhanced transparency. Experienced legal professionals should be given an equal chance to join the bench.

Any eligible candidate may apply directly for a vacancy.[11] There is no separate system of promotion; judges apply directly for positions in higher courts under similar conditions as other candidates.[12] Presidents, court colleges and general assemblies of judges of relevant courts assess candidates' qualifications and submit opinions to the National Council of the Judiciary through the Minister of Justice.[13] Alternatively, the Minister can propose candidates to the Council directly.[14] The Council selects nominees for appointment by the State President.[15] In practice, however, most judges enter the judiciary through the apprenticeship process.[16]

---

[11] The eligibility criteria include Polish citizenship, legal capacity, good character, possession of a law degree, adequate health, and specific professional experience; in addition, candidates must be at least 29 years old. Act on Ordinary Courts, Art. 61.

[12] Act on Ordinary Courts, Art. 57.

[13] Act on Ordinary Courts, Art. 57-58.

[14] Act on Ordinary Courts, Art. 59.

[15] Decree of the President of the Republic of Poland of 22 December 2001 on Detailed Mode of Operation of National Council of the Judiciary and Proceedings before the Council, chapter 2.

[16] *See, e.g., Report on performance of supervision over administrative activity of the courts*, Chief Board of Supervision/Department of Public Administration (document No. 150/2001/P00/003/DAE), Warsaw, December 2001.

The key component of the selection procedure for an apprenticeship is a written and oral exam administered by the appellate courts. Appellate court presidents establish examination commissions consisting of regional and appellate judges and a representative of the Ministry of Justice,[17] although in practice the Ministry representative almost never sits on the commission.[18] Thought should be given to developing mechanisms for input or participation by legal professionals or representatives of interested civil society organisations. In addition, judges who serve on selection commissions are not trained for this task. These shortcomings diminish the value of the exam as a legitimate means of verifying professional aptitude.

Lack of outside representation, input and participation can be partly remedied by detailed and uniform examination criteria and procedures so that selection committees are prevented from exercising undue discretion. Certain positive steps have been taken to standardise and unify exams for admittance to apprenticeship. In 2001 the Ministry of Justice for the first time prepared the written section of the exam and provided general topics for questions during the oral section. Written exams took place on the same day in the whole country. Efforts to specify eligibility criteria and standardise admittance procedures should continue, especially as the actual decision on admissibility can take into account not only the exam but also candidates' performance during their studies and opinions from former superiors.[19]

Over-reliance on the apprenticeship programme is a source of concern. In practice the selection process clearly gives preference to apprentices – who almost inevitably become judges – and thus even judicial aspirants with extensive legal experience may be excluded in favour of less experienced apprentices. While apprenticeship programmes are certainly valuable and give participants relevant training and practice, selection of the most qualified judicial candidates should be the goal, in order to ensure the highest possible level of professionalism in the judiciary.

2. Evaluating and Regulating Performance

The existing procedure for monitoring judicial performance is insufficient to assist judges in their professional development; it is not systematic and is not based on clear criteria or transparent procedures. Consistent with the requirements of judicial

---

[17] Ministry of Justice Decree of 25 June 1998 on Judicial and Public Prosecution Apprentices, para. 14 (1) J.L. 1998, No. 86, item 550 (amended).

[18] There are not enough Ministry employees available to take part in each exam, especially since exams take place at the same time. Information from the Ministry of Justice, May 2002.

[19] Ministry of Justice Decree of 25 June 1998 on Judicial and Public Prosecution Apprentices, para. 16 (3), J.L. 1998, No. 86, item 550 (amended).

independence, new legislation or regulations should establish an efficient system for periodic evaluation of judicial performance.

Monitoring and evaluating judges' performance is incorporated within regular and *ad hoc* inspections of court activities conducted by judge-inspectors.[20] Regular inspections are supposed to be carried out every three years,[21] but this rule is not followed in practice.[22] A judge's court president or the National Council of the Judiciary may request an *ad hoc* inspection if a judge changes positions or if a complaint has been lodged against that judge.[23]

Inspectors are required to evaluate the efficiency of court proceedings (including preparation of sessions and length of time for preparation of judgements), supervision of execution of judgements, and work culture;[24] however, the quality of adjudicative work is not listed as a subject for evaluation. Moreover, the criteria for both regular and *ad hoc* evaluations are imprecise and afford broad discretion to the judge-inspectors, and results of inspections are not made public.

An inspection may result in a judge being censured either by the Ministry of Justice or the court president for failure to conduct court proceedings efficiently.[25] If the inspection reveals a disciplinary violation, the judge can be sanctioned in a disciplinary procedure.[26]

The appellate procedure allows another kind of check on unsatisfactory or unprofessional work by trial court judges. If an appellate or regional court, when considering an appeal, finds an obvious breach of law by a court of first instance, it censures this breach, irrespective of the appellate ruling. Before the censure, the appellate or regional court may demand an explanation from the judge who presided

---

[20] Act on Ordinary Courts, Art. 38.

[21] Ministry of Justice Decree of 18 September 1995 on the Mode of Performing Supervision over the Administrative Activity of Courts, para. 5 (5), J.L. 1995, No. 111, item 538.

[22] *Report on performance of supervision over administrative activity of the courts*, Chief Board of Supervision/Department of Public Administration (document No. 150/2001/P00/003/DAE), Warsaw, December 2001.

[23] Written and oral complaints may be handled by either the Ministry of Justice or courts presidents; complaints may lead to censure or disciplinary proceedings. Ministry of Justice, Information about Manner of Receiving and Serving Complaints and Motions of Citizens to the Ministry of Justice in 2001, Warsaw, January 2002.

[24] Ministry of Justice Decree of 18 September 1995 on Mode of Performing the Supervision over Administrative Activity of Courts, para. 10. J.L. 1995, No. 111, item 538.

[25] Act on Ordinary Courts, Art. 37 (4).

[26] Act on Ordinary Courts, Art. 114.

over the trial in the first instance court.[27] The censure is recorded in the judge's personnel file. However, the effectiveness of this tool in guiding judges' performance is limited, as it applies only to trial court judges and to those particular cases that reach an appellate instance. In addition, this evaluation tool is seldom used; although encouraged by court presidents, appellate judges are often reluctant to reproach their colleagues in the lower courts.[28]

The media cover the courts extensively and provide informal public feedback on judges' performance. However, there is continuing controversy over the degree to which the general public and the media should have access to court files.[29] Clear rules are needed to reconcile the right of access to information with the right to protection of personal data, but in general court files should be more readily accessible.

3. Training for a Professional Judiciary

There is no comprehensive system for judicial training. Training of judicial apprentices is insufficiently standardised and lacks professionalism. Although continuing training for serving judges is offered by a number of organisations in connection with specific projects of limited duration or on an *ad hoc* basis, the already limited amount of unsystematic State-sponsored training has been dramatically reduced as a part of the recent financial austerity measures. Training of both apprentices and sitting judges is generally narrow in scope and does not contribute to the development of sustained improvements in the judiciary's level of professional capacity, for which comprehensive, integrated training on a long-term basis is required.

The Ministry of Justice's Department of Personnel and Training is responsible for judicial training.[30] The relevant section of the Department has a staff of six who are responsible for training of judges and public prosecutors as well as apprenticeship examinations – quite a limited capacity in light of the number of judges and apprentices.[31]

---

[27] Act on Ordinary Courts, Art. 40 (1).

[28] Interviews with regional court presidents.

[29] Lech Gardocki, "Should court files be made available to journalists", *Rzeczpospolita*, 14 May 2001; Prof. Piotr Winczorek, "A press reporter is asking for files", *Rzeczpospolita*, 6 August 2001.

[30] Act on Ordinary Courts, Art. 82.

[31] At the beginning of 2002 there were 8,350 posts for judges and assessors (assessors may perform judicial functions) and 2,830 apprentices.

The training of apprentices is largely conducted by judges,[32] who are not trained for this task. Training is conducted on a weekly basis in regional courts under the supervision of appellate court presidents. The training manager, a regional court judge, develops a training programme that must be approved by the relevant appellate court president; the Ministry of Justice is also notified.[33]

There are no national standards addressing the principles, scope and methods of training for judicial apprentices. In practice, seminars concentrate on analysis of legal norms. Trainers are almost exclusively judges of regional and appellate courts who have no training in teaching techniques.[34] There is a need for standardisation of training for judicial apprentices to include skills-oriented topics and judicial ethics, *inter alia*.

Continuing judicial training likewise generally concentrates on imparting substantive legal knowledge, ignoring administrative and managerial skills. Even this limited training was dramatically reduced as part of the financial austerity measures;[35] at present the Ministry of Justice conducts training only sporadically,[36] and the selection of topics is haphazard.[37]

It might be advisable to transfer authority for training to an autonomous administrative institution in which judges are well represented. So long as the Ministry of Justice retains authority for training, however, it needs to develop a clear and coherent conceptual framework – including funding, organisational principles, and

---

[32] The Ministry of Justice provides only the regulatory framework for training apprentices. *See* Ministry of Justice Decree of 25 June 1998 on Judicial and Public Prosecution Apprentices, J.L. 1998, No. 86, item 550 (amended).

[33] Ministry of Justice Decree of 25 June 1998 on Judicial and Public Prosecution Apprentices, para. 18–21, J.L. 1998, No. 86, item 550 (amended).

[34] Interviews with Ministry of Justice employees and judges in regional courts.

[35] *See* Section B.2., "Austerity Measures Imposed by the Ministry of Justice".

[36] Training programmes organised or co-organised by the Ministry of Justice have been suspended for over a year. Exceptionally, training courses are organised in response to pressing needs, such as for district court judges who took over misdemeanour cases. The Ministry of Justice's Department for International Cooperation and European Law also implements EU-sponsored training projects, primarily in the framework of the PHARE and TAIEX programmes. These projects also concentrate on delivering specific legal knowledge rather than on building long-term capacity for judicial training.

[37] The Human Rights Ombudsman has twice approached the Ministry of Justice with a request to "take action for launching a post-graduate study in psychology and pedagogy for judges from family departments." Letters of the Human Rights Ombudsman to the Minister of Justice of 13 June 2001 and 7 November 2001. In reaction to the second letter the Ministry contracted the University of Warsaw to develop a relevant training programme, which took place in May 2002. On another occasion, the Ministry of Culture requested that judges be trained in intellectual property law; training courses on this topic have not taken place.

training priorities – and to take immediate practical steps to improve coordination of existing NGO training efforts as well as to build institutional capacity. Training should focus not only on substantive law, but also on developing judges' adjudicative and administrative skills.

D. INSTITUTIONAL CAPACITY OF THE JUDICIAL BRANCH

The judiciary continues to rely on the Ministry of Justice for administrative support, which unnecessarily introduces opportunities for indirect interference with adjudication, and contradicts the principle of judicial capacity that courts should have a meaningful institutional role in organising their own work. Moreover, the Ministry has failed to provide the kind of leadership and support that would enhance courts' competence; whatever body has the authority to administer the courts system – whether an autonomous judicial institution or the Ministry – needs to be more transparent and to develop more regularised and inclusive procedures. Court administration lacks professionalism. Training judges in management techniques should be an immediate priority; in the longer term, managerial tasks should be transferred to professional staff, leaving judges free to focus on adjudication. The recent introduction of court directors, financial managers, and legal assistants is a positive step; if these measures are to succeed, reforms must be supported by clear implementing regulations.

1. Governance and Administration of the Judicial Branch

The judiciary continues to rely on the Ministry of Justice for strategic planning, identification of priorities, and administrative support. This model of governance and administration unnecessarily introduces opportunities for indirect interference with adjudication, and contradicts the principle of judicial capacity that the courts should have a meaningful institutional role in organising their own work. Moreover, the Ministry has failed to provide the kind of strategic leadership and operational support that would enhance the competence and efficiency of the courts.

The Ministry of Justice supervises administration of all courts[38] except the Supreme Court and Chief Administrative Court, which are independently administered. In practice, the Ministry is the only State institution with competence to develop and implement standards for the operational support of courts. There is an autonomous National Council of the Judiciary, but it has quite limited powers and only minor

---

[38] Act on Ordinary Courts, Art. 9.

influence on the court operations; the powers of the Council include assessing candidates for judgeship, appointing the disciplinary prosecutor, issuing opinions on legal acts concerning courts and judges, and adopting a code of ethics.[39]

Despite its undivided standard-setting and administrative responsibilities, the Ministry of Justice has failed to develop a clear strategy for the development of the judicial branch – as demonstrated by the sweeping cuts in the budget for judicial training and the absence of an effective system for periodic performance evaluations.[40] In addition, the Ministry has not developed standard norms for caseloads, standards and procedures for modernisation of court technology and equipment, norms for court facilities, or a system for assessing training needs. This lack of clear standards often puts court presidents in the potentially compromising position of lobbying for funds and other material necessities.

The budgeting process in particular still largely excludes judges' participation; however the Act on Ordinary Courts has given the National Council of the Judiciary the right to comment on draft budgets prepared by the courts and present them to the Ministry of Justice,[41] which is a step towards some judicial representation in a process still marked by a lack of standardisation and transparency. Nonetheless, as noted above, the Ministry's authority to impose fiscal austerity measures on the judiciary raises concerns about risks to the courts' adjudicative and administrative independence.[42]

Among the causes contributing to the inadequate performance of the Ministry are frequent changes of Minister[43] and rotation of staff[44] – both of which introduce an element of instability into the Ministry's operations – and poor cooperation and supervision within the Ministry.[45] There is a perception among judges that the current

---

[39] Act on National Council of the Judiciary, Art. 2–3.

[40] *See* Sections C.2., "Evaluating and Regulating Performance", and C.3., "Training for a Professional Judiciary".

[41] Act on Ordinary Courts, Art. 178.

[42] *See* Section B.2., "Austerity Measures Imposed by the Ministry of Justice".

[43] There have been five Ministers of Justice over the last 25 months. A change of Minister usually causes other personnel changes as well.

[44] *See* "*Report on performance of supervision over administrative activity of the courts*", Chief Board of Supervision/Department of Public Administration (document No. 150/2001/P00/003/DAE), Warsaw, December 2001. The problem of frequent rotation hindering effective operations has been directly linked to the practice of short-term employment of judges at the Ministry, which not only contradicts the principle of judicial independence but also negatively affects the efficiency of the Ministry of Justice and, consequently, of the judicial system.

[45] "*Report on performance of supervision over administrative activity of the courts*", Chief Board of Supervision/Department of Public Administration (document No. 150/2001/P00/003/DAE), Warsaw, December 2001.

model of judicial administration on the national level is ineffective and needs to be reformed.[46] Whatever body has the authority to administer the courts system – whether an autonomous judicial institution or the Ministry – needs to be more transparent and to develop more regularised and inclusive procedures.

2. Court Administrative Capacity

Court administration lacks professionalism. Judges who act as managers are neither required to have management skills before being appointed nor trained accordingly thereafter. Training in areas such as court and personnel management techniques should be an immediate priority; in the longer term, courts' professionalism and capacity would benefit from transferring major managerial tasks to professional managers, leaving judges free to focus on adjudication.

The overall responsibility for court management and supervision rests with court presidents; their duties include preparation of requests for numbers of judges and court staff, employment and dismissal of court personnel, court-level training, execution of the court budget, and provision of supplies.[47] Presidents of immediately superior courts and the Minister of Justice supervise lower court presidents.[48]

Despite their broad managerial responsibilities, neither court presidents nor the vice-presidents and chairs of departments who assist them are required to have any managerial experience; moreover, there is no system for providing them with relevant training after their appointment. The Minister of Justice appoints court presidents from among the judges of each court after receiving the non-binding opinion of the general assembly of the relevant court.[49]

---

[46] *See, e.g.,* "What should we improve in the Polish justice system? Report from the conference in the Poznan Regional Court", *Gazeta Wyborcza,* 8 April 2002 ("...[citing a judge's comments that] it is already so bad, that something must be done... The image of the courts can not be good when there are immense backlogs... Representatives of the Ministry of Justice explained that every year they have been requesting to employ additional judges, but there is a lack of money... We mean the reform of the entire system... [Another judge said] the main issue was the efficiency of the judges' work and of the judicial administration, so that the judges could devote themselves to adjudication. Judicial procedures should also be changed as now they hinder the efficiency of the judicial process").

[47] Ministry of Justice Decree on Regulation of Internal Operations of Ordinary Courts, 19 November 1987.

[48] The Minister of Justice may quash administrative orders issued by court presidents. Law on Ordinary Courts, Art. 37 (3).

[49] Act on Ordinary Courts, Art. 23–27.

Having judges perform managerial tasks is obviously not the most effective use of their judicial skills. The recent introduction of court directors in regional courts and the possibility to employ financial managers in district courts[50] are positive steps towards professionalising courts management. If they are to succeed, these legislative reforms must be supported by implementing regulations – currently being prepared – that grant court directors meaningful and clearly delineated powers, and court presidents must be persuaded to concede managerial powers to carefully selected court directors, who should remain under their supervision.

A number of other operational problems continue to limit the courts' ability to focus on effective adjudication. Judges are overburdened with technical tasks that could be performed by court personnel if they were better qualified, but the Ministry of Justice has been unable to set up a coherent system of training for court staff. Training is left to regional courts, which results in significant disparities in the quantity and quality of training offered.

In addition, the courts, and especially their secretariats, are not sufficiently computerised; for instance, both case registration and statistical reporting are performed manually. At the same time, the number of incoming cases is steadily growing,[51] and court delays remain a serious problem.[52] There is also a shortage of space.

The new Law on Ordinary Courts introduced a new position of legal assistant,[53] which may assist judges in concentrating on adjudication rather than technical work. However, more concentrated effort is needed to improve work conditions in courts and to speed up court proceedings. Besides training and technical modernisation, more attention should be paid to legal reform – such as alternative methods of dispute resolution – as a way of easing the pressure on an insufficiently professionalised court system.

---

[50] Act on Ordinary Courts, Art. 21 (2).

[51] Ministry of Justice/Department of Ordinary Courts, *Yearly Information about Activity of Ordinary Courts in 2001*, (doc. No. DSP/60/80/2002), indicating that the courts received 17 percent more cases in 2001 than in 2000.

[52] Poland has a high number of cases before the European Court of Human Rights alleging violation of the right to a fair trial within a reasonable time; as of April 2002, 213 such cases have been communicated by the Court to the Government. Information provided by the Office of the Agent of the Polish Government to the European Court of Human Rights.

[53] Act on Ordinary Courts, Art. 155 (2).

E. RECOMMENDATIONS

1. To the Polish Government and Legislature

- Continue judicial reform by further strengthening the institutional independence and administrative capacity of the judiciary as a separate branch.

- Reduce the administrative authority of the Ministry of Justice; ensure that the courts have sufficient, stable funding that is reasonably insulated from discretionary political interference.

- Improve the system for selecting apprentices by further rationalising criteria and procedures for examinations, providing specialised instruction for members of selection committees, and making the procedure more transparent.

- Make changes to the system for selection of new judges to ensure that experienced legal professionals are given an equal chance to join the bench.

- Consistent with the requirements of judicial independence, develop a system for periodic evaluation of judges' performance that is comprehensive and transparent and that will assist judges in their professional development.

- Develop a clear and coherent conceptual framework for judicial training – including funding, organisational principles, and training priorities – and take immediate practical steps to improve coordination of existing efforts; prioritise specialised training for court managers and support personnel.

- Consider transferring authority for training from the Ministry of Justice to an autonomous body in which judges are well represented.

- Increase the role of professional managers in court administration. Develop clear, merit-based criteria for selection of court directors and financial coordinators.

- Develop operational standards and a comprehensive plan to improve work conditions in courts, modernise court operations, and decrease court delays; consider encouraging wider application of alternative forms of dispute resolution.

2. To the European Union

- Facilitate exchanges with other EU candidate and member States that have created self-governing and self-administering judicial branches in order to transfer knowledge about how to realise the principles of separation of powers, judicial independence, and judicial capacity.

- Encourage steps to reduce the residual administrative and fiscal powers exercised by the Ministry of Justice over the courts, perhaps by vesting broader authority in the National Council of the Judiciary or another truly autonomous administrative institution.

- Emphasise the pressing need to develop a comprehensive plan for judicial training within a sustainable institutional framework; in existing support programmes, focus more on contributing to the development of long-term capacity to provide comprehensive training.

Judicial Capacity in Romania

Table of Contents

A. INTRODUCTION

Romania has made little progress in realising greater independence or professionalisation of the judiciary during the last year. Several major structural problems – the Ministry of Justice's continued administrative authority, the General Prosecutor's power to file extraordinary appeals, the Superior Council of Magistracy's mixed composition and joint jurisdiction over judges and prosecutors – have not been addressed, preventing the effective and independent functioning of the judicial system and contributing to the high level of public mistrust in the courts. Government, Parliament, and society as a whole need to commit to comprehensive and sustained reform of the judiciary's internal structuring and its relationship to the rest of the State, if judges' necessary independence and their professional capabilities are to be fully realised.

The Ministry of Justice continues to exercise unnecessarily broad and overly centralised authority over the courts and over the selection, promotion and evaluation of judges, raising concerns about potential political interference. In particular, provisions allowing politicians and senior bureaucrats to be appointed judges without passing standard examinations unnecessarily blur the separation of powers and risk replacing professionalism with political cronyism as a criterion for judicial service. Training programmes need considerable improvement and a long-term funding commitment. Court-level administration – which is also subject to the Ministry's supervision – is not transparent; poor working conditions seriously interfere with efforts to professionalise the judiciary.

B. Current Developments Affecting Judicial Independence and Capacity

Little improvement in the judiciary's position has occurred in the last year. The Ministry of Justice continues to exercise unnecessarily broad authority over the courts. Other major problems – the General Prosecutor's power to file extraordinary appeals, the Superior Council of Magistracy's mixed composition and joint jurisdiction over judges and prosecutors – have not been addressed. The process of drafting a new Act on the Judiciary lacks transparency, making it less likely that a version addressing public concerns and taking account of judges' need for increased professionalisation and independence will come out of Parliament; serious and broad-based commitment to reform is essential if judges' independence and professionalism are to be realised.

1. Little Significant Progress

The situation of the judiciary has not noticeably improved in the last year. The Ministry of Justice continues to exercise unnecessarily broad supervisory and regulatory authority over judicial administration and the career path of judges. The Ministry's judicial inspectors continue to exercise an intrusive authority to evaluate judges' performance, and allegations concerning their undue interference have increased during the past year.

Several particular threats to the independence and professional capacity of judges have not been addressed: the power of the General Prosecutor to file extraordinary appeals against final judgements in civil and criminal cases remains in force and, moreover, has been intensively used in practice.

These serious, structural shortcomings contribute to the high level of public mistrust in courts and judges that brings the legitimacy of the judicial system into question. The percentage of citizens indicating that they have little or very little trust in the judiciary increased from 62 percent in 1998 to 74 percent in 1999 and to 77 percent in 2000.[1] There is a public perception that corruption is widespread in the judiciary; the judiciary is ranked second among governmental structures that are perceived as the

---

[1] For a comprehensive discussion of corruption in Romania, including its judiciary, *see* EU Accession Monitoring Program, *Monitoring the EU Accession Process: Corruption and Anti-Corruption Policy in Romania* (Open Society Institute, Budapest, October 2002), available at <http://www.eumap.org>, (accessed 26 September 2002); *see also* World Bank, *2000 Diagnostic Survey.*

most corrupt.[2] The media often accuse judges of lacking professional preparation, of misconduct, and of unfair or even unlawful rulings;[3] they also frequently refer to political intrusion in the functioning of the system of justice.[4] However, this broad-based dissatisfaction has not generated public discussion about structural problems such as working conditions in courts, the causes for a high caseload or the institutional situation of the judicial branch.

2. Recent and Pending Legislative and Regulatory Changes

The Ministry of Justice is drafting a new Act on the Judiciary; however, the drafting process lacks transparency. Reportedly, the Ministry of Justice sent the draft law to the courts as well as to the prosecutors' offices in late June 2002 in order to get magistrates' input on the draft law. However, this draft is not available to other legal professionals or to civil society. A secretive drafting process may further contribute to public scepticism and makes it less likely that the draft will sufficiently address the problems underlying the courts' present lack of independence and low level of professionalisation.

In the meantime, an Emergency Ordinance has modified the existing Act on the Judiciary[5] by, *inter alia*, changing the composition of the Superior Council of Magistracy.[6] Two additional members – one regional court judge and one prosecutor – were added, raising the membership from 15 to 17. The system of appointment by

---

[2] EU Accession Monitoring Program, *Monitoring the EU Accession Process: Corruption and Anti-Corruption Policy in Romania* (Open Society Institute, Budapest, October 2002), available at <http://www.eumap.org>.

[3] *See, e.g.,* "Corrupted magistrate at the Supreme Court of Justice", *Jurnalul National,* 11 February 2002; "Lawsuit of corrupted magistrates", *Romania Libera,* 8 May 2002; "Motorola case was buried", *Evenimentul Zilei,* 13 April 2002; "Magistrates from Constanta legalised the international poaching", *Adevarul,* 27 July 2002.

[4] *See, e.g.,* "Justice accuses to be subjected to political pressure", *Jurnalul National,* 12 February 2002; "Political Power controls magistrates by occult mechanism", *Curentul,* 22 April 2002; "The two vice-presidents of the Iasi Tribunal have been dismissed", *Romania Libera,* 27 April 2002; "Magistrates' revolt. 28 judges want to leave the Bucharest Tribunal", *Romania Libera,* 27 April 2002; "Political appointments in the judiciary", *Adevarul,* 12 June 2002; "The president of the Supreme Court of Justice exposes political pressures on the Supreme Court justices", *Adevarul,* 17 June 2002.

[5] Act 92/1992 on the Judiciary, republished *Official Gazette* 259, 30 September 1997. The Act on the Judiciary was also previously modified through Government Emergency Ordinance 179/1999 for the modification of the Act 92/1992 on the Judiciary, *Official Gazette* 559, 17 November 1999.

[6] Government Emergency Ordinance 20/2002 on the Modification of the Act 92/1992 on the Judiciary, *Official Gazette* 151, 28 February 2002.

Parliament was also changed; Parliament is now obliged to vote on one candidate only for each position in the Council, whereas previously the Parliament chose from three candidates for each position. These changes do not address the main issue related to the Council's composition, however, which is the presence of prosecutors in a body empowered to take decisions on the career of judges.

The Emergency Ordinance is currently being debated in the Parliament. Government, Parliament, and society as a whole need to commit to comprehensive and sustained reform of the judiciary's internal structuring and its relationship to the rest of the State, if judges' necessary independence and their professional capabilities are to be fully realised.

One positive development is that the jurisdiction of the military courts over police has been restricted. With one exception, police officers will now be prosecuted by civil prosecutors and tried in civil courts.[7] In addition, new Regulations for the Admittance to the National Institute of Magistrates[8] and for the Promotion of Judges[9] were adopted without, however, bringing significant changes.

C. PROFESSIONAL COMPETENCE OF JUDGES

The Ministry of Justice's continued influence over the selection and promotion of judges raises concerns about potential political interference with the judiciary. Provisions allowing politicians and senior bureaucrats to be appointed judges without passing standard examinations unnecessarily blur the separation of powers and risk replacing professionalism with political cronyism as a criterion for judicial service. The intrusive role of the Ministry of Justice and superior judges in evaluating judges' performance may slow down the development of a capable and independent cadre of judges. Training programmes need considerable improvement; the National Institute for Magistrates, which is heavily reliant

---

[7] Act 360/2002 on Police, Official Gazette 440, 24 June 2002. The exception from civil jurisdiction over police officers applies when they commit criminal offences endangering the national security of the State, in which case they remain under the jurisdiction of military courts.

[8] Order of the Minister of Justice 1478/C for approving the Regulation for Admittance to the National Institute of Magistrates, 13 July 2001. *See* Section C.1., "Selection and Promotion", and Section C.3., "Training for a Professional Judiciary".

[9] Ministry of Justice Order 2958/C for approving the Regulation on the Organisation of the Promotion Examination for a Vacant Position or Within the Same Working Place in Courts and Prosecutors' Offices, *Official Gazette*. 18, 15 January 2002. *See* Section C.1., "Selection and Promotion".

on the Ministry of Justice for its budget and managerial direction, is poorly funded, which in turn threatens the long-term sustainability of training.

1. Selection and Promotion

The Ministry of Justice's continued influence over the identification, selection and appointment of candidates for judgeships, and over the promotion of judges to higher courts, raises concerns about the potential for political interference with the judiciary.

The Ministry of Justice continues to act as a gatekeeper for judges' appointment and promotion prospects. Judges are appointed by the State President upon the proposal of the Superior Council of Magistracy, but only following the recommendation of the Minister of Justice; the Council may not consider a candidate not recommended by the Minister.

The initial selection and training process is largely controlled by the Ministry of Justice. Since 2000, candidates for judgeship in the district courts must complete a two-year training course at the National Institute of Magistracy and pass an examination jointly organised by the Ministry and the Institute.[10] Admittance to the Institute is, however, effectively in the hands of the Ministry, which appoints the members of the admittance and examination commissions and establishes their powers and duties.

Candidates for the Institute who meet basic requirements[11] must pass a written examination;[12] apparently no evidence with regard to the candidate's good reputation is required.[13] This failure to verify the integrity of candidates may contribute to a lack of professionalism.

A potentially serious problem involves the discretionary appointment of more experienced individuals without any training or standardised vetting. Individuals with five years of relevant legal experience can be appointed as judges of district courts by

---

[10] Order of the Minister of Justice 1478/C, for approving the Regulation for Admittance in the National Institute of Magistrates, 13 July 2001.

[11] Candidates must be Romanian citizens, have a law degree, a clean criminal record and good reputation, know Romanian, and be medically and psychologically fit. Act 92/1992 on the Judiciary, republished *Official Gazette* 259, 30 September 1997, Art. 46 (as modified by Government Emergency Ordinance 179/1999 for the Modification of the Act 92/1992 on the Judiciary, *Official Gazette* 559, 17 November 1999).

[12] Ministry of Justice Order 1478/C, for approving the Regulation for Admittance in the National Institute of Magistrates, 13 July 2001.

[13] There is no specification of the term and no clear procedure on how this legal requirement can be verified either in the Act on the Judiciary or in subsequent legislation.

passing an examination organised by the Ministry of Justice.[14] Moreover, individuals who have served in a specified range of legal positions for five to ten years can be appointed "exceptionally" without any examination.[15] In addition, Members of Parliament, the Minister of Justice, State Secretaries and employees of the Ministry with a legal background may also be appointed without examination.[16]

In all these cases, there are no recruitment procedures or standards other than time served, and the process effectively takes place without any possibility for external scrutiny. In practice, it is not unusual that a court president with an urgent vacancy finds a candidate for whom the president himself supplies a recommendation. The procedures lack clarity and transparency, while the professional associations of lawyers and revelant civil society organisations have no say about the process.

While opening the lower ranks of the judiciary to more experienced candidates is itself a welcome initiative, the particular procedure employed here creates opportunities for excessively broad discretion; the practice of making appointments without a prior examination jeopardises the merit-based process for the selection of judges. The high number of exceptional appointments to the bench without an examination – 45 out of 53 between July 2000 and June 2001, and 70 out of 70 between September 1999 and June 2000 – raised the concern of the Superior Council of Magistracy, which criticised the procedure as lacking clear criteria and transparency.[17] The provisions allowing Members of Parliament and the employees of the Ministry of Justice to be appointed without any standardised vetting unnecessarily blur the separation of powers and risk replacing professionalism with cronyism as a criterion for judicial service.

---

[14] The list of eligible categories includes private-practice lawyers, notaries, law professors, legal counsellors, experts, forensic assistants, researchers with the Romanian Academy, and legal staff members in various organs who have served at least five years. Act 92/1992 on the Judiciary, Art. 65. The Government pledged, in a letter sent to the EC Delegation, not to apply Art. 65; however, Art. 65 is still in force and might be applied at any time.

[15] The list includes individuals who have served at least five years as judges, prosecutors, or general inspectors or legal counsellors at the Ministry, other legal counsellors who have served for ten years, and individuals who hold a PhD in law. For individuals who hold a PhD in law there is no requirement of practical legal experience. Act 92/1992 on the Judiciary, Art. 67.

[16] As well as "consultant magistrates" serving in labour cases; see Government Emergency Ordinance 20/2002 on the modification of the Act on the Judiciary, *Official Gazette* 151, 28 February 2002. Although not judges, consultant magistrates enjoy most of the rights granted to judges by the Act on the Judiciary. Being appointed by the Minister of Justice for a four-year term, they lack independence. Nonetheless, they take part in the hearings and deliberation having a "consultative" vote.

[17] *See* Superior Council of Magistracy annual reports, 1999–2000 and 2000–2001; *also* interview with Lucian Popescu, supervising judge and former director in the Ministry of Justice, Bucharest Court of Appeal, 13 April 2002.

Promotions are decided by the Superior Council of Magistracy, but again only after the recommendation of the Minister of Justice. For promotion, judges must serve in the magistracy a minimum number of years and have "meritorious activity proven by the qualifying grades given by the hierarchical superiors"[18] The presidents of the courts of appeal have to issue an opinion whether a judge can participate in the examination for promotion; to this end, they take into account the annual qualification grades and the reports done by the supervising judges. In case of a negative opinion, the interested judge can complain to the Superior Council of Magistracy, whose Secretary General takes the final decision.

2. Evaluating and Regulating Performance

The intrusive role of the Ministry of Justice and superior judges in evaluating judges' performance may be slowing the development of a capable and independent corps of judges.

Judges' performance is evaluated annually by their court presidents[19] and further verified by judges from the higher courts; the performance of appellate court presidents and vice-presidents of the courts of appeal is evaluated by a commission appointed by the Minister of Justice. District and regional court judges may appeal the results of their evaluations to their appellate court president; regional court presidents and vice-presidents themselves may appeal the results of their evaluations to a commission appointed by the Minister, while appellate court presidents and vice-presidents may appeal directly to the Minister. Reportedly, there is a general opinion among judges that there is little real interest in appealing results of evaluations.[20]

Judges may also be dismissed for "obvious professional incompetence."[21] However, there is no procedure detailing the criteria to be used for assessing professional incompetence and it is unclear which body or official makes such decisions. These criteria need to be clarified to ensure that judges are not subject to improper pressures masked under the evaluation procedure.

---

[18] Act on the Judiciary, Art. 66. The detailed conditions and procedure for the organisation of the promotion examination are laid down in the Regulation on the Organisation of the Promotion Examination in a Vacant Position or Within the Same Working Place in Courts and Prosecutors' Offices, approved by Ministry of Justice Order 2958/C, *Official Gazette* 18, 15 January 2002.

[19] There is a standard evaluation form produced by the Ministry of Justice that includes guidelines on filling in the form.

[20] Interviews with judges wishing to remain anonymous, 2002.

[21] Act on the Judiciary, Art. 97 (2).

Judicial inspectors play a significant and problematic role in performance evaluation. There are two categories of inspectors: supervising judges[22] at each court of appeal and general judicial inspectors[23] in the Ministry of Justice. There have been reports of instances when general inspectors have extended their evaluation to the substantive reasoning of judgements under the rubric of verifying how the law is applied in particular cases;[24] many judges have expressed concern that the Ministry is using inspections to control the judiciary. The Minister's power to order both preliminary investigations in cases of alleged misconduct and periodical verifications through the general inspectors[25] poses a real danger to judicial independence.

The internal evaluation of judges takes place strictly inside the system; other legal professionals and civil society have no meaningful opportunity to comment upon matters related to judges' performance.

3. Training for a Professional Judiciary

Training programmes need considerable improvement. The main organ for training, the National Institute for Magistrates, is heavily reliant on the Ministry of Justice for its budget and managerial direction. It is also poorly funded, which threatens the long-term sustainability of training.

The Ministry of Justice coordinates the professional training of judges.[26] The National Institute for Magistrates actually organises the initial two-year training of future magistrates – judges and prosecutors – and the continuing training of serving magistrates. However, the Institute is legally dependent on the Ministry of Justice[27] for

---

[22] The attributions of the supervising judges are listed in the Regulation for the Organisation and Administrative Functioning of Courts, approved by Ministry of Justice Order no. 125/C, 17 January 2000, Art. 14 (unpublished).

[23] The qualifications and authority of general judicial inspectors are listed in the Regulation for the Organisation and Functioning of the Ministry of Justice, approved by the Minister of Justice, Order no. 39/C, 6 January 1999, Art.20, (unpublished).

[24] *See, e.g.,* Interview with a judge from the Bucharest Tribunal (regional court), Bucharest, 5 March 2002.

[25] Regulation for the Organisation and Administrative Functioning of Courts, approved by Ministry of Justice Order no. 125/C, 17 January 2000 (unpublished). The legal basis for the Ministry's exercise of these powers is questionable.

[26] Government Decision 212/2001 on the Organisation and Functioning of the Ministry of Justice, *Official Gazette* 59, 5 February 2001, modified by Government Decision 553/2001, *Official Gazette* 328, 19 June 2001, Art. 4, (1 p. 14).

[27] Act on the Judiciary, Chapter 2, Section III, Art. 70–85.

its funding, decisions about the numbers of trainees, approval of its programmes, approval of its top management and trainers (who are largely judges and prosecutors), and approval of all decisions adopted by the Institute's Council.

The National Institute for Magistrates is insufficiently funded. Foreign donors, primarily the EU, have borne the principal financial burden for sustaining the Institute's programmes, and its long-term domestic sustainability remains unclear. The recent renovations to the Institute's premises were financed largely from foreign sources, including EU funds, and continuing training for judges in 2002 has been organised exclusively under the aegis of international assistance programmes. This also raises concerns about the long-term sustainability of judicial training.

The National Institute for Magistrates also needs to adopt a more professional and inclusive approach in developing and running its programmes, especially for continuing training of judges. Curricula for both initial and continuing training are almost exclusively concentrated on imparting immediately relevant legal knowledge and are only infrequently complemented by topics aiming at improving judicial skills such as legal reasoning and writing and reflecting on the new role of judges in a democratic society. Only occasionally are such topics developed, generally by foreign experts, and mostly within the PHARE programme. Input from the larger legal community, especially court consumers and academics, would assist in improvement of the curricula.

Continuing training is especially problematic. At least every five years judges must attend a training session either with the National Institute for Magistrates or with the courts of appeal or some other educational body.[28] In practice both the Institute and the Ministry organise such trainings,[29] which are not based on any long-term programming, and attendance has been haphazard. Quite often, for example, the only criteria by which the courts' presidents designate which judges participate is the schedule of judicial hearings on the training day; this leads to participation by judges whose work is unrelated to the training topics. In general, judicial education is in need of a comprehensive strategy that includes retraining for serving judges and a clear plan for developing the pre-service education system.[30]

---

[28] Act on the Judiciary, Art. 119. There is however no sanction mentioned either in the Act or in subsequent regulations if judges do not comply with this requirement. Moreover, there is no database with information about magistrates' participation in trainings.

[29] There is no clear legal provision that would entitle the Ministry of Justice to organise and conduct continuing judicial training.

[30] *See, e.g.*, W. Rusch, PHARE project RO9905.01-01 Inception report, 7 December 2001.

The Training Centre for Clerks was set up in 1999[31] and began operations in December 2000. The Centre is subordinated to the Ministry of Justice[32] and is responsible for developing initial and continuing training for the auxiliary specialised personnel working in courts and prosecutors' offices, in coordination with the National Institute of Magistrates. So far, the Centre has only dealt with the initial training of 44 persons, in part due to lack of funds, office space, staff and teaching facilities. Considering that 2,286 judicial clerks are currently working in the courts, the Centre's impact in producing trained supporting staff is still insufficient and should be expanded.

D. INSTITUTIONAL CAPACITY OF THE JUDICIAL BRANCH

The judiciary is still administered primarily by the Ministry of Justice, in a highly centralised and hierarchical system; the Ministry has the authority to supervise and control any matter within the lower courts' administration, which discourages the development of an independent and professionally capable judiciary. Court-level administration – which is also subject to the Ministry's supervision – is not transparent and is lacking professionalism; conditions in the courts are so poor as to seriously interfere with efforts to professionalise the judiciary.

1. Governance and Administration of the Judicial Branch

The system of governance and administration of the judicial branch fails to ensure the appropriate degree of judges' participation needed for an independent judiciary. The judiciary is still administered primarily by the Ministry of Justice, in a highly centralised and hierarchical system. While court presidents conduct day-to-day operations, the Ministry has the authority to supervise and control any matter within the lower courts' administration; this discourages the development of an independent and professionally capable judiciary.

---

[31] Government Decision 423/1999 for Setting up the Training Centre for Court Clerks and Other Auxiliary Specialised Personnel, *Official Gazette* 250, 2 June 1999, modified by Government Decision 985/2000, *Official Gazette* 529, 27 October 2000.

[32] The Decision reserves to the Ministry of Justice numerous responsibilities including budgetary details and internal organisation of the Training Centre for Clerks. Government Decision 423/1999 for Setting up the Training Centre for Court Clerks and Other Auxiliary Specialised Personnel, *Official Gazette* 250, 2 June 1999, modified by Government Decision 985/2000, *Official Gazette* 529, 27 October 2000.

The Ministry of Justice develops and supervises the policy of the entire judicial system and exercises governing and representative powers in respect of the judiciary.[33] The General Inspection Department in the Ministry and appellate-level supervising judges exercise broad monitoring powers with regard to the organisation and functioning of the judicial system. The Ministry's Economic, Investments and Administrative Department makes decisions concerning courts' capital investments and financial matters. Court presidents are obliged to fulfil any administrative order issued by the Ministry or its departments. The Supreme Court, however, is largely self-managing.

The judiciary does not include any self-governing body formed of judges. The Superior Council of Magistracy is only responsible for judges' careers and even in this area its powers are limited by the Minister of Justice's power to make proposals. The Council's ability to express opinions on draft laws and matters concerning courts' administration[34] is not an effective check, as the Council only expresses such opinions at the Minister's request, and the opinions offered are not binding; in practice the Council's opinions often have not been taken into account.[35] The authority of the Council does not extend to such broad areas as administering the judiciary or developing and implementing the policies related to its organisation.

Despite its substantial supervisory powers, the Ministry of Justice has not developed national standards in areas such as distribution of funds among courts, norms for caseloads, use of technology or allocation of court space and facilities. This leaves the courts both unable to function effectively and unable to take any initiative to address their problem themselves.

The judiciary has almost no authority over its own budget process, which is in the hands of the Ministry of Justice.[36] The judiciary has little direct influence on the process of drafting and adopting the budget; courts provide initial figures but are not consulted further in the process.[37] The Ministry of Justice distributes allocated funds, for which there are no relevant legal guidelines.[38] In part because budgeting decisions

---

[33] Act on the Judiciary, Art. 18 (2); Government Decision No. 212/2001 on the Organisation and Functioning of the Ministry of Justice, *Official Gazette* 59, 5 February 2001, nodified by Government Decision 553/2001, *Official Gazette* 328, 19 June, Art. 4.

[34] Act on the Judiciary, Art. 88 (g).

[35] Superior Council of Magistracy annual reports 1999–2000 and 2000–2001.

[36] See EU Accession Monitoring Program, *Monitoring the EU Accession Process: Judicial Independence*, Open Society Institute, Budapest, October 2001), pp. 374–375.

[37] Interview with Viorica Costiniu, President of the National Association of Magistrates, April 2002; interview with the president of a regional court, April 2002.

[38] The Ministry also determines the spending of judicial fees and taxes used for investments in the courts' infrastructure, such as renovation of buildings.

depend on the executive and legislative powers, the judiciary has had insufficient financial support for developing into a strong and independent authority capable of providing a check on the other branches.

2. Court Administrative Capacity

Court-level administration is not transparent and is unnecessarily cloaked from public scrutiny. For instance, courts statistics are only available upon filing a request with the relevant department in the Ministry of Justice; the Ministry then determines if there are any grounds for granting the request. The administration of particular courts is assessed by the judicial general inspectors of the Ministry of Justice and the supervising judges of the courts of appeal but results of assessments are not made public. Court administration is not subject to any general or public evaluation outside of the Ministry's processes.

The day-to-day administration of individual courts is conducted by court presidents, who administer procurement issues, control court space, distribute materials to judges and staff, manage the caseload, and organise court records and statistics.[39] In addition, presidents of regional courts are secondary financial administrators for the funds distributed to all courts within their territorial jurisdiction. Court presidents reportedly devote 90 percent of their time to handling administrative matters,[40] and consequently have little time for adjudication or for assisting judges. When exercising their management functions, presidents are obliged to fulfil any administrative order of the Ministry of Justice and its departments.[41]

---

[39] Act on the Judiciary, Art. 18 (3); Ministry of Justice Order 125/C for Approving the Regulation on the Organisation and Administrative Functioning of District Courts, Regional Courts and Courts of Appeal, 17 January 2000, Art. 9-13.

[40] World Bank Diagnostic Review, *Legal and Judicial Systems in Romania* (2002), Section III, p. 41, quoting M.B. Zimmer and R. St. Vrain, *Administrative and Management Reform in the Romanian Courts*, (ABA-CEELI Implementation Plan, August 1999) (unpublished report):

> "The administrative burdens placed on presiding judges verge on being oppressive. On average, the presiding judge of the *judecatorie* spend 90% of their working day handling administrative matters that include assigning new and remanded cases; instructing the day's 'duty judges' in the registry office on current matters; reviewing the large proportion of cases that are appealed; responding to complaints from the bar, the public, other judges, and court staff on a myriad of matters; supervising building renovations; and answering correspondence from other courts or the Ministry."

[41] Ministry of Justice Order 125/C for Approving the Regulation on the Organisation and Administrative Functioning of District Courts, Regional Courts and Courts of Appeal, 17 January 2000, Art. 8 (6).

Court presidents are appointed to four-year terms with the possibility of renewal, on the initiative of the Minister of Justice. Considering the broad powers they exercise, court presidents should be selected with regard to their management capacity. However, there is no initial or continuing training in administrative and financial matters for court presidents, and it appears that their renewal is related to shifts in political power rather than to managerial skills; for example, a number of court presidents were replaced soon after the November 2000 elections, reportedly on political grounds. To enhance the efficiency of court management, introduction of professional management should considered; in the interim, court presidents should be trained in court and case management techniques.

Judges are also involved in court administration. Court presidents designate judges to perform administrative functions, such as supervising the activities of judicial clerks,[42] courts' archive offices,[43] registration and recording offices,[44] and enforcement.[45] In practice, judges are overloaded with both cases and administrative tasks and they cannot deal adequately with any of them. Trained supporting staff could replace judges, thus freeing judges up to focus on core adjudicative activities.

The shortage of judges and supporting staff and their insufficient training has led to inefficient case management. Clerks are crowded into small offices and lack necessary professional equipment; as noted above, clerks do not benefit sufficiently from the available legal training and therefore their ability to offer assistance is very limited. This in turn contributes to extremely slow and lengthy court proceedings. Significant case backlogs affect the quality of judgements, encourages parties to seek extra-judicial remedies or to turn to corrupt practices, and generally affect public trust in courts. Reduction of case backlogs should a priority addressed through improved case management, including automation, re-assignment of non-judicial tasks to trained clerks, and introduction of alternative dispute resolution.

The courts' physical infrastructure and the circumstances in which judges work give rise to very serious concerns. Although in 2001 and 2002 the judiciary received 11 new buildings and another 35 are under construction, a recent analysis found that in Bucharest in particular and in other regions of the country "judges have to work in

---

[42] Ministry of Justice Order 125/C for Approving the Regulation on the Organisation and Administrative Functioning of District Courts, Regional Courts and Courts of Appeal, Art. 15.

[43] Ministry of Justice Order 125/C for Approving the Regulation on the Organisation and Administrative Functioning of District Courts, Regional Courts and Courts of Appeal, Art 17.

[44] Ministry of Justice Order 125/C for Approving the Regulation on the Organisation and Administrative Functioning of District Courts, Regional Courts and Courts of Appeal, Art. 18.

[45] Ministry of Justice Order 125/C for Approving the Regulation on the Organisation and Administrative Functioning of District Courts, Regional Courts and Courts of Appeal, Art. 20 and 21.

buildings that are totally inadequate and sometimes even on the verge of collapse."[46] Court buildings and courtrooms are constantly crowded, and courts often lack necessary professional equipment; the majority of courts have only one or two computers for all their judges and supporting staff, and court libraries are inadequately supplied. A computerised database for legislation and an automatic case-file management system has recently started, but will not cover all courts in the near future.[47]

The case information system in particular needs reform. It is based on an archaic series of manually maintained and overlapping case registers; there is an urgent need for a docket-based system and automated case information, which would lead to administrative efficiency, time savings, and greater certainty with regard to the data registered.

E. RECOMMENDATIONS

1. To the Romanian Government and Legislature

- Make the creation of an independent and capable judiciary a clear and public priority. Commit to a timely and transparent process for developing a comprehensive plan of reform to address the major structural problems limiting judicial independence and judges' professional capacity.

- Ensure that reforms comprehensively reduce the Ministry of Justice' powers to manage and control the courts.

- Reform the Superior Council of Magistracy, in particular to establish a clear division between the responsibilities of prosecutorial and judicial representatives on the Council to ensure that judges' independence is not compromised, and that the Council or its successor can fairly represent and defend society's legitimate interests in an independent judiciary, without unnecessary conflicts of interests.

---

[46] PHARE Horizontal Programme on Justice and Home Affairs, *"Reinforcement of the Rule of Law"*, *Republic of Romania, Recommendations* (revised version 1 May 2002), p. 3. (unpublished report).

[47] The first 1997 PHARE project – RO 9705.02 – for the Romanian judiciary aiming at the automation of the courts system installed specific software in only nine locations (four courts, four prosecutors' offices and the Ministry of Justice) and procures licenses for another 100 locations. A 2000 PHARE project aims to procure equipment for 35 locations; all the rest will have to be covered by the Ministry of Justice and the Public Ministry from their own budgets. Interview with Emil Zahan, local project manager for PHARE project RO 9705.02, 15 July 2002.

- Expand the powers of a reformed Superior Council of Magistracy to represent and administer the judicial system, and provide it with a separate budget, staff and adequate facilities.

- Decentralise budgeting for the courts and give individual courts financial autonomy.

- Introduce standardised and transparent mechanisms for selecting judicial candidates and for evaluating judges' performance; reduce involvement of the Ministry of Justice in matters related to judges' careers.

- Eliminate or radically restrict the system of judicial inspectors controlled by the Ministry of Justice.

- Strengthen judicial training by providing sufficient funding and giving more autonomy to the National Institute of Magistrates to develop curricula, make staffing decisions and manage its own budget; consider transferring authority over the Institute to the Superior Council of Magistracy.

- Strengthen the Training Centre for Clerks in order to enable court clerks to perform non-judicial tasks efficiently.

- Enhance the professional level of court management. Consider introducing professional management in courts; in the interim, court presidents should be trained in court and case management techniques.

- Reduce the backlog of cases through improved case management, including automation, re-assignment of non-judicial tasks to trained clerks, and introduction of alternative dispute resolution.

2. To the European Union

- Stress that an independent and capable judiciary is an essential aspect of the continuing obligations of EU membership. In this connection, assist Romania in developing an effective reform programme by clarifying the values common to the Union and essential for membership with regard to an independent and functioning judiciary, and consequently the minimal expressions of those values, in concrete policies, that continuing membership requires.

- Ensure that judicial reform is made a priority; assist the Government and Parliament in making changes that will lead to effective legal and institutional guarantees for the independence of the judiciary. Press for a speedy commitment to structural, constitutional and legislative reforms, in particular of the roles of the Ministry of Justice and the Superior Council of Magistracy.

- Assist in the modernisation of the Romanian courts, in particular by supporting introduction of professional management, and facilitating the transfer of knowledge from other EU candidate and member States that have already undertaken such efforts.

- Increase support for professional training throughout judges' careers; encourage solutions that will ensure sustained, domestic commitment to training.

Judicial Capacity in Slovakia

Table of Contents

A. INTRODUCTION

In the past two years Slovakia has made significant progress in clarifying the equality of the judicial branch and in strengthening the independence, competence, and efficiency of courts.

Still, further improvements are clearly needed in several areas. Although recent constitutional and legislative changes have transferred certain powers to the new Judicial Council, the Ministry of Justice retains extensive responsibilities for the operation of the judicial sector. Independence and capacity concerns alone argue for a more thoroughgoing transfer of policy-making and administrative powers to an autonomous body with judicial representation. To the degree that it does retain such authority, however, the Ministry – or whatever body ultimately exercises administrative control over the courts – needs to develop more professional administrative capacity and expertise. Comprehensive implementation of the new Act on the Judicial Council would do much to further enhance the autonomy and efficiency of the judiciary.

There continue to be significant and serious delays in case resolution that require a more committed response; some recent initiatives have improved the situation, and should be pursued more comprehensively. In addition, the procedural framework for selecting new judges should be further clarified to eliminate undue discretion and increase transparency. New evaluation methods are imprecise and should be reassessed. Training efforts are in need of stronger institutional support, stable funding, and effective mechanisms to implement decisions once adopted.

B. CURRENT DEVELOPMENTS AFFECTING JUDICIAL CAPACITY AND INDEPENDENCE

The passage of the Act on the Judicial Council should increase judges' participation in managing their own affairs, in particular in resolving many of the problems concerning selection and promotion of judges, but the establishment of the Judicial Council is still in the initial stages. Meanwhile, case backlogs continue to be a serious problem, and more must be done to address them, especially by transferring non-adjudicative functions to legal and technical staff under judges' supervision.

1. Act on the Judicial Council

The passage in April 2002 of the Act on the Judicial Council[1] resolved the legal stalemate over how to regulate judges' career paths that had existed since the passage, in February 2001, of a constitutional amendment mandating judicial reform.[2] The Act creates a Judicial Council with significant responsibilities for personnel matters including the selection, transfer and removal of judges;[3] the Council became operational in August 2002. The Act will also facilitate the filling of vacancies and ease the serious problem of case delays.[4] Passage of the Act was a major step forward; effective implementation of the Act is essential if it is to have a positive effect on judges' career paths.[5]

2. Initiatives to Address Case Delays

There continue to be significant and serious delays in case resolution. A considerable number of cases alleging a violation of the right to a court hearing within a reasonable time are pending before the European Court of Human Rights.[6] In December 2001, the Court found Slovakia in violation of the European Convention on Human Rights

---

[1] Act on the Judicial Council, No. 185/2002 Coll.

[2] Act 90/2001 Coll., amending CONST. SLOVAK REP. Complete version of the Constitution that include all amendments was published as Act No. 135/2002 Coll.

[3] *See* Section D.1., "Governance and Administration of the Judicial Branch".

[4] *See* Section B.2., "Initiatives to Address Case Delays".

[5] *See* Section C.1., "Selection and Promotion".

[6] Slovakia reportedly has the highest number of complaints before the Court per capita, with the most frequent cause being delays in court proceedings. *See RFE/RL NEWSLINE*, Vol. 6, No. 128, Part II, 11 July 2002.

for excessive delay.[7] Endemic case delays seriously undermine public confidence in and support for the judiciary.

Recent initiatives to reduce court delay have been encouraging. Caseload norms have been changed from a purely numerical system, by which each judge was required to close up to 25 cases per month, to a point system designed to account for the complexity of individual cases.[8] In addition, shortened proceedings have been made available for certain civil cases, and the Government is developing a probation and mediation service that will allow conditional dismissal of criminal charges; these initiatives may reduce the burden on judges, allowing them more effective use of time for adjudication.[9]

In addition, the establishment of an Office of the Ombudsman[10] may enhance access to courts and encourage more expeditious processing of cases. The Ombudsman has the authority to initiate disciplinary proceedings on behalf of citizens against judges at all levels;[11] this may be useful in allowing the public to challenge courts in cases of delay – assuming, of course, that the Ombudsman's independent powers are themselves only exercised subject to the strictures required by the judiciary's independence. The new Ombudsman was appointed in March 2002; the Office became operational at the end of July 2002. The office commenced its activities with about 1,000 motions on its docket, many of which concern the work of the judiciary and in particular court delays.[12]

These steps, while commendable, are still not sufficient to address the underlying causes of endemic delays; the Ombudsman's punitive powers, for example, will not directly contribute to an increase in courts' capacity. More must be done to transfer non-adjudicative workloads to technical professionals under judges' supervision, so that judges are free to focus on their core adjudicative functions.

---

[7] Finding a violation of Article 6 (right to a fair and public hearing within a reasonable time by an independent and impartial tribunal established by law) in *Gajdúsek v. Slovakia,* Judgement ECHR 40058/98, 18 December 2001.

[8] Each judge must achieve at least 1,000 points a month. *See* Section C.2., "Evaluating and Regulating Performance".

[9] *See* also Section D.2., "Court Administrative Capacity".

[10] Act on Public Protector of Rights, No. 564/2001 Coll.

[11] Act on the Judicial Council, Art. 61.

[12] Information provided by the Ombudsman's Office on 6 August 2002.

C. Professional Competence of the Judiciary

The creation of the Judicial Council should lead to improved selection and promotion procedures. The current regulatory framework is underdeveloped, and the continuing lack of clear standards encourages arbitrary or even biased selections that reinforce a closed institutional culture detrimental to judges' professional development. New evaluation procedures, though as yet untested, appear insufficiently clear and may create risks for judges' independence. Inadequate training poses a serious impediment to ensuring the competence of individual judges.

1. Selection and Promotion

Slovakia has taken steps to improve judicial selection procedures. For example, the Judicial Council now nominates candidates for an appointment, and authority for making appointments has been transferred from the Parliament to the State President,[13] which might help depoliticise the process. Beyond that, however, judges' career paths are still subject to unduly discretionary procedures that both introduce risks to judges' independence and limit opportunities to increase professionalism.

One source of concern is over-reliance on the three-year long apprenticeship programme that precedes the judicial exam and entry to the profession.[14] The judicial selection process gives preference to judicial apprentices: a public tender for a vacant judge's position at the entry level is announced only if a vacancy cannot be taken by an apprentice;[15] applicants with extensive legal experience are therefore excluded in favour of less experienced apprentices.[16] This practice unnecessarily narrows the field of qualified candidates. While apprenticeship programmes are certainly valuable, selection of the most qualified judicial candidates should be the goal.

Since apprentices have such a preferential position in the ultimate selection of new judges, the manner in which apprentices are themselves selected is crucial. However,

---

[13] CONST. SLOVAK REP., Art. 145

[14] Act on Courts and Judges, No. 335/1991 Coll., Section 6.

[15] Provided an apprentice has passed a judicial exam. Act on Judges and Lay Judges, No. 385/2000 Coll., Art. 28 (1).

[16] The number of judicial apprentices routinely exceeds the number of vacant positions; this both excludes applicants who are not apprentices, and allows for broad discretion in selecting which apprentices will receive judgeships.

the regulatory framework for selection of judicial apprentices is poorly developed.[17] The criteria for granting apprenticeships are not sufficiently defined, leaving significant decisional discretion to involved officials.

Eligible applicants for apprenticeship[18] must pass written and oral tests before *ad hoc* selection committees[19] that include four judges (a regional court president and three judges designated by the relevant judicial council) and one representative of the Ministry of Justice.[20] The Ministry prepares the written test,[21] but there are no clear criteria for the oral interview, which is based rather on the vaguely defined purpose of examining candidates' personality and ability to apply the law.[22] The procedure and the content of the system by which apprentices are selected need further improvement; in particular, the content and the purposes of the oral interview need to be clarified. Inclusion of representatives of legal professions and academicians in the process, better preparation for members of selection committees, and more transparent proceedings are all advisable measures.

Additionally, the value of apprenticeship as a legitimate means to verify the abilities of candidates and prepare them for the profession is undermined by the fact that the Minister of Justice is entitled to assign other, non-judicial work to apprentices during the apprenticeship period.[23] This gives the Minister significant discretion, allowing the possibility for improper exemptions from apprenticeship on subjective grounds.

The process of selection for vacant judges' positions is also ambiguous. After completing their apprenticeships, candidates for a judgeship are entitled to take a judicial exam and apply for vacant entry positions.[24] Five-member committees, consisting of judges

---

[17] *See* Principles of Tendering Procedure, Promotion to Higher Courts and Higher Judicial, 19 April 2001 The Principles are signed by President of the Supreme Court (and concurrently *ex officio* President of the Council of Judges) and the Minister of Justice. *See* <http://www.justice.gov.sk.>, (accessed 25 September 2002).

[18] Eligibility requirements for apprentices include: Slovak citizenship, a law degree, full legal capacity, permanent residence in the Slovak Republic, and integrity and "moral characteristics" that guarantee "correct performance." Act on Courts and Judges, Art. 62. These are similar to the requirements for judges, who in addition must be at least 30 years of age and must have successfully completed the judicial examination. *See* CONST. SLOVAK REP., Art. 145 (1-2) and Act on Judges and Lay Judges, Art. 5 (1).

[19] Principles of Tendering Procedure, Promotion to Higher Courts and Higher Judicial Offices.

[20] Principles of Tendering Procedure, Promotion to Higher Courts and Higher Judicial Offices.

[21] Principles of Tendering Procedure, Promotion to Higher Courts and Higher Judicial Offices; interview with Anna Hesková, Personnel Department of the Ministry of Justice, 27 March 2002.

[22] Principles of Tendering Procedure, Promotion to Higher Courts and Higher Judicial Offices.

[23] Act on Courts and Judges, Art. 63.

[24] Act on Courts and Judges, Art. 63.

appointed by the relevant regional court president, select candidates for judicial nominations.[25] There is no legal requirement to invite outside comment during this process, nor is it the practice. Selection committees base their decisions on the results of judicial exams,[26] evaluations of the apprenticeship periods by court presidents, evaluations of candidates by relevant judicial councils and oral interviews with candidates.[27] The criteria for evaluating candidates are vague, and thus members of selection committees have a significant, and perhaps unnecessarily broad, degree of discretion. (This is also true of the oral interviews for promotions to regional courts and the Supreme Court.) At the same time, members of selection committees, who are all judges, lack specialised training that might help guide their decisions.

This combination of a rigid career system and vague decisional criteria that concentrate significant discretionary powers over selection and promotion in the hands of the Minister of Justice and judges, while not affording any opportunity for input from professional groups or civil society organisations, may reinforce a closed institutional culture detrimental to the continuing renewal of the judiciary and to judges' professional development.

2. Evaluating and Regulating Performance

A system of periodic evaluation of judges' performance has been introduced, which is still under development. The Act introducing the system[28] is insufficiently precise, and the adoption of detailed legal regulations is advisable both to encourage professionalism and to prevent potential abuses that might threaten judges' adjudicative independence. The system for filing a complaint against a judge is overly insulated from public critique and scrutiny, and is thus limited in its potential to effect institutional change; public access to court files and judicial opinions continues to be limited.

A mandatory system of performance evaluation was established in 2000,[29] and is being tested during 2002. The law prescribes periodic evaluations of judges every five years; in addition, evaluations are mandated during every selection procedure, or in connection with disciplinary proceedings or whenever a judge so requests. The president of the court to which the judge is assigned conducts the evaluation; in

---

[25] Act on Judges and Lay Judges, 385/2000 Coll., Art. 29.

[26] The Minister of Justice is entitled to recognise other examinations, such as the prosecutorial examination, or waive this requirement altogether. Act on Judges and Lay Judges, Art. 5 (2).

[27] Principles of Tendering Procedure, Promotion to Higher Courts and Higher Judicial Offices.

[28] Act on Judges and Lay Judges, 385/2000 Coll.

[29] Act on Judges and Lay Judges, Art. 27.

preparing their appraisals, court presidents are supposed to rely on a review of the judge's decisions prepared by the judicial council, the opinions of appeals courts, and their own observations.[30]

Because the system is only now being tested, it is too early to estimate its efficacy. The mandatory evaluation system might become a valuable tool for deciding promotions and assisting judges in their professional development, provided the process is reasonably transparent; considering the important role of court presidents in the evaluation process, implementing regulations ought to be designed to minimise the potential for abuse of judges' adjudicative independence.[31]

In February 2002, the Ministry of Justice expanded an experimental system of continuous monitoring based on points allocated for work accomplished; the system now applies to all courts and judges.[32] In accordance with this system, judges' work is continuously monitored against a pre-determined number of points for specific procedural acts. While primarily intended as a tool to confront court delays, this system might also prove an important element in performance evaluation, provided it is used in coordination with qualitative criteria. The system has been criticised as having a negative impact on the quality of court decisions;[33] obviously, any evaluation system must also conform, in intent and in implementation, to the principles of judicial independence and accountability, and should not create incentives for judges to produce busy-work or in any way limit the quality of their decisions simply to fulfil a quota.

The public complaint system provides an imperfect check on judges' behaviour. Anyone may file a complaint against a judge in cases of delays, unsuitable behaviour or misconduct detrimental to the dignity of court proceedings.[34] In response, the authorised State official – commonly the court president, but sometimes the Minister of Justice – is obliged to investigate the facts and, if necessary, interview the parties. Complaints must

---

[30] Act on Judges and Lay Judges, Art. 27.

[31] Court presidents, except the President of the Supreme Court, are appointed and dismissed by the Minister of Justice. *See* Section D.2., "Court Administrative Capacity".

[32] Interview with Alena Roštárová, Director of Civil and Administration Law Section of the Ministry of Justice, 5 April 2002.

[33] *See, e.g.,* Dušan Konček, "Points Swing the Scales of Justice", *Nový deň*, 23 January 2002, arguing that some judges are more concerned about the collection of points than about justice. Specifically, the point values assigned to specific procedural acts do not necessarily relate rationally to their difficulty or the time required (Interview with Juraj Majchrák, President of the Slovak Association of Judges, 4 April 2002), and thus may provide a distorted picture of judges' performance. *See also* Section B.2., "Initiatives to Address Case Delays".

[34] Act on Seats and Jurisdiction of Courts, State Administration of Courts, Settlement of Complaints and Election of Lay Judges, No. 80/1992 Coll., Art. 17.

be resolved within two months and may lead to a disciplinary procedure.[35] However, judges generally resolve complaints themselves, with court presidents taking final decisions; this entirely inward orientation tends to limit the value of the complaint procedure in encouraging institutional change. The introduction of the Ombudsman to this process may improve the effectiveness of the complaint procedure and enhance judicial performance.[36]

Public access to court files and judicial opinions is limited. Case files are available only to parties to a case and their legal representatives, as well as community representatives or others who can demonstrate a justified legal interest.[37] There is no system for publication and general circulation of judicial opinions to the public or on the Internet. Wider distribution of judicial decisions would enhance transparency and encourage constructive public debate, providing an informal source of feedback on courts' performance.

3. Training for a Professional Judiciary

Insufficiencies in the judicial training system pose a serious impediment to ensuring the competence of individual judges over time. While training of judicial apprentices appears satisfactory, training for serving judges is uneven and inadequate. The amount of funding devoted to training is insufficient, in part because the judicial branch has not been effective in winning support for increasing resources and for the creation of a permanent institution for judicial training.

There is no centralised, dedicated training centre for judges or judicial staff; training is managed by the Ministry of Justice.[38] While the training of apprentices appears satisfactory,[39] continuing training of serving judges is inadequate. There are no standards for determining the allocation of funding for training programmes, and no long-term budgetary commitment. Consequently, the implementation of training programmes has been poor. For example, the judicial education plan adopted in 1995 (the *System of Training of Judges and Other Staff in the Sector of the Ministry of Justice*[40]),

---

[35] Act on Courts and Judges, Art. 6.

[36] *See* Section B.2., "Initiatives to Address Case Delays".

[37] Criminal Code, No. 141/1961 Coll., Art. 65.

[38] Act on Judges and Lay Judges, Art. 35 (2).

[39] Apprentices attend semi-annual week-long seminars organised by the Ministry of Justice, periodic seminars organised by regional courts (approximately four times a year), and work in district courts under the supervision of a tutor appointed from among district court judges. Interviews with Anna Hesková, Personnel Department of the Ministry of Justice, 27 March 2002, and Tibor Kubík, Deputy President of Bratislava Regional Court, 11 April 2002.

[40] Ministry of Justice Decree No. 3381/1995-30.

which mandated training for certain categories of judges and court staff, has remained largely unimplemented. Instead, the Personnel Department of the Ministry plans and organises *ad hoc* seminars for judges on a voluntary basis. Apparently, there is a lack of clear system for selection of judges for specific training events and no system that would track participation of judges in different trainings, whether organised by the Ministry or other providers.

Dissatisfied with the State-sponsored system of judicial training, the Association of Slovak Judges organises parallel seminars. In addition, a PHARE project aimed at training of judges has been underway since 2001 to introduce topics relevant to future EU membership.[41] However, these projects do not contribute to the long-term sustainability of judicial training: the Association has been unable to secure support from the Ministry of Justice for the establishment of a permanent judicial training institution,[42] and until now the EU programmes have merely served to reinforce the practice of *ad hoc* judicial training. Whether administered by a professional, dedicated department within the Ministry or a stand-alone judicial training centre, a capable judiciary requires a long-term mechanism for training judges throughout their careers.

The new Act on the Judicial Council increases the role of the Judicial Council in judicial training.[43] The specific tasks the Council will undertake remain to be specified in secondary regulations.

D. INSTITUTIONAL CAPACITY OF THE JUDICIAL BRANCH

The new Act on the Judicial Council transfers some powers to the new Judicial Council, although the Ministry of Justice retains broad responsibility for courts' administration. To date, the Ministry has not developed clear and objective administrative policies. Budget processes likewise still give courts too little involvement. Independence and capacity concerns alone argue for a more thoroughgoing transfer of policy-making and administrative powers to an autonomous body with judicial representation. To the degree that it does retain such authority, however, the Ministry of Justice — or whatever body ultimately exercises administrative control over the courts — needs to develop more professional administrative capacity and expertise. Court presidents have significant managerial responsibilities for which they are generally not adequately prepared. Work conditions remain inadequate, and backlogs are a problem.

---

[41] PHARE SR 99/IB/JU 03.

[42] Interview with Juraj Majchrák, President of the Slovak Association of Judges, 4 April 2002.

[43] Act on the Judicial Council, Art. 4.

1. Governance and Administration of the Judicial Branch

Although the 2001 Constitutional amendment[44] and the Act on the Judicial Council have transferred certain powers, especially in personnel matters, to the new Judicial Council, the Ministry of Justice retains large responsibilities for the operation of the judicial sector. Independence and capacity concerns alone might argue for a more thoroughgoing transfer of policy-making and administrative powers to an autonomous body with judicial representation. To the degree that it does retain such authority, however, the Ministry of Justice – or whatever body ultimately exercises administrative control over the courts – needs to develop more professional administrative capacity and expertise.

As the new Judicial Council became operational only in August 2002, its role and ability to provide leadership and expertise to guide the judiciary remain unclear. The change may lead to improvements in policy-making and administration, provided the Council receives sufficient resources and competent staff.

In the meantime, the Ministry of Justice continues to act as the policy-making and administrative body for regional and district courts, a position that unnecessarily introduces risks to the judiciary's independence. Moreover, despite exercising this authority, the Ministry has failed to develop standards and guidelines to support certain areas of court operations necessary to the judiciary's efficient and professional development.

The extensive powers retained by the Ministry of Justice include: drafting relevant laws, representing the judiciary in relations with the political branches, preparing and defending the judiciary's budget, administering allocated funds, determining the numbers of judges and support staff in courts, participating in the selection and disciplining of judges, appointing and dismissing court presidents, and developing and overseeing the implementation of standards and guidelines for court operations.

Despite exercising authority over such a broad range of issues, to date the Ministry has failed to develop clear and objective criteria concerning the numbers of judges and support staff in courts or norms for technology and equipment that are necessary to support competent and efficient adjudication. This results in inconsistencies and shortages among and within courts. Often, efforts to remedy shortfalls in staff, equipment and material are dependent upon the personal relationships and skill of the court president rather than objective norms and need. Selection of court presidents is also not based on clear standards.

---

[44] Act No. 90/2001 Coll.

In July 2002, members of the Judicial Council[45] were appointed,[46] and in August 2002 the Council became operational.[47] The powers of the Council include:

- nominating judges;

- assigning judges to the various courts;

- recommending judges' recall;

- electing and recalling members of disciplinary committees;

- issuing opinions on the draft budget for the judiciary;[48]

- receiving reports on budget implementation;

- coordinating local judicial councils; and

- providing comments on draft legal regulations concerning the organisation of the judiciary, procedural rules, and status of judges.[49]

The Ministry of Justice will also need to coordinate with the new Judicial Council on formulating the rules for judicial appointments and promotions, performance assessment, appointments of court presidents, principles of judicial ethics, and determination of the content of judicial training.[50]

However, the issue of funding for the Judicial Council's operations remains to be resolved, and the Council does not yet have either premises or staff. In large part, the success of the Council will depend on the resources and quality of staff it receives.

More broadly, the budgetary process does little to encourage courts' involvement in their own effective administration. The national budget for the judiciary is included within the budget for the Ministry of Justice, with the exception of the Supreme Court, which has its own budget chapter. The system for preparing the budget and distributing allocated funds is not based on a clear methodology and is insufficiently transparent.

---

[45] The Judicial Council consists of the President of the Supreme Court, three members appointed by the Parliament, three by the State President, three by the Government, and eight members elected by judges from their own ranks.

[46] *See* "Judges elected eight members of the Judicial Council", SME, 1 July 2002, and "Schuster decided on judges in his own way", SME, 6 July 2002.

[47] *See* Súdna Rada už začala pracovať, SME, 7 August 2002.

[48] CONST. SLOVAK REP., Art. 141a (4).

[49] Act on Judicial Council, Art. 4.

[50] Act on Judicial Council, Art. 4.

District and regional courts currently have little input into the budgeting process, although this process has an important impact on court operations. The Ministry of Justice compiles an annual budget, primarily based on the prior year's expenditures. There is no link, in law or practice, between caseload and budget.[51] Regional and district courts' allocations are filtered through the Ministry for later disbursement. This creates conditions for budget decisions that depend more on the personal skill and relationships of the court president in dealings with the Ministry than on any objectively determined need.

The new Judicial Council will be entitled to express its opinion on the draft budget for the judiciary, which constitutes a positive development. In addition, creating a stronger connection between allocation of funds and caseload would help reduce case delays and enhance courts' adjudicative capacity.

2. Court Administrative Capacity

Court presidents have significant managerial responsibilities, for which they are generally not adequately prepared; they are neither trained for administrative work nor is such work the best use of their judicial skill and training. Professionally trained court management teams in district and regional courts are needed to free court presidents to focus on delivery of justice and to enhance the capacity of local courts. At a minimum, court presidents should be given managerial training, and court personnel should be given specialised training in case management and use of modern technology.

Managerial responsibilities of court presidents range from human resources management – such as determining the numbers of lay judges and hiring and supervising administrative staff – to supervising the budget, overseeing case management, overseeing vocational training of apprentices, and dealing with complaints.[52] Regional court presidents must, in addition, supervise the administration of all district courts within their regions.[53] The judicial councils in regional courts are merely advisory bodies, and their limited role is most often not directed at the kinds of local court management that constitutes the bulk of the administrative responsibility placed on court presidents.[54]

---

[51] Interviews with Juraj Majchrák, President of the Slovak Judges Association, 4 April 2002, and Alena Roštárová, Director of Civil and Administrative Law Section of the Ministry of Justice, 5 April 2002.

[52] Act on Seats and Jurisdiction of Courts, State Administration of Courts, Settlement of Complaints and Election of Lay Judges, Art. 15.

[53] Act on Seats and Jurisdiction of Courts, State Administration of Courts, Settlement of Complaints and Election of Lay Judges, Art. 14.

[54] Act on Courts and Judges, Art. 58.

Despite these extensive managerial responsibilities, the Ministry of Justice selects court presidents from among judges according to unclear criteria, which in any event do not appear to include an assessment of candidates' managerial capacity. Court presidents do not receive training for managerial work.

An increasingly heavy caseload has caused significant delays in court proceedings. One of the major reasons for this problem is the weak system of support for competent and timely adjudication; a shortage of support staff forces judges to devote precious time to technical tasks related to case preparation rather than to substantive judicial matters. By some estimates, such tasks take about 50 percent of judges' work time.[55] As noted above,[56] transferring more administrative and technical responsibilities to support staff would free up judges to focus on adjudication – but this would also require a concomitantly greater commitment to developing the capacity of support staff. The recent Act on Court Officers[57] was adopted with the aim of taking some of the administrative burden off judges.[58]

Several pilot projects are addressing the problem of court delays by various means. For example, since January 2002 an experimental project has established a Probation and Mediation Service in certain courts, which allows conditional dismissal of criminal charges upon acceptance of responsibility and payment of damages. This system is purely voluntary for both offender and victim, available only for less serious crimes and subject to approval by the court or prosecution.[59] If successful, and implemented nation-wide as planned by April 2003, this project has the potential to reduce caseloads dramatically.

Other initiatives have introduced summary proceedings to speed up cases in court,[60] while in January 2001 an Internet-based commercial register was introduced,[61] which should expedite case processing. An important legal remedy against court delays is the

---

[55] Interviews with Alena Roštárová, Director of Civil and Administrative Law Department of the Ministry of Justice, 5 April 2002, and Juraj Majchrák, President of Association of Judges, 4 April 2002.

[56] *See* Section B.2., "Initiatives to Address Case Delays".

[57] Act No. 425/2002 Coll.

[58] Interview with Alena Roštárová, Director of Civil and Administrative Law Department of the Ministry of Justice, 5 April 2002.

[59] Interview with Martina Tabačíková, Criminal Law Department of the Ministry of Justice, 9 April 2002.

[60] Rules of Civil Procedure, Act No.99/1963 Coll., Art. 172, 175; Criminal Order, Act No.120/2001 Coll., Art. 314e.

[61] Report of the Ministry of Justice on Conditions in the Judicial System, available at: <http://www.justice.gov.sk.>, (accessed 25 September 2002).

possibility for individuals to lodge complaints with the Constitutional Court. In July 2002, the Constitutional Court adopted its first two decisions awarding a monetary penalty for delay in court proceedings.[62]

Although the judiciary's facilities are currently undergoing technical modernisation,[63] in several courts reporters continue to take trial minutes by hand, or use dictaphones for later transcription; an improved system of court recording would increase significantly the amount of time available for hearing cases and limit the possibility for abuse.

E. RECOMMENDATIONS

1. To the Slovak Government and Legislature

- Improve the regulatory framework for selecting judges by making judgeships more accessible to qualified legal professionals, clarifying criteria for examinations and interviews, restricting undue discretion, providing specialised training for selection committees, and allowing some public scrutiny of the selection process.

- Consistent with the principle of judicial independence, further define the details of the new evaluation system to ensure that risks of arbitrariness and abuse are minimised.

- Take steps to ensure a stable institutional and financial framework for the conduct of judicial training. Establish and support strong training programmes for judges at all stages of their careers, as well as for court managers and court personnel.

- Provide the new Judicial Council with sufficient resources and expertise to ensure efficient execution of its tasks and responsibilities.

- Consider introduction of professionally trained court managers in district and regional courts to free court presidents to focus on delivery of justice and to enhance the capacity of local courts. As an immediate priority, court presidents should be given systematic managerial training, and court personnel should be given specialised training in case management and use of modern technology.

---

[62] Svjatoslav Dohovič, "Courts shall pay thousands", Pravda, 10 July 2002.

[63] The Ministry of Justice, with EU PHARE support, has developed an initiative to reduce the technical workload of judges by equipping each judge with a computer and internet access during 2002.

- Continue efforts aimed at reducing the administrative load of judges so that they may focus their efforts on substantive judicial matters; increase training and support for court staff.

- Continue and expand pilot projects and legal reforms aimed at the reduction of court backlogs and length of proceedings.

2. To the European Union

- Support strengthening of judicial training; ensure that EU-sponsored programmes contribute to sustained, comprehensive training of judges throughout their careers.

- Emphasise the need to enhance the level of professional management in the judiciary at the national and court levels. Draw on the experiences of other EU candidate and member States to provide technical assistance to Slovakia in its efforts.

Judicial Capacity in Slovenia

Table of Contents

A. INTRODUCTION

Slovenia has made considerable progress in establishing an independent and capable judiciary. Professional and political commitment has kept improvement of the judiciary at the top of the reform agenda.

Certain discrete areas remain in need of further improvement. More effective judicial representation in the budgetary process needs to be secured. Greater transparency and professionalisation are still needed in the selection and promotion of judges – especially in the implementation of recent improvements in the Judicial Act – and in evaluation, where quantitative measurements need to be balanced by qualitative indicators. Judicial training needs to be institutionalised. Further professionalisation would streamline court management practices, where case delays continue to pose a serious obstacle to efficiency and limit citizens' access to meaningful justice; programmes aimed at reducing the case backlog should be continued and expanded.

Legislative efforts to address some of these concerns are currently underway. However, some recently adopted legislative changes and proposed constitutional amendments would actually reduce the scope of judicial independence and their impact on capacity is unclear. In particular, the proposed five-year probationary period, mandatory dismissal of judges in cases of constitutional violations, and the system for setting judges' salaries should be reconsidered.

Because the domestic debate over these particular measures has centred in large part on what Slovenia's proposed accession to the European Union does or does not require, it would be particularly beneficial for the Union to clarify its understanding of the obligations membership entails for the organisation of a member State's judiciary.

B. CURRENT DEVELOPMENTS AFFECTING JUDICIAL CAPACITY AND INDEPENDENCE

In July 2002 Parliament enacted amendments to the Judicial Service Act; in addition, the Government has proposed amendments to the Constitution that enact some of its wide-ranging reform proposals. While mostly beneficial, certain of these amendments could reduce the scope of judges' independence and hinder efforts to increase the judiciary's professional capacity. In particular, proposals creating a five-year probationary period for new judges and introducing mandatory dismissal of judges, as well as a previously enacted provision allowing judges' salaries to be determined by parliamentary decree, may reduce the scope of judicial independence without improving judges' capacity to adjudicate or to administer their own affairs.

1. Amendments to the Judicial Service Act

In July 2002 the Parliament adopted amendments to the Judicial Service Act.[1] According to the Government, the purpose of these amendments is to address the European Commission's concerns about case backlogs. In fact, the amendments are broader in scope. The amendments:

- allow judges who believe that someone's action has infringed their independence to lodge a complaint with the Judicial Council;[2]

- introduce more expeditious and to some extent more transparent selection and promotion procedures;[3]

- elaborate more detailed criteria for the assessment of judicial performance;[4]

- introduce stricter and more detailed rules for supervision of judges' work;[5]

- provide that supervision and discipline are now performed exclusively by judges;[6]

---

[1] Act on the Amendments to the Judicial Service Act, Official Gazette No. 66/2002.

[2] Judicial Service Act (amended), Art. 3.

[3] For details *see* Section C.1., "Selection and Promotion".

[4] *See* Section C.2., "Evaluating and Regulating Performance".

[5] The amendments identify 27 typical violations of judicial duties, the most serious of which may lead to termination of judicial office. *See* Judicial Service Act (amended), Art. 79a – 80.

[6] The Minister of Justice may initiate disciplinary procedures. *See* Judicial Service Act (amended), Art. 79a – 80.

- allow judges to be transferred, with their consent, to overburdened courts and other State organs and to receive increased remuneration for additional work; in certain cases, they also allow transfer without the judge's consent.[7]

For the most part, the amendments incorporate the views expressed by members of the judicial community during parliamentary discussions.[8] However, the provisions on productivity-based remuneration and involuntary transfer are potentially harmful to principles of judicial independence and impartiality. It is important, therefore, that these principles are given due consideration when these provisions are elaborated in secondary regulations and in actual practice.

2. Public Sector Wage System Act

The Public Sector Wage System Act, adopted in June 2002, allows judges' salaries to be defined by parliamentary decree rather than determined by statute.[9] This provision makes it easier for the political branches to alter judges' salaries, and arguably contradicts international standards that judges' remuneration be stable and secured by law.[10] Moreover, if judges' salaries are perceived as unpredictable and unstable, it may become more difficult to attract qualified judicial candidates, which in turn may have serious repercussions for the judiciary's professional capacity.[11] The Presidents of the

---

[7] Judicial Service Act (amended), Art. 3, 29, 38–45.

[8] *See, e.g.*, "Odbor za notranjo politiko o sodniški službi", *Delo*, 8 March 2002.

[9] Public Sector Wage System Act, Official Gazette No. 56/2002, Art. 10.

[10] *See* Basic Principles on the Independence of the Judiciary, Art. 11, *endorsed* by UN General Assembly Resolutions 40/32 of 29 November 1985 and 40/146 of 13 December 1985; Recommendation No. R (94) 12 On the Independence, Efficiency and Role of Judges, Art. 2 ii. Committee of Ministers of the Council of Europe, *adopted* 13 October 1994; Judges' Charter in Europe, Art. 8, European Association of Judges, *adopted* 20 March 1993; Universal Charter of the Judge, Art. 13, International Association of Judges, *adopted* November 1999; European Charter on the Statute for Judges, Art. 6.1., Council of Europe, *adopted* 8-10 July 1998. *See also* Consultative Council of European Judges, Opinion No. 1 (2001) for the Attention of the Committee of Ministers of the Council of Europe on Standards Concerning the Independence of the Judiciary and the Irremovability of Judges, Strasbourg, 21 November 2001 (noting that especially in the new democracies it is important to adopt specific legal provisions guaranteeing that judicial salaries are not reduced).

[11] In addition, the actual wages of judges are often lower than those of comparable public officials in other branches; for example, a salary of a district Court Judge is lower than the salary of an assistant to the State Prosecutor.

Supreme Court, Judicial Council, and Slovenian Association of Judges all opposed the new wage provision during deliberation of the Act.[12]

3. The Proposed Constitutional Amendments

Constitutional amendments proposed by the Government include both salutary improvements and elements that may actually harm judges' independence. The amendments would:

- replace the present system of lifetime appointment with an initial five-year term, with the possibility of lifetime tenure only after this period, reviewed by court personnel councils and the national Judicial Council;

- remove the minimum age requirement for entering judicial office;

- transfer authority to appoint judges from Parliament to the State President on the recommendation of the Judicial Council;

- make the President of the Supreme Court and the Minister of Justice members of the Judicial Council *ex officio;*

- allow Parliament to appoint six of the 15 Judicial Council members directly, instead of acting upon a motion of the State President as it presently does;

- allow the Judicial Council to authorise criminal prosecution and detention of judges suspected of criminal offences;

- mandate the dismissal of judges who have committed constitutional violations, serious violations of laws, or deliberate abuse of judicial office amounting to a criminal offence.[13]

In particular, proposals to create a five-year probationary period and to mandate the dismissal of judges for a broad and ill-defined range of conduct seem to be a step back from existing guarantees for judicial independence, while their usefulness for enhancing judicial capacity and professional responsibility is uncertain.

Any probationary period places individual judges in a dependent position, in which they may feel incentives to rule based on the interests of those who hold the power to approve or deny tenure, rather than on their professional appreciation of the facts and

---

[12] Proposed Public Sector Wage System Act, National Assembly *Poročevalec* ("Reporter"), No. 9, 2002.

[13] Proposal to Commence the Procedure to Amend the Constitution of the Republic of Slovenia, National Assembly *Poročevalec*, ("Reporter"), No. 69, 2001.

the law. While in certain circumstances probationary periods may be necessary to ensure that a new judge possesses the requisite professional competence, in general there are less intrusive alternatives that mean it is seldom legitimate to employ extended probationary periods.[14]

The proposed probationary period of five years would place judges in a dependent position for a significant portion of their professional careers, far more than any legitimate concern with initial evaluation could justify. The explanatory note to the proposed Constitutional amendments provides no substantiation for the new probationary period, stating only that it will make the system for assessing new judges more inclusive by incorporating the national Judicial Council's input.[15] However, this goal can be achieved by adopting less invasive procedures for evaluating new judges' performance,[16] and by developing more rigorous screening and training of candidates before they first become judges.

Likewise, the Government has not explained why the existing system that provides for the possibility of dismissal from judicial office should be replaced by mandatory dismissal. Moreover, the grounds for mandatory dismissal are not clearly defined, which could lead to uncertainty and interference with judicial decision-making. For example, it might be possible to violate the Constitution – one of the grounds for mandatory dismissal – by issuing a judgement that comported with national legislation but violated international human rights standards incorporated into the Constitution. If this provision remains, it is essential that guidelines and implementing regulations clearly define the content of the conduct that lead to mandatory dismissal in a manner consistent with the principles of judicial independence and accountability.

Judges have been critical of the proposed amendments, arguing that probationary periods and mandatory dismissal potentially contradict the principles of judicial independence.[17] The Government has countered that such measures are necessary for Slovenia's accession to European Union membership – a posture that highlights the

---

[14] *See* "Overview: Judicial Independence in the EU Accession Process," in *Monitoring the EU Accession Process: Judicial Independence,* (Open Society Institute, Budapest, October 2001). pp. 51–53, available at <http://www.eumap.org.>, (accessed 26 September 2002).

[15] Proposal to Commence the Procedure to Amend the Constitution of the Republic of Slovenia, National Assembly, *Poročevalec* ("Reporter"), No. 69, 2001.

[16] See Section C.2., "Evaluating and Regulating Performance".

[17] *See, e.g.,* critical remarks by the President of the Supreme Court: Mile Dolenc, "Neznosna lahkost razlogov za ustavne spremembe glede sodstva" (The Unbearable Lightness of Reasons for the Constitutional Amendments Concerning the Judiciary), *Pravna praksa* 31, 11 October 2001.

need for the Union to clarify its presently undefined standards relating to organisation of the judiciary.[18]

C. Professional Competence of Judges

The recent amendments to the Judicial Service Act have introduced potentially important improvements in the selection and promotion procedures; provided that new legislation will be effectively implemented and those responsible for making decisions are appropriately instructed, the new procedures will make selection and promotion more transparent. The current evaluation criteria and procedures require further elaboration to reduce a possibility of arbitrariness and an overemphasis on quantitative criteria. The present system of training is insufficient; training infrastructure should be improved, and stable funding for training ensured.

1. Selection and Promotion

Court personnel councils, the Ministry of Justice, and the national Judicial Council all participate in the system for judicial selection and promotion. This cooperative organisational structure has certainly contributed to judicial independence and accountability, but has lacked transparency; until recently selection and promotion procedures have been opaque. Neither applicants nor the general public have been able to determine how the general criteria for assessing candidates' knowledge and abilities or fitness for promotion[19] are interpreted and applied in practice. The recent amendments to the Judicial Service Act,[20] if effectively implemented, would make selection and promotion processes more transparent.

The present process involves various branches. The Ministry of Justice screens applicants for formal eligibility requirements[21] and then submits candidates, together with its opinion, to the relevant court's personnel council for its opinion. According to

---

[18]   *See* "Overview: Judicial Independence in the EU Accession Process," in *Monitoring the EU Accession Process: Judicial Independence,* (Open Society Institute, Budapest, October 2001).

[19]   Assessment criteria include professional knowledge, ability to deal correctly with legal issues, conscientiousness, reliability, diligence, oral and written expression, ability to communicate and work with parties, attitude towards colleagues, and behaviour outside work. Judicial Service Act, Art. 29–30.

[20]   Judicial Service Act (amended), Art. 10–24.

[21]   Candidates must be Slovenian citizens, possess a university law degree, have completed of the State law exam, have a suitable personality and be at least 30 years of age.

recent amendments of the Judicial Service Act, candidates and the relevant court president receive copies of the opinions of the personnel council and the Ministry of Justice; both in turn have the right to append their own comments – changes that will increase transparency.

After considering these opinions, the personnel council forms a final opinion and ranks all candidates in order of priority, with justifications; the Judicial Council then decides on appointment,[22] though it is not bound by the opinion of the personnel council. Finally, a rejected candidate may file a lawsuit in administrative dispute against the decision of the Judicial Council.[23]

The amended system, though improving the previous system by providing better access to information about decisions, would further benefit from better preparation of members of the personnel councils that formulate opinions and take decisions in the process; currently, neither members of court personnel councils nor members of the Judicial Council receive special training to perform their responsibilities.

2. Evaluating and Regulating Performance

Judges' performance is subject to regular monitoring and assessment. However, although the recent amendments to the Judicial Service Act have introduced improvements, the criteria and procedures for evaluating judges' performance require further elaboration to reduce certain risks of arbitrariness and the present overemphasis on quantitative data.

With the adoption of the amendments to the Judicial Service Act, judges are assessed twice during their first four years in office;[24] thereafter, the personnel councils evaluate the professional performance of their colleagues every six years or upon the request of the Judicial Council, the court president or president of the relevant higher court, or the judge himself.[25] The Judicial Council's decisions on the personnel council assessments can affect the career path of judges, such as promotions to higher courts

---

[22] For vacancies on the Supreme Court, the National Assembly appoints judges upon the proposal of the Judicial Council.

[23] CONST REP. SLOVENIA, Art 157. However, the effective use of this right may be limited since the Judicial Council is not obliged to issue a formal decision that includes reasoned arguments.

[24] Under the previous system new judges were assessed during each of their first two years in office.

[25] Judicial Service Act (amended), Art. 31.

and higher pay brackets; a negative assessment may result in removal from office by the Judicial Council.[26]

Despite certain improvements, the evaluation criteria are still overly general.[27] A positive change is that court presidents, personnel councils, the Judicial Council, and judges being evaluated are all now entitled to present relevant information during the process. However, the procedure and assessment results are still confidential, and outside input into the process is minimal.[28]

In 1999, the Judicial Council adopted its *Criteria for Determining the Projected Amount of Judicial Work.*[29] In accordance with this resolution, judges' performance is continuously monitored against pre-determined norms for disposition of cases.[30] While primarily intended as a tool to reduce court delays,[31] this regulation is also used in the performance evaluation process; failure to achieve projected goals in caseload has a negative effect upon evaluation of judges' performance.

Judicial and academic commentators have criticised the *Criteria* and its influence on judges' careers, arguing that the quantitative indicators for judicial work are not balanced by clear, qualitative evaluation criteria. Moreover, the indicators are not linked to specific circumstances in which different courts operate – such as location, space, and human resources – or the differing complexity of cases that appear before

---

[26] For example judges may be removed from office if, based on an assessment of their judicial work, it is considered that they are not suited to judicial service. Judicial Service Act (amended), Art. 33.

[27] Assessment is based on the same criteria that apply to the initial selection of a candidate for the judicial service discussed above. The amendments do somewhat clarify criteria for the assessment of the performance of judges in areas not directly related to adjudication, such as teaching, training, participation in the legislative drafting, or active role in reducing case backlogs. *See* Judicial Service Act (amended), Art. 20 (6).

[28] Five members of the Judicial Council are appointed by Parliament to represent it and the community of lawyers.

[29] *Adopted by* the Judicial Council on 3 June 1999, *in force* 1 July 1999.

[30] The *Criteria* mandate that a Supreme Court justice has to resolve eight cases per month or 80 cases per year, a regional court judge 16 cases a month or 160 per year, and a district court judge 18 cases per month or 180 per year.

[31] *See also* Section D.2., "Court Administrative Capacity".

judges.[32] Performance indicators should be based on broader and more comprehensive techniques of case-flow management that take into account relevant circumstances such as differences in case-flow structure in different courts, and the complexity of specific cases.

Without further changes in the evaluation of performance consistent with the principles of judicial independence and accountability, the current system employed to decide judges' promotion, remuneration, and, especially, removal may degrade the quality of judgements as well as the reputation of the judicial profession.

There are also channels for public scrutiny and criticism of judicial performance. Parties in a specific case may lodge a supervisory appeal with the president of the court before which a specific procedure is in progress complaining of delay in the proceedings[33] or with the Administrative Court;[34] they may also lodge complaints with the office of the Human Rights Ombudsman, which can also intervene in judicial actions at its own initiative.[35] Courts are required to comply with the Ombudsman's request for information irrespective of the level of confidentiality.[36]

Through regular and special reports the Human Rights Ombudsman reports to the National Assembly and to the public.[37] Special reports can be issued if the Ombudsman commences an investigation in connection with a specific case and the court does not comply within the time limit or does not explain its reasons for failing to do so. In this case, Ombudsman informs the higher court immediately,[38] and can report this to the National Assembly and the public.[39] These measures help to ensure some level of public access to information about judicial behaviour, which in turn

---

[32] *See, e.g.*, Drago Škerget, *Analyses of the causes for court backlogs*, 29 March 2002, Ljubljana (written notice to the Supreme Court); Mateja Končina Peternel, *Analyses of the causes for court backlogs*, 29 March 2002, Ljubljana (written notice to the Supreme Court); Franc Rupret, *Analyses of the causes for court backlogs*, 29 March 2002, Ljubljana (written notice to the Supreme Court); Marjan Pogačnik, *Analyses of the causes for court backlogs*, 29 March 2002, Ljubljana (written notice to the Supreme Court); and Aleš Zalar, *Analyses of the causes for court backlogs*, 2 April 2002, Ljubljana (written notice to the Supreme Court).

[33] Courts Act, Art. 72.

[34] Constitutional Court decision Up-369/97 of 21 January 1998, OdlUs VII, 116, Nova revija. *See* Section D.2., "Court Administrative Capacity".

[35] Human Rights Ombudsman Act, Art. 9 (1). *See* Section D.2., "Court Administrative Capacity".

[36] Human Rights Ombudsman Act, Art. 6.

[37] Human Rights Ombudsman Act, Art. 5, 8.

[38] Human Rights Ombudsman Act, Art. 33 (2–3).

[39] Human Rights Ombudsman Act, Art. 33 (5).

allow non-intrusive feedback that increases judges' accountability and their incentives to improve their professionalism.

3. Training for a Professional Judiciary

The Centre for Judicial Training is the primary mechanism for judicial training,[40] in the development of which judges, prosecutors, academics, and representatives of the Ministry of Justice all participate.[41] However, due to lack of supporting infrastructure,[42] the Centre acts as an intermediary rather than provider of judicial training, and since 2000, governmental financial support for judicial training has declined steadily.[43] In addition, the selection of providers of training services is not based on public tenders,[44] which would encourage both more efficient use of limited funds and assist the professionalisation of judicial management. These factors do not favour further institutionalisation or professionalisation of judicial training.

Currently, judicial training focuses on imparting legal knowledge and only minimally includes topics relevant to enhancing judicial skills or changing the attitudes and behaviour of judges and court staff. Training of court staff is provided only irregularly and there is no training for court managers.[45] Furthermore, there is a lack of institutional incentives motivating judges to attend training. For example, the *Criteria for Determining the Projected Amount of Judicial Work* seem to discourage participation in training: while the *Criteria* provide for reduction in workload for judges with administrative responsibilities, it does not make any accommodation for judges attending professional development seminars.

---

[40] The Centre for Judicial Training is also responsible for training prosecutors, lawyers in the State attorneys office, and misdemeanour judges.

[41] The Centre includes a Program Council and an administrator. The Program Council consists of 12 members representing the judiciary, the State prosecution office, the State attorney office, and the Ministry of Justice; it is responsible for both programming and implementation of judicial training.

[42] The Centre does not have its own premises. The Program Council meets periodically at the Supreme Court, while its administrator is located at the Ministry of Justice.

[43] Interview with Alenka Jelenc-Puklavec, President of the Programme Council of the Centre for Judicial Training, 27 February 2002.

[44] *See* EU Accession Monitoring Program, *Monitoring the EU Accession Process: Corruption and Anti-Corruption Policy in Slovenia* (Open Society Institute, Budapest, October 2002), Section 7, "Public Procurement", available at <http://www.eumap.org.>, (accessed 26 September 2002).

[45] In the absence of any State-sponsored training, in 2001 the Slovenian Association of Judges organised two seminars on strategic planning, personnel management and media relations.

D. INSTITUTIONAL CAPACITY OF THE JUDICIAL BRANCH

Coordination of the various bodies responsible for representing and administering the judiciary is a problem, especially in the budget process. Management training for court presidents and secretaries should be an immediate priority, although in the long term a corps of professional managers should be developed. Work conditions are generally satisfactory, although case delays remain a problem; some initiatives to address case delays may have the incidental effect of harming judicial independence while not contributing to improved judicial capacity.

1. Governance and Administration of the Judicial Branch

The Supreme Court, Judicial Council, and Ministry of Justice all have significant roles in representing, administering and setting policy for the judiciary. On occasion, this division of authority causes coordination problems, especially with regard to the budget process.

Each of these three bodies has important influence or authority over the judiciary. The Supreme Court generally represents the judiciary in its dealings with the executive and legislative authorities, especially in financial matters, although there is no clear constitutional or statutory basis for it to do so. The Judicial Council plays an important role in personnel matters and in certain policy areas such as court workloads.[46] The Ministry of Justice is responsible for the overall administration of the judiciary.[47] In particular, the Minister prescribes the Court Rules, the document that determines the internal organisation and operation of courts, and supervises their implementation.

Lack of clarity in responsibilities leads both to gaps and overlap in overall management and is especially evident (and detrimental) during the budgetary process. The Supreme Court, in coordination with the Ministry of Justice, formulates the budget for the judiciary on the basis of courts' financial plans and presents it to the Government; the Judicial Council also provides its opinion on the proposed budget. However, the judiciary is rarely represented during the crucial stage when the State budget is deliberated within the executive branch. Although the Minister of Justice is a member of the Government, he has no responsibility to represent the judiciary. In combination

---

[46] The Council has adopted Criteria for Determining the Projected Amount of Judicial Work. *See* Section C.2., "Evaluating and Regulating Performance", and Section D.2., "Court Administrative Capacity".

[47] Courts Act, Art. 10.

with the absence of predetermined standards for funding levels, this makes funding for the judiciary uncertain.[48]

2. Court Administrative Capacity

Court presidents have considerable managerial autonomy, but lack necessary management skills; management training should be an immediate priority, although in the long term a corps of professional managers should be developed.

Court presidents are responsible for the day-to-day administration of courts, including personnel policy, internal organisation, financial and material operations, staff training, public relations, building management, and safety.[49] Despite this extensive managerial workload, applicants for the post of court president are not required to have any management skills; once appointed by the Minister of Justice, court presidents receive no training in court and case-flow management. Court secretaries – who hold managerial positions in all but district courts – are lawyers, not trained managers.[50] Over time, the capacity of courts will suffer if more professional management is not encouraged.

Individuals responsible for management should receive immediate training to perform these duties. A more long-term solution would be to concentrate resources on the introduction of a corps of professional court managers under the supervision of the court president.

Overall, courts are fairly well equipped; in most cases court presidents express satisfaction with present levels of access to databases and professional literature. However, some courts lack space and certain court buildings are not fit for their purpose. Several courts face a particular need for professional court staff. Because of the shortage of qualified support and professional staff, judges often have to deal with technical and procedural matters, such as checking the payment of fees and sending court documents, which reduces the time available for substantive judicial matters. Professional staff should be sufficiently trained and equipped to allow judges to concentrate on the administration of justice.[51]

---

[48] Interview with Aleš Zalar, President of the Ljubljana Regional Court, 17 March 2002.

[49] Court Rules, *Official Gazette*, 1995–2001.

[50] Interview with Jasna Šegan, Deputy President of the Administrative Court of the Republic of Slovenia, 25 March 2002.

[51] *See* Survey of Slovenian Court Presidents, conducted by Boštjan Zalar, Institute of Social Sciences, Centre for Evaluation and Strategic Studies, Faculty of Social Sciences, University of Ljubljana, March 2002 (based on responses submitted by 58 of the 67 courts).

Court workloads remain high, although the inflow of cases decreased during the 1990s and is now relatively stable;[52] in 2001, the number of unresolved cases decreased slightly.[53] Still, unreasonable delays remain a concern. For example, the most frequent cause for complaint to the Human Rights Ombudsman asserts a violation of the right to a hearing within a reasonable time.[54]

Recent initiatives aimed at reducing case backlogs and shortening the length of proceedings have contributed to this improvement. The electronic land register installed in all courts has helped to decrease the backlog in this area, which had been especially high.[55] The regional court in Ljubljana – the largest court in Slovenia – launched a project in 2001 to resolve backlogs by using alternative forms of case resolution; the Judicial Council has recently endorsed the project.[56] There is also a legal tool to challenge court delays: parties have the right to lodge complaints at the Administrative Court against lengthy proceedings in pending cases.[57] In a case following this decision, the Administrative Court found a violation of the right to a trial within a reasonable time.[58]

Two additional initiatives have raised controversy. Under the 2001 *Herkules* project, proposed by the Supreme Court, 20 judges would be transferred, with their consent, to overburdened courts for a period not exceeding one year. So far, two judges have been transferred for six months from the Higher Court in Ljubljana to district courts; the effects of this project are not yet clear. The project has come in for criticism because it also introduces productivity-based rewards for judges solving more cases, which arguably contravenes the principle of judicial impartiality by encouraging speedy resolution of cases for personal reward.[59] The Human Rights Ombudsman has

---

[52] 1990 there were 592,505 new cases, in 2000 – 527,856 new cases, and in 2001 – 529,981 new cases.

[53] The number of unresolved cases grew from 199,893 in 1990 to 533,225 in 2000. In 2001 however, the number of unresolved cases dropped 0.04 percent to 532,937.

[54] Human Rights Ombudsman, Annual Report of the Human Rights Ombudsman for 2001. *See also* Section C.2., "Evaluating and Regulating Performance".

[55] 35 percent of court data is now recorded in the electronic land register; it estimated that the project will be completed in 2003. Delo, "Elektronska zemljiška knjiga" (Electronic Land Register), 21 March 2002, p. 3.

[56] Resolution of the Judicial Council, 31 May 2002.

[57] Constitutional Court decision Up-369/97 of 21 January 1998, OdlUs VII, 116, Nova revija. *See* Section C.2., "Evaluating and Regulating Performance".

[58] Judgement in case U 836/98-25 of 7 March 2000. The judgement has not been published, as the case is pending before the Supreme Court.

[59] *See, e.g.*, The Executive Committee of the Slovenian Association of Judges, *Inappropriate* Herkules, Pravna Praksa, 31/2000.

suggested that in the long run the *Herkules* project will not efficiently contribute to reduction of court delays.[60]

Criticism has been directed also at the evaluation measures adopted under the *Criteria for Determining the Projected Amount of Judicial Work* established by the Judicial Council. The measures favour numerical goals over qualitative assessments of effectiveness in managing case flow, which critics believe will not improve judicial capacity in the long term.[61] Both the *Herkules* and *Criteria* projects should be reassessed with an eye to their possible effects on judicial independence and the real effects they have on promoting judicial capacity.

E. RECOMMENDATIONS

1. To Slovenian Government and Legislature

- Re-evaluate the recently enacted legislative amendments and the proposed constitutional amendments to ensure that they in fact will enhance judicial capacity and not jeopardise judicial independence; in particular:

- Withdraw the proposal to introduce a five-year probationary period for new judges, and develop instead non-intrusive means of checking judges' qualifications, preferably by employing methods that more rigorously screen and train candidates before they become judges.

- Review the proposed changes requiring the mandatory dismissal of judges in cases of Constitutional violations, and at a minimum ensure that implementing regulations clearly define the content of the conduct that would lead to mandatory dismissal in a manner consistent with the principles of judicial independence and accountability; and

- Reconsider the changes to the system for setting judges' salaries made by the Public Sector Wage System Act, to ensure that the political branches may not improperly alter judges' salaries.

---

[60] Human Rights Ombudsman, Annual Report of the Human Rights Ombudsman for 2001.

[61] There is also concern over the fact that numerical data collected as a result of the *Criteria* is used for making evaluation and promotion decisions. *See* Section C.2., "Evaluating and Regulating Performance".

- Clarify responsibility for policy-making and administration at the national level, especially with regard to the budget process, which should incorporate judges' input more effectively.

- Ensure greater transparency and professionalism in the process of judicial selection and promotion of judges performed by the Judicial Council and personnel councils to ensure that competent judges are chosen in a manner that reinforces public confidence in the judicial system.

- Re-evaluate the principles and content of the *Criteria for Determining the Projected Amount of Judicial Work*; in particular, performance evaluation should balance quantitative performance indicators with clear qualitative criteria, and link these measures to a more sophisticated model of case-flow management.

- Strengthen training for judges by institutionalising the Centre for Judicial Training to guarantee stable funding and professional staffing. The performance evaluation system should not create disincentives for judges to attend training.

- Transfer managerial responsibilities to professional managers in order to reduce the burden on court presidents. Prioritise training in court and case-flow management for court presidents and court secretaries.

- Continue efforts to reduce court backlogs and case delays by increasing the corps of professional court staff and improving the training of court support personnel. Expand alternative dispute resolution programmes. Reassess the effects of the Herkules and Criteria projects' potential to harm judicial independence.

2. To the European Union

- Clarify the Union's presently undefined standards regarding the obligations that membership properly imposes on States in organising their judiciaries, both generally and as they relate to the disputes over the proposed amendments to Slovenia's Constitution and the Public Sector Wage System Act.

- Assist with continued efforts to reduce court backlogs by increasing emphasis on more sophisticated means to address delays rather than focusing purely on numerical systems that may undermine the quality of court decisions.

- Support development of the Centre for Judicial Training with technical expertise from candidate and member States.